FORGE OF FREEDOM

American Aircraft Production in World War II

V. Dennis Wrynn

Motorbooks International
Publishers & Wholesalers ®

First published in 1995 by Motorbooks International Publishers & Wholesalers, PO Box 2, 729 Prospect Avenue, Osceola, WI 54020 USA

The information in this book is true and complete to the best of our knowledge. All recommendations are made without any guarantee on the part of the author or Publisher, who also disclaim any liability incurred in connection with the use of this data or specific details We recognize that some words, model names and designations, for example, mentioned herein are the property of the trademark holder. We use them for identification purposes only. This is not an official publication

Motorbooks International books are also available at discounts in bulk quantity for industrial or sales-promotional use. For details write to Special Sales Manager at the Publisher's address

Library of Congress Cataloging-in-Publication Data

Wrynn, Dennis.
    Forge of freedom/Dennis Wrynn.
    p. cm.
    Includes index.
    ISBN 0-7603-0143-3 (pbk.)
    1. Airplanes, Military--United States--History. 2. Airplanes, Military--United States--Pictorial works. 3. Aircraft industry--Military aspects--United States--History. 4. World war, 1939-1945--United States. I. Title.
TL685.3.W77   1995
623.7'46'0973--dc20   95-35619

On the front cover: A row of new Douglas Dauntless SBD-3s are moved down the production line. Once finished, SBDs were sent all over the Pacific to carry out dive-bombing and scouting missions. *Northrop*

On the back cover: These B-17Gs are participating in their April 1944 roll-out at Boeing's plant Two in Seattle. Strategic bombing missions over Germany became almost a daily chore for B-17s in Europe. Their Four 1,200hp Pratt & Whitney R-1820-97 engines could be throttled up for a lumbering take-off with over eight tons of bombs on board. *Boeing*

Printed and bound in the United States

Contents

Introduction and Acknowledgments

To the thousands of American men and women, mostly anonymous, who built and flew the greatest armada of aircraft ever assembled, this book is most sincerely dedicated.

Their contribution to victory in World War II was most significant and remains a glorious chapter in the annals of the American people, forever free.

When the editors at Motorbooks International first discussed this book concept with me, I naively suggested that such a history encompass the entire spectrum of US defense production during World War II (WWII). It did not take long to realize that this topic was immense, and could not be adequately addressed in a dozen books.

Most historians of the period agree that America's industrial might was a major, if not deciding, factor in the Allied victory in WWII. On examination, the immensity of this manufacturing miracle boggles the mind. Thousands of companies dedicated all their resources to winning the war. The millions of individual men and women in the military needed dozens of items, from shoelaces to helmets, plus everything in between, in order to be personally equipped to carry out their missions. Weapons systems required thousands of parts. Food and fuel have always been vital components of warfare, and were demanded in tremendous quantities. Training equipment requirements were huge, and the expected wastage of war as well as battlefield losses resulted in the paradox of overproduction of thousands of items in order to provide adequate reserves.

Millions of civilians participated in defense production with patriotic fervor, not just with an eye toward a significant and hard-earned paycheck at the end of the week. These working men and women accepted shortages, rationing, relocation, separation, and loss while producing every imaginable commodity and weapon for the military. Their sacrifices and successes are well-documented.

The aircraft industry by itself was an overwhelming part of the production war. There were thirty-five major facilities in the United States producing airplanes for fifteen major corporations, employing hundreds of thousands of American workers. Subcontractors operated from hundreds of additional locations and employed additional thousands of workers. American companies manufactured more than 300,000 aircraft from 1939 to 1945. Each year from 1942 to 1945 the United States produced more aircraft than Germany and Japan combined. Aircraft manufacture was the largest industry in the world, and was truly an economic marvel. This book is a tribute to that success, and its significant contribution to victory in WWII.

Before deciding to restrict *Forge of Freedom* to a study of US aircraft production, I contacted by telephone and letter more than 200 American companies that were involved in defense production during WWII. The results were discouraging. Very few of them responded in a positive fashion, and most ignored my requests for information. Archives were closed or nonexistent. In cases of foreign ownership there was a distinct lack of interest in the companies' involvement in WWII. The surviving partners in mergers were usually not interested in the history of the non-survivors. In some instances companies demanded more than $50 an hour for research assistance. In other cases the company archives had been donated to local museums or historical societies, and these non-profit organizations, usually confronted with financial limitations, understandably charged fees for research, further complicating the situation. There were some positive exceptions to this dismal perspective, but corporate attitudes toward preservation were not encouraging. It appears the business community needs to be reminded that we ignore our past at our peril.

Happily, the aviation industry proved to be a notable exception to this discouraging corporate trend.

While there were some instances of constraints and limited responses, these were usually the result of the work load and volume of requests that these archivists face on a daily basis. In those instances where the information requested was not available for whatever reasons, several very professional aviation writers, with far more expertise than this writer, cordially offered their assistance, which was gratefully accepted. Thus there are many people for me to thank, and I trust I will not neglect any of them for their generous contributions to this book. There has been no attempt to prioritize or even alphabetize these acknowledgments, and I hope that no one takes offense with the manner in which he or she is listed. They were all generous and helpful, but I would begin by thanking several independent aviation historians and friends who offered their assistance.

My gratitude, therefore, to Pete Bowers of Seattle, Washington; Steve Pace of Tacoma, Washington; Phil Kaplan of Hershey, Pennsylvania; Bob Dorr of Oakton, Virginia; Alan McNally of Port Jefferson, New York; Rick Netherton of Falls Church, Virginia; John Talmadge of Haydenville, Massachusetts; Margie McVey of Port Jefferson, New York; Margaret Rayll of Farmingdale, New York; Ray Lewis of Washington, D.C.; Bill Foster of Brewster, Massachusetts; and Jim Dacey of Arlington, Virginia. Special thanks to Wendell S. Storms of Long Island, New York, for his P-47 poem. Also thanks to my editors, Mike Dapper and Greg Field, who as usual were affable, helpful, and understanding as this volume progressed.

Responding for their corporations and offering their assistance were J. J. Frey of EDO Corporation, College Point, New York; Tom Lubbesmeyer and Marilyn Phipps of Boeing Company, Seattle, Washington; Jean Ross and Kim Ethridge of Martin Marietta Corporation, Baltimore, Maryland; Lynn McDonald of the Cradle of Aviation Museum, Garden City, New York; Michael Starn of the US Marine Corps Aviation Museum, Quantico, Virginia; Brian Nicklas of the Smithsonian Air & Space Museum, Washington, D.C.; Ray Wagner of the San Diego Aerospace Museum, San Diego, California; Sue Petre of General Motors, Detroit, Michigan; Tom Garver of Rayovac, Madison, Wisconsin; Ed Kalail of General Tire, Akron, Ohio; Georgia Maddox Engle of Vought Aircraft Company, Dallas, Texas; Lois Lovisolo of Grumman Corporation, Bethpage, New York; John Amrhein of Northrop Corporation, Los Angeles, California; Leslie Stegh of Deere & Company, Moline, Illinois; David Letourneau of Burlington Northern Railroad, Ft. Worth, Texas; Doug Horstman & Orville Butler of Maytag Company, Newton, Iowa; George Braatz of Cooper Champion Spark Plug, Toledo, Ohio; John Taylor of Zenith Electronics Corporation, Glenview, Illinois; Robert Hood, Daniell Schaeffer, and Harry Gann of McDonnell Douglas, Long Beach, California; Brandt Rosenbusch of Chrysler Motors, Highland Park, Michigan; Mary Edith Arnold of Motorola Museum of Electronics, Schaumburg, Illinois; Jeannie Ng of Girl Scouts of the USA, New York, New York; Pat Reilly of the Aviation Hall of Fame of New Jersey, Teterboro, New Jersey; Mark Renovitch of the Franklin Delano Roosevelt Library, Hyde Park, New York; Joe Stout of Lockheed, Ft. Worth, Texas; Harold Sherman of Yankee Air Force Library, Belleville, Michigan; Jeff Rhodes of Lockheed Aeronautical Systems, Marietta, Georgia; Erik Simonsen of North American Aviation Rockwell International, Los Angeles, California; Eric Dickerson of the Allison Gas Turbine Division of General Motors, Indianapolis, Indiana; Tom Campbell of Cooper Industries, Houston, Texas; Eugene Moore of Armstrong World Industries, Lancaster, Pennsylvania; Nancy Sherbert of Kansas State Historical Society, Topeka, Kansas; Sam Salem of Loral Goodyear Aircraft, Akron, Ohio; Jim Smart of Brown Forman Corporation, Louisville, Kentucky; Barbara Brennan and Delores Goulet of Post Street Archives (Dow), Midland, Michigan; Charles Foster and Eric Schulzinger of Lockheed Corporation, Calabasas, California; Holly Reed and Ruth Dicks of National Archives, Washington, D.C.; Mark Sullivan of Pratt & Whitney (UTC), East Hartford, Connecticut; John Mayo and George Rosen of Hamilton Standard (UTC), Windsor Locks, Connecticut; Fred Hartman of Sikorsky Aircraft (UTC), Stratford, Connecticut; John Houser of Aeronca Incorporated, Middletown, Ohio.

Without their contributions I could not have completed this book.

—V. Dennis Wrynn
Fairfax Station, Virginia
November 1994

Aircraft Classifications

The manner in which the US Army Air Corps (USAAC; the name was changed to the US Army Air Forces [USAAF] in 1941) designated aircraft was developed in the 1920s and was rather straight-forward. The first letter referred to mission type.

A—Attack
B—Bomber
C—Cargo
F—Photo Reconnaissance
G—Glider
L—Liaison
O—Observation
P—Pursuit (Fighter)
R—Rotary Wing (Helicopter)
BT—Basic Trainer
PT—Primary Trainer
AT—Advance Trainer

An *X* in front of the mission designator indicated experimental; a *Y* signified service testing; and a *Z* meant the aircraft was obsolete. The number following the letter designator was assigned by the Air Corps to that aircraft type in order of acceptance, although some types were never accepted and therefore numbers are missing. The letter following the type number represented modifications to the aircraft type. Thus a B-17F was the sixth revision in B-17 production. Some confusion occurred when a P-38 was converted to photo reconnaissance and became an F-5, or a P-51 used as a dive bomber was designated an A-36.

Navy classification of aircraft was somewhat different. The first letter or two letters signified aircraft type and the following number was assigned to aircraft from the manufacturer.

F—Fighter
OS—Observation Scout
PB—Patrol Bomber
SB—Scout Bomber
SN—Trainer
TB—Torpedo Bomber

The letter following the number represented the manufacturer and the next number indicated revisions.

A—Brewster
B—Boeing
C—Curtiss
D—Douglas
F—Grumman
G—Goodyear
J—North American
M—Martin or General Motors
U—Chance Vought
Y—Consolidated

An F4F Wildcat was a fighter built by Grumman, and a PBY was a patrol bomber built by Consolidated, while an OS2U was an observation scout produced by Chance Vought and an SBD was a scout bomber (dive bomber) built by Douglas. An Avenger built by Grumman was a TBF, and the same plane built by General Motors was a TBM, which could be confused as a Martin-built aircraft because for some unknown reason Martin and General Motors aircraft were both designated by the letter *M*. Some other anomalies also existed. A Wildcat built by General Motors was an FM-1. The F4U-2 Corsair was built by Chance Vought; exactly the same plane built by Goodyear was the FG-1, and those manufactured by Brewster were F3As. The letter *N* was the US Navy designator for a trainer. The SNJ was a Navy trainer built by North American Aviation (J).

Chapter I

Beginnings

The two decades between the two World Wars were known as the Golden Age of aviation in the United States, and indeed they were just that to the nation's fledgling aircraft industry. Measured by the standard of the Wright Brothers' first flight in 1903, the technical advances in the 1920s and 1930s were enormous, and daring aviators of both sexes were constantly setting records and performing feats considered impossible only a few years earlier.

While various aviation "firsts" garnered newspaper headlines, many serious commercial enterprises and experiments were being conducted in the offices and factories of American aircraft manufacturers. Such disparate men as Lockheed's technical genius Clarence "Kelly" Johnson and eccentric millionaire Howard Hughes designed aircraft to fly higher and faster than their predecessors, while others such as James "Jimmy" Doolittle worked to improve fuel performance and initiated technical innovations, including instrument flying, that would have a tremendous impact in the coming war. There were many such pioneering aviators, men like Charles Lindbergh, Roscoe Turner, Wiley Post, C. R. Smith, and Eddie Rickenbacker. American women led by Louise Thaden, Amelia Earhart, Blanche Noyes, Ruth Nichols, Elinor Smith, and Fay Gillis Wells were also advancing the cause of aviation around the world. There were many more of these trailblazers, most of them forgotten today. Their contributions were important, and collectively they laid the groundwork of an entirely new industry.

These innovations resulted in bigger and faster airplanes carrying higher payloads at greater altitudes. For the commercial airlines this meant greater passenger comfort and the opportunity to compete with the railroads and automobiles as a legitimate transportation option. For the military, these major changes required a significant strategic adjustment, which was somewhat slow in coming to an essentially isolationist nation confident in the deterrent of its ocean barriers and its battleship navy.

The air battles on the Western Front during World War I (WWI) had become major confrontations involving dozens of aircraft by the time that war ended. American pilots participated in the air war over the Continent in their own squadrons as well as those of the French and British air forces, but no American-manufactured aircraft entered combat in the skies of Europe before the Armistice was signed on November 11, 1918. There had just not been enough time to convert the American civilian manufacturing base to war production in the 19 months of US participation in the war, even though many American industries had been supplying the munitions needs of the British, French, and Russians since 1915. Despite the dramatic reduction in military funding that occurred in the United States after the war, and over the opposition of many land-bound soldiers

A decade before Pearl Harbor the US Navy was flying the Curtiss F8C-4 Helldiver, powered by the 450hp Pratt & Whitney R-1340-C engine, shown here in a promotional photograph for MGM's 1931 movie entitled, predictably, *Hell-divers*. Stars Clark Gable and Wallace Beery are the middle two men in this group. Designed as a fighter in 1927, the F8C had a top speed of 137mph. *National Archives*

Powered by the same engine as the Helldiver was Boeing's P-26A Peashooter, delivered in 1933. However, this low-winged monoplane had a metal skin and was the first USAAC pursuit plane that used wing flaps due to its high landing speed. The aircraft cruised at 205mph and had a top speed of 234mph. Its ceiling was 27,400ft. With its open cockpit and fixed landing gear the P-26A was already obsolete when assigned to the Philippines in 1940, and was decimated in combat against the Japanese early in the war. *USAF*

and water-bound sailors, progress in the air went forward, due mostly to the determined efforts of junior officers of the regular services. Army fliers under the leadership of William "Billy" Mitchell, Henry H. "Hap" Arnold, George Kenney, Carl "Tooey" Spaatz, and Ira Eaker, as well as Marc Mitscher, Raymond Spruance, and William "Bull" Halsey of the Navy, led the way in reducing the scientific and physical barriers to military aviation, often at great cost to the personnel involved. Navy experiments with aircraft-carrying dirigibles ultimately proved unsuccessful, but aircraft carrier development flourished, along with new operational tactics involving ship-based torpedo planes, fighters, and dive bombers. At the same time Army visionaries evolved the concept of strategic bombing that became a mainstay of US policy during WWII, and led directly to the development of four-engined bombers such as the B-17, the B-24, and the B-29.

In the late 1930s, Adolph Hitler's aggressive actions against his European neighbors and Japan's war against China had not gone unno-

The *USS Macon* over lower Manhattan in 1933. The US Navy experimented heavily with rigid airships, known as dirigibles, in the 1920s and 1930s. Used for long-range reconnaissance, this 785ft, long airship, which used pockets of helium for lift, had an internal hangar with storage for several Curtiss F92-C Sparrowhawk biplane fighters used for scouting and protection against enemy aircraft. They were lowered and recovered on a trapeze gear suspended through a T-shaped door in the floor of the dirigible. The *Macon* crashed into the sea off Point Sur, California, in February 1935, killing two of the crew of eighty men. The wreckage was discovered in 1,450ft of water 13mi off the California coast in 1991, with two of its Sparrowhawks still intact. Her sister ship, *Akron*, crashed 30mi off the New Jersey coast during a storm in April 1933, killing seventy-two crew members. Her wreckage was discovered in August 1986 in 150ft of water. The loss of these two ships effectively ended the Navy dirigible program. *National Archives*

Realizing that the standard Douglas TBD-1 Devastator torpedo bomber on active service was quickly becoming obsolete, the US Navy sought a faster replacement. The Vought Aircraft Company produced the experimental XTBU-1 Sea Wolf pictured here, but lost the contract award to the Grumman TBF Avenger. *Vought Aircraft Company*

ticed by the US government. By the Fall of 1940, a year after the German invasion of Poland, all the countries of Europe on Hitler's planned list of conquest had been defeated and occupied except Great Britain. As a result, the American Congress instituted military draft registration for all men between eighteen and thirty-five years old, and actually drafted the twenty-one year olds. President Franklin Delano Roosevelt also mobilized the reserves; Army, Navy, and Marines. He announced that the United States was the "Arsenal of Democracy" and embarked on a defense spending program designed to upgrade the nation's military preparedness for war. Roosevelt's production agenda also provided military equipment and munitions to Great Britain and the Soviet Union, ultimately through LendLease.

Although isolationism was a legitimate political position embraced by many respectable national leaders and by the great majority of the US population, other officials, including the President and most of his Cabinet, viewed American involvement in the two major wars then raging as inevitable. Thus various industries were privately directed by the US government to prepare for conversion of their plants to defense manu-

As production materials were diverted into defense programs, manufacturers of civilian goods faced peacetime shortages, which led to the curtailment of their main product lines. In this September 1941 letter from the president of Maytag, he informed his employees that the company's most successful and famous clothes washer was discontinued "for the duration," a full three months before the war began! *Maytag Archives*

THE MAYTAG COMPANY
EXECUTIVE OFFICES
NEWTON, IOWA

FRED MAYTAG II
PRESIDENT

General Letter No. 1091
September Ninth
1 9 4 1

TO ALL FIELD REPRESENTATIVES:

      The growing shortage of materials has forced us to discontinue manufacture of the Model 32 for the duration. Our last 32's are being shipped this week. None will be available hereafter.

      Please pass this information to your dealers and obtain from them revised specifications for all unfilled orders containing Model 32's. Submit these new specifications to your branch office in the usual manner.

      Insofar as is practicable the entire aluminum washer allotment previously divided between 32's and E's will now apply to the Model E. Barring unforeseen developments, E's will be available to the extent that both E's and 32's have been available up to now.

      The scheduling of shipments is in charge of your branch office. Your branch manager will continue to work closely with you in determining the portion of his branch allotment which is available for your territory.

Very truly yours

Fred Maytag II

President

Fred Maytag II-MW

Martin Aircraft's twin-engined bomber known as the A-22 Maryland was developed for the USAAC but never ordered by that service. However, the French Armee de l'Air, which called the plane the Glenn, bought 115 of them and then placed a second order for 100 additional Marylands, but only twenty-five aircraft from the follow-up order were delivered before France fell in June 1940. Several of these escaped to England while others were flown against the Allies by the Vichy French forces. The RAF took over the remnant of the French contract, totaling seventy-five planes and ordered 185 more. The A-22 carried a crew of three, 2,000lb of bombs, and ten machine guns at a top speed of 305mph. The aircraft featured here at the Martin plant near Baltimore are in final assembly. *Martin Marietta*

facture. The western railroads were given incentives to build new track and enlarge yards in Southern California in preparation for a Pacific conflict, and the aviation industry was asked to design and produce planes able to defeat the Axis aircraft then ruling the skies. Increased demand for raw materials as well as finished goods generated a vigorous boost to the nation's economy. Some

manufactured goods were suddenly in short supply. Ironically, it was determined that a national scarcity of scrap metal resulted from the sale of 200 million tons to Japan between 1935 and 1940 by American junk dealers. Depending on your point of view, this was a direct result of the hard times businessmen faced during the Depression or, conversely, reflected the desire of unscrupulous in-

dividuals to profit at the nation's expense.

While many conservative businessmen decried the President's obsession with the war in Europe, they had no aversion to the profits that resulted from this massive infusion of government spending in the economy. However, the American automobile industry, which became heavily involved in defense production

The British asked Martin for an updated version of the A-22, which resulted in the A-30 Baltimore twin-engined bomber. Slightly faster than its predecessor at 320mph and powered by two 1,700hp radial engines, the A-30 carried a crew of four and was armed with eleven machine guns. Its bomb load was 2,000lb and the "Balt" was equipped with self-sealing gas tanks and 211lb of additional armor. The British government ordered 1,575 A-30s from 1940 to 1942, the first 975 of them through LendLease. The Baltimore was highly praised by its RAF crews and was also flown by the Royal Australian Air Force (RAAF) in the Pacific war as well as several other Allied air forces. It is curious that neither the A-22 nor the A-30 was ever ordered by the US government. The RAF aircraft pictured here features the famous low-silhouette Martin top gun turret. *Martin Marietta*

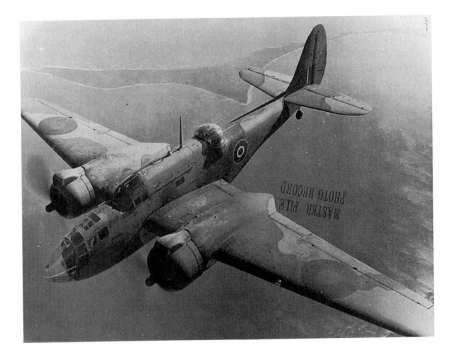

With the institution of the peacetime draft in 1940 and the mobilization of the Reserves at the same time, military camps were filled to overflowing. In many instances there was not enough room in the permanent barracks on base and the men lived in canvas tents. The sides of these army tents could be raised to allow fresh air to circulate in temperate climes. *Dow Chemical*

after the United States entered the war, was acutely aware that 1940 and 1941 had produced the best car sales since before the Depression. These companies were very reluctant to divert peacetime resources to military production while they had the opportunity to cash in on civilian sales. The car manufacturers also expected government restrictions on automobile production if America entered the war, and sought to maximize profits while the nation was still at peace. Henry Ford was a declared pacifist and refused a contract for his company to build military aircraft engines for Great Britain, announcing he would only participate in programs for the US armed services. Incidents such as this received significant publicity, but the mood of the country grew more receptive to President Roosevelt's interventionist policies as the global media reported on the scope and the savagery of Axis conquests. Economically America's isolationism paid off handsomely in the two years before the war, just as it had done when supplying armaments to the belliger-

Prewar 1940 scrap iron, in this case surplus rails from the rebuilding of the nation's railroads, accumulated in Duluth, Minnesota, prior to being reforged for use in America's expanding defense initiative. Although much negative publicity was directed toward the sale of 200 million tons of US scrap metal to Japan in the years before the war, American industry was also busily procuring the precious resource. *National Archives*

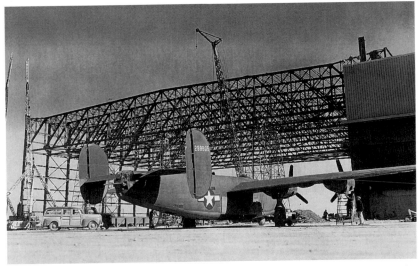

Ground was broken for the government-owned Consolidated Aircraft factory in Fort Worth, Texas, in April 1941. Finished 100 days ahead of schedule, the plant was twelve city blocks long and six stories high, and contained 27,000 tons of steel. The 30,547 employees, including 11,577 women, built 3,034 B-24 Liberator bombers and at peak production delivered 175 B-24s per month. A San Diego-built B-24 is featured here along with a Ford "woodie" station wagon. *Lockheed Fort Worth*

After America entered the war, the tempo of rearmament increased dramatically. In August 1942 an Allegheny-Ludlum mill train hauled tons of scrap iron and steel to the open-hearth furnaces in the Pennsylvania mill yard, after which it was poured as alloy steel. *National Archives*

ents prior to America's entry into WWI some twenty-three years earlier. Opportunities for employment expanded dramatically, and American workers moved to the new job locales in ever-increasing numbers.

As a direct result of the experimental nature of aviation development in the United States, the actual manufacture of aircraft was excruciatingly slow when contrasted with mass production in other industries. This was especially true when compared to automobile manufacture, where the Ford Motor Company and others had been refining their assembly line procedures for twenty-five years. A realistic evaluation of the US aviation industry in 1940 indicates production of approximately 6,000 planes, even while President Roosevelt was calling for 50,000 military aircraft a year. *Fortune Magazine* referred to the American aviation industry in August 1940 as "a spectacular experimental laboratory," but not the major mass production industry it needed to become in time of war. Indeed, that year the nation's airlines had only 450 aircraft in their fleets, operational military aircraft totaled less than 6,000 in all categories, and most manufacturers had barely survived the Depression. It usually took several years for a new aircraft to advance from the initial contract through design to the experimental stage, with the test models essentially built by hand. After modifications, the aircraft were accepted by the ordering agency, an assembly line had to be designed, jigs and machine tools ordered and installed in the factory, and workers trained for the specifics of this new manufacturing. When the new plane was ready for deployment, instructors had to be trained on the aircraft in order to in turn prepare thousands of young, inexperienced pilots for combat. When one considers the number of different aircraft under development just prior to and during WWII, it is understandable that things didn't happened overnight in the American aircraft industry.

The British, who were in desperate straits as they stood alone in the

West against Hitler's Germany, turned to America for manufacturing assistance, and siphoned off the increasing American defense production, especially aircraft, at a great rate. Great Britain had bolstered Lockheed Aircraft's position in the industry by contracting in 1938 for a military version of the manufacturer's Model 14 passenger transport, redesignated the B-14 Hudson bomber. Indeed, by the end of 1939, Lockheed, located in Burbank, California, led the aircraft industry financially with $35 million in sales. The British also ordered 800 of Lockheed's P-38 Lightning twin-engined, twin-boomed fighters. In order to accommodate the factory floor space requirements of this very lucrative contract, the company purchased a nearby whiskey distillery known as "3-G" from Aaron, Lou and Moe Greenberg and converted it into the needed factory. In 1932 Lockheed had been mired in bankruptcy and could boast only one employee. By the summer of 1940 the company was hiring sixty new workers a day and employed 10,000 people.

Northrop was another American company that benefited from Great Britain's rearmament program, receiving a $17 million order in September 1940 for the Vengeance dive bomber which had been designed by Vultee Aircraft. Ten months later the USAAC ordered 200 of these rather cumbersome aircraft, designated the A-31, for $16 million from Northrop.

As the United States shored up its defenses, contracts between the government and American aircraft manufacturers proliferated: Boeing Aircraft was building the B-17 Flying Fortress heavy bomber, Consolidated Aircraft was producing the B-24 Liberator bomber, and Douglas Aircraft was busy manufacturing its legendary C-47 (DC-3) and the SBD Dauntless dive bomber, a Navy mainstay throughout the war. Grumman Aircraft on New York's Long Island was producing the F4F Wildcat fighter and the TBF Avenger torpedo plane for the US Navy. Work was underway at North Ameri-

An abandoned panel truck in a Fort Worth, Texas, scrap yard proclaimed a defiant message to America's enemy in the Pacific in October 1942. The character of scrap became rather personal as the civilian population responded to the government's call for all available surplus metals. On the cardboard box in the front center of this photograph is printed "WON'T YOU HAV-A-TAMPA CIGAR?" In addition, the name Fred Harris, Fort Worth, Texas, has been scrawled across the box. *National Archives*

The South Works of the Carnegie-Illinois Steel Works in Chicago, Illinois, worked at full capacity as production escalated at an incredible rate. In the background are blast furnaces and the finishing end of the 40in Blooming Mill and Sintering Plant. The railroad cars are waiting under the 89th Street bridge for their next haul. *National Archives*

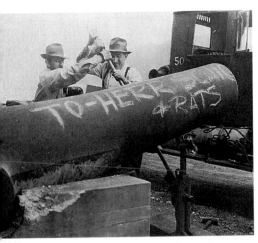

Scrap collection was no respecter of sentimentality or even history. At Fort Point, California, workers removed a nineteenth-century cannon from its concrete emplacement. It is inscribed "To Schikel and Rats" and was reforged into usable metal for the war effort. "Schikel" was a derogatory name for Hitler. *Ray Lewis Collection*

Very ordinary individuals participated on the local level in various promotions designed to aid the war effort. Led by a uniformed band, the American Legion in West New York, New Jersey, paraded down Bergenline Avenue with two dozen "jalopies" on their way to an auto wrecking yard for conversion into war material.

It was the beginning of a New York and New Jersey American Legion Jalopy Drive sponsored by the War Production Board involving 150,000 legionnaires. The phrase "Sorry Please" on the marchers' sign mocked the Japanese tendency to apologize profusely after offending a person or a country. *National Archives*

PLEASE DRIVE CAREFULLY.
V BUMPERS ARE ON THE SCRAP HEAP

Actress Rita Hayworth exhibited her shapely legs in this 1942 publicity appeal for scrap metal. Westbrook Pegler, whose column appeared in 177 newspapers across the country, suggested that instead of small items donated for scrap, 28 million car owners in America should contribute 300,000 tons of car bumpers. Pegler donated the bumpers from his 1942 Chrysler. *National Archives*

can Aviation on the B-25 Mitchell bomber and the P-51 Mustang fighter, while Martin Aircraft of Baltimore, Maryland, built the B-26 Marauder bomber, and Curtiss turned out the P-40 Warhawk fighter, made famous by the "Flying Tigers" in China after the United States entered the war. It was also used successfully by the British in North Africa. The French government ordered 1,000 fighters from Curtiss, but France was defeated before seventy percent of them could be delivered. Many other

American companies eagerly accepted government contracts, including the Ford Motor Company, which built a new factory at Willow Run, Michigan, to accommodate production of Consolidated Aircraft's B-24 Liberator bomber. The $15 million tab for construction was picked up by Uncle Sam.

As encouraging as these production developments appeared, when war came to Pearl Harbor on December 7, 1941, US forces were woefully unprepared to withstand the onslaught of well-trained enemy units operating combat-proven equipment, especially aircraft. In the case of the Navy's F4F Wildcat fighter, new tactics had to be developed to counter the superior speed and maneuverability of the Japanese Mitsubishi A6M Zero fighter. One of these was the Thach Weave, a defensive maneuver pioneered by US Navy Lt. Comdr. John "Jimmie" Thach in which pairs of criss-crossing fighters provided rear cover for each other while still continuing offensive maneuvers against enemy aircraft. In the case of the P-40 Warhawk, it entailed using the aircraft's superior diving speed to attack and escape, rather than dogfighting against the Zero. This was achieved by gaining position above the enemy fighter, attacking it in a dive, and continuing the dive out of the action. An experienced aviator never tried to out-climb this Japanese

Individuals showed their support for the war effort in a variety of ways. In July 1942, citizens who made a pledge to The Greater New York War Bond Pledge Campaign autographed bombs, in this case a 2,000lb blockbuster, for airborne delivery to enemy installations. John Harvilas, shown signing the missile, bought a $1,000 bond for himself and $100 bonds for his sisters. He announced he was leaving his job as a rigger for military service in the near future. *National Archives*

As part of the effort to conserve gasoline, workers were urged to carpool when commuting to their jobs. Negative but effective publicity was generated when police handed out summonses to persons who used their vehicles for recreation, such as a drive in the country, to the beach, or to the ballpark. This 1943 government poster equated riding alone to Hitlerism—a tough message to oppose. The second poster was somewhat more positive and pushed conservation. *Advertising Council–National Archives*

fighter, nor did a knowledgeable pilot attempt to "turn into" the Zero, which had a superior turn radius to the P-40. Bomber tactics included the Combat Box, designed by Curtis LeMay, which brought the massed firepower of the .50cal machine guns of ten B-17s to bear against enemy fighters that attacked this formation. However, the box lost its effectiveness when the unit did not maintain tight formation flying discipline. Some US aircraft, such as the Brewster F2A Buffalo fighter, the Douglas TBD-1 Devastator torpedo plane, and the Chance Vought SB2U-3 Vindicator dive bomber, were hopelessly out-classed and withdrawn from combat after a series of calamitous defeats in the first six months of American in-volvement in WWII. Obsolete Army aircraft in the US arsenal at this time

Gasoline rationing was originally decreed to save scarce rubber by reducing the need for civilian tires. However, German U-boats sank such large numbers of tankers along the East Coast in early 1942 that gas shortages became a sud-den reality. As US forces took the offen-sive later in the war, gasoline was used in enormous quantities by the military. Fea-tured here is a Washington, D.C., gas station on July 21, 1942, the day before gasoline rationing went into effect in the nation's capital. *Library of Congress*

In New York City gasoline rationing began on May 15, 1942. As a result of panic buying, many stations ran out of gas before the midnight deadline and closed down until ration coupons went into effect the next day. This station was located on 1st Avenue at 33rd Street, very close to the Manhattan end of the Queens-Midtown Tunnel under the East River. *National Archives*

The Girl Scouts demonstrated their devo-tion to the cause by collecting household fats to be used in the manufacture of munitions. These young ladies at their Painted Post and Corning, New York headquarters have loaded up a "Red Racer Express" with coffee cans full of the important substance. Prominently displayed are Beech-Nut and Premier Coffee containers. *National Archives*

were the Douglas B-18 Bolo bomber, Martin's B-10 bomber, Republic's P-35A fighter, and the Curtiss P-36C. They were used only in last-ditch efforts.

While American soldiers and sailors fought desperate delaying actions in the Pacific early in 1942 and German U-boats sank US merchant ships at will in the Atlantic, the nation's huge industrial potential was gearing up for war production. Civilian car production was halted by government decree in February 1942. The automobile manufacturers led the nation in building tanks, airplanes, trucks, engines, artillery pieces, rifles, and almost anything else needed to further the war effort. There were shortages everywhere, most notably in raw materials. As the war continued and production surged, it became evident that not everyone could be a soldier. Trained personnel were needed to operate the assembly lines. People involved in essential defense work were not allowed to enlist, and if workers did so in defiance of these regulations, the Federal Bureau of Investigation (FBI) came looking for them. Women were recruited from their homes into the factories, and unskilled laborers had the chance to become skilled if they could avoid the draft. Millions of people crossed state lines in search of better salary opportunities. Black Americans were offered access to jobs in the manufacturing sector unheard of a few short years earlier.

Gasoline was rationed, initially along the East Coast but ultimately across the nation. Rubber, tungsten, oil, and tin from the Far East were early casualties as the Dutch and the British lost their colonial empires in Malaya and Java to the victorious Japanese Army and Navy in rapid and decisive military campaigns. In the United States, the civilian population vigorously supported the war effort, holding metal and rubber scrap drives and participating in patriotic rallies and bond drives. Children collected aluminum foil and newspapers for the war effort while housewives saved cooking fats for munitions production.

Another major industry heavily impacted by Japanese successes in the Pacific was the manufacture of rubber. Scrap drives resulted in the reclamation of millions of tires, but in itself this effort was insufficient. The situation was exacerbated by a suspicious fire that had broken out on the night of October 11, 1941, at the Fall River, Massachusetts, plant of the Firestone Rubber Company that destroyed 12 percent of the nation's rubber stockpile. Sabotage was suspected. *National Archives*

During 1942 the government instituted a national rubber campaign that generated prodigious enthusiasm and insignificant results. Citizens made a great effort to collect scrap rubber, but most of the items collected were already made of reconstituted rubber and were useless for the needs of the military. A storekeeper in Rockbridge City examined donated rubber items in this almost whimsical photograph. *National Archives*

Many segments of the population felt the repercussions of the scarcity of rubber, including farmers who needed to increase their output of foodstuffs for the war effort. Manpower was unavailable due to the draft and also the desirability of defense-plant jobs, and aging equipment could not be replaced. These Baltimore County, Maryland, farm boys rode a home-assembled tractor using telephone cable rolls to replace unavailable wheels and tires. *National Archives*

Although Americans exhibited a resolute determination to resist their enemies and win the war, there was a degree of panic as well. Japanese aliens and Japanese-American citizens were forced to leave the "red zone," which consisted of military districts Arizona, California, Oregon, and Washington as a security measure. Because most of them had nowhere to go on such short notice, they were forced into relocation camps in bleak, deserted areas of the West. Those suspected of subversion were not allowed to leave these camps; ultimately 5,600 Japanese-Americans renounced their American citizenship. In contrast, thousands of others enlisted in the US Army. A Japanese submarine shelled an oil refinery near Santa Barbara and enemy agents were landed on both coastlines. There were fears of air attacks on West Coast cities and defense factories by the enemy, resulting in elaborate camouflaging of many manufacturing plants. During the 1930s there had been a concerted effort to create a national system of air markings to assist pilots in locating their destinations from the air. The program was very successful, and resulted in thousands of rooftops and water towers being marked with information concerning locations and compass headings. These air markings were now obliterated within 50mi of both coasts to thwart enemy bombers that might penetrate the country's rather porous defenses. The Warner Brothers Movie Company sound stage in Burbank, which could be mistaken from the air for a defense plant, displayed a 20ft arrow and the cryptic

Rationed Firestone tires fill a rack at a service station in an unnamed American community. Although alleviated to some extent by the manufacture of synthetic rubber, the scarcity of this invaluable raw material remained a critical problem throughout the war. As a result of their Pacific conquests, the Japanese controlled 92 percent of the world's rubber supply by mid-1942. Tires for civilian use were rationed in the United States, and a certificate entitled Replenishment Part of Mileage-Rationing Program was required to buy new tires or recap worn tires. In order to buy a pair of shoes with rubber soles a civilian needed a Rubber Footwear Purchase Certificate. *National Archives*

message, "Lockheed-ThatAway," painted on the roof.

In retrospect, the economic depression that gripped the entire world in the 1930s, coupled with the hubris displayed by the Axis nations, led to a serious and ultimately fatal miscalculation by Germany and Japan of America's industrial potential and the will of the American people. Both Japan and Germany postulated the theory of the master race (each concluding that their race was it), and this clouded their ability to view potential opponents objectively. Their official policies toward the peoples and nations they subjugated were often genocidal. Any attempts to deal with Axis aggression in a restrained or reasoned manner was viewed by these nations as weak and cowardly. The Japanese especially never understood the nonchalant manner in which Americans often reacted to threats and international belligerence, and considered them decadent and unwilling to defend their political and economic positions or possessions. Germany's brilliant military success in overrunning Europe and Japan's rapid advances during the first five months of the Pacific war only served to strengthen these nativist delusions. Some leaders, men like Adm. Isoroku Yamamoto, the architect of Japan's surprise attack on Pearl Harbor, who had lived in the United States, cautioned against "awakening the sleeping giant." However, many of his country's political and military leaders were guilty of the same type of racism they criticized in the Western mentality. It was their belief that the United States would be forced to accept peace on Japan's terms, and boasted that their envoys would sign the treaty document in the White House. Nazi Germany, however, faced with Great Britain's refusal to capitulate and its huge commitments on the Eastern Front against the Soviet Union, did not want a confrontation with America.

President Roosevelt's provocative efforts to assist Britain in 1940 and 1941, as evidenced by the "destroyers for bases" agreement, the oc-

Fear of enemy air attacks was very real on the West Coast after the Japanese attack on Pearl Harbor. These before-and-after views of the Lockheed Aircraft plant in Burbank, California, in early 1942 reflected the country's anxieties. The camou- flage effort was very ingenious and included cloth houses painted in different colors and fabric bushes scattered throughout this bogus community constructed atop large nets suspended from poles. *Lockheed Aeronautical Systems*

cupation of Iceland as a North Atlantic weather station, LendLease, and the use of American destroyers to track German U-boats, were downplayed by Hitler's government. For Germany, war with the United States was both undesirable and unnecessary. The underlying assumption of the Axis leaders was that the war would soon be concluded, and that Germany and Japan would create a new world order. Germany would deal with the Western Hemisphere after it completed its conquest of Great Britain and the Soviet Union.

Another Navy plane of little value against the Japanese was the SB2U-3 Vindicator dive bomber, which had joined the fleet in December 1937. With a top speed of only 182mph, it was outperformed by the Douglas SBD Dauntless dive bomber, which became operational in April 1938. As part of a mixed force, eleven Vindicators were dispatched from Midway Island to attack the approaching enemy fleet in June 1942. Three of them were shot down by the Japanese combat air patrol and no hits were registered on the enemy ships. *National Air & Space Museum*

The Brewster F2A Buffalo fighter was a prime example of an obsolete aircraft still on operational status when war broke out. Powered by a Pratt & Whitney R-1820-40 engine, its top speed was 284mph. This antiquated fighter, while armed with four .50cal machineguns, had a very poor rate of climb and limited maneuverability. Marine fighter squadron VMF-221 on Midway Island was equipped with twenty Buffaloes in June 1942. Ordered to intercept incoming Japanese dive bombers escorted by Zero fighters during the opening stages of the pivotal Battle of Midway, thirteen of the fourteen Buffaloes involved were lost to enemy action, and the lone survivor was declared unserviceable upon its return to Midway. The export version of the Brewster fighter suffered the same misfortune when used by the British and Dutch in the early days of the Pacific War. It was removed from US Navy combat status in mid-1942. *USMC*

This miscalculation resulted in a lack of the industrial planning needed to defeat the United States. Aircraft production in Germany and Japan never came close to that of the United States, without even taking into consideration the added production of Great Britain and the Soviet Union. From 1941 to 1945 Japan produced 69,000 aircraft compared to 298,000 planes manufactured in America. During the same five year period, Germany produced approximately 100,700 aircraft, which were deployed against the Soviets in the East as well as British and Americans in the West. In addition, German and Japanese aircraft factories were priority targets in the strategic bombing campaign initiated by the Allies, and both Axis countries (Italy was out of the war by September 1943) were forced to concentrate on the fighter production needed to protect their homelands from the constant battering of Allied bombing raids. At the same time neither Germany nor Japan had developed the long-range aircraft capable of reaching and then returning from the coastline of America, no less any industrial production centers located inland. German V-1 and V-2 rockets were able to hit Great Britain, but not with a great deal of accuracy nor in sufficient numbers to seriously affect either production or operations. Faced with America's superior manufacturing capability and larger population, it was essential for Germany and Japan to triumph quickly, as they had no chance of winning a war of attrition. This they failed to accomplish.

Another important factor contributed to Allied air superiority as the war progressed. American aircraft manufacturers were able to maximize production without unduly restricting design changes, positions often considered mutually exclusive and unusually difficult to achieve in mass production. Proponents of design freeze (often those responsible for supply) argued that theirs was the only way to achieve mass production and also sustain materiel reserves while providing maintenance on existing equipment. Mass production specialists such as the automobile industry promised manufacturing miracles if design specifics were not changed after a final production schedule was in place. Early in the war the demand for more aircraft inevitably exceeded production capabilities, and there were attempts by the planners to meet these operational needs by minimizing changes in design and thus facilitating production. On the other hand, commanders in the field had to balance the problems created by too many equipment changes against the failure to upgrade systems necessary to improve performance and to defeat the enemy. It was classic quantity versus quality. Fortunately American manufacturers and military specialists were able to adroitly compromise in most situations, providing essential improvements throughout the war to US aircraft while the enemy was forced to accept design freezes in order to come anywhere near their production goals. From the United States' point of view, it was necessary "to improve procedures to minimize changes," and it worked.

Throughout the war years the US aircraft industry incurred production setbacks due to scarcities in raw materials, unavoidable changes in equipment design, and unwarranted government interference in the manufacturing process, as well as labor unrest and shortages of available workers when and where they were needed. However, the airplanes needed to defeat the Axis powers had been mainly designed prior to Pearl Harbor and America's aircraft manufacturers were eager to enter full-scale production. That they successfully overcame the difficulties of the existing marketplace, just as their aircraft successfully confronted the nation's enemies abroad, is a matter of record.

Douglas TBD-1 Devastator torpedo planes took part in the Battle of the Coral Sea in May 1942 without suffering excessive casualties, but during the Battle of Midway the following month, three squadrons of these US Navy aircraft were decimated by enemy fighters and antiaircraft fire from the Japanese fleet. Only four of forty-one TBDs returned to their carriers, a serious loss of experienced naval aviators. When used as a bomber the Devastator carried a crew of three; as a torpedo plane the crew was reduced by one enlisted man. First ordered in 1934, 130 Devastators were delivered to the fleet by 1939. This lumbering plane's top speed was 192mph, and it was taken off combat status in June 1942. *National Archives*

Devastators from Torpedo Squadron Six on board *Enterprise* prepare to engage the enemy in the May 1942 Battle of the Coral Sea. While they scored no torpedo hits on the Japanese fleet, they endured only a few casualties, mainly because of good protective cover provided by US Navy Wildcat fighters. During the confused Battle of Midway a month later, the TBDs attacked without fighter cover and were nearly exterminated by the enemy. *National Archives*

The Bombers

Chapter **II**

I n the years following WWI the seagoing battleship was the "Queen of Battle," and the bomber was initially developed to counter the threat and power of these massive ships. Later the concept of destroying the enemy's ability to wage war by attacking his means of production became the prime moving force behind bomber development. However, aircraft in the 1920s and early 1930s were not big enough nor powerful enough to carry the bomb load and the fuel necessary to attack an enemy fleet with any hope of success, and certainly did not have the range needed to carry the fight to the enemy's homeland. The Barling bomber, built in 1920, had three wings and six engines, but could only

One of 605 B-17Fs built by McDonnell Douglas Aircraft Company. Powered by four 1,200hp Wright R-1820-97 engines, it had a maximum speed of 299mph. Much heavier than its predecessors, it took 25min, 42sec to climb to 20,000ft. The B-17F carried a crew of ten and was armed with eleven .50cal machine guns. *Douglas*

President Franklin D. Roosevelt visited the Boeing Plant in Seattle, Washington, on September 20, 1942. His car, surrounded by Secret Service agents, is stopped under the wing of a B-17 in final production, and another nearly completed aircraft is located behind the president. *FDR Library*

travel at 90mph, and its range was just 300mi.

Boeing Air Transport built the Model 214 twin-engined bomber in 1930, which the USAAC designated the B-9. It was an all-metal monoplane based on Boeing's commercial mail plane. Although it could fly nearly 100mph faster than the current Army bomber, the B-9 had several flaws and was quickly superseded by Glenn Martin's B-10 bomber. Boeing continued to design both civilian and military aircraft. The four-engined XB-15 was underpowered but was followed by the famous B-17, originally conceived as the Model 299. As this bomber moved through its various stages of development, there were forces at work in the military that tried to limit the role of aircraft to support of ground forces, and after three B-17s successfully located the Italian ocean liner *Rex* while still 700mi off the American coast, the USAAC was ordered to restrict its over-ocean flight operations to within 100mi of the coastline. Despite the successes of these four-engined heavy bombers, the USAAC did not order any in fiscal 1939 and 1940. Boeing had only received one follow-up order for thirty-nine B-17Bs, and was losing money due to price quotes based on an assumption of much larger orders. This frustrating saga was repeated in the production of the B-24 Liberator, as well as with other important US bombers being developed in the prewar years.

Ultimately the Army did invest significantly in its bomber force. The best known heavy bombers of WWII were the B-17 and the B-24, and of course the super heavy B-29, which was a very different aircraft from its wartime predecessors. America's

Rows of B-17F forward fuselages with exposed wiring panels fill a section of the main-body assembly line at the Boeing plant. The banners on the wall proclaim "Remember Pearl Harbor" Shop 306 and "Builders of Victory" Shop 301. *Boeing*

The same section of the main-body assembly line, but in this case the fuselages are for the later G models. Note the cutout for the navigator bubble just forward of the cockpit. The cutout behind the cockpit was for the top turret and the rearmost cutout was located above the radio operator's position. Completed fuselages with tails installed are positioned in the rear of this photograph. "Let's Get 'em Flying" is the message on the banner in the far corner of the plant. *Boeing*

The B-17Gs in the foreground are awaiting cockpit installation, while those in front progress step by step toward completion. The aircraft in the center of the picture have the inner wings and engines in place as well as the tail sections. Propellers and outer wing sections are visible on the planes farthest from the camera. *Boeing*

medium, two-engined bombers were led by the B-25 Mitchell and the B-26 Marauder and the less well known A-20 Havoc and the A-26 Intruder.

The medium bomber was used most often in a tactical role; that is, in support of ground or sea forces attempting to take specific objectives. These aircraft became more and more diversified as the war continued. Many continued as level bombers, but other models used massed machine guns, specialized bomb loads, even airborne artillery pieces, to achieve their objectives. Fast and powerful, US medium bombers and attack aircraft relentlessly pounded the enemy, and were a major component of victory over the armies of the Axis.

The long-range bomber achieved prominence, perhaps better described as notoriety, during WWII, and ushered in a new type of warfare directed against the civilians and the economic infrastructure of the belligerents. When war broke out in Europe, Presi-

In October 1943 this industrious female worker at Lockheed's Vega plant in Burbank installed the chin turret containing two .50cal machine guns on a B-17G, working both inside and outside the plane. The guns were operated remotely from the bombardier's position, situated in the plexiglass nose above the turret. The white rectangle on the fuselage was a wartime censorship effort, blanking out any identifiers in a photograph that might aid the enemy. *Lockheed–Phil Kaplan Collection*

Looking at the assembly line from the opposite end clarifies the process. The first B-17G is nearly complete, with outer wings, engines, and propellers installed, while the second aircraft is lacking propellers. The third B-17 in line has not yet acquired wings. Only the tail has been attached to the fuselage. *Boeing*

Two women workers riveting an aluminum panel to the stringers in the nose section of a B-17. One uses the rivet gun while the woman inside the fuselage employs a bucking bar to flatten the end of the rivet, while also securing and tightening it in the process. Long hair was a popular fashion during the war years but could be hazardous if it tangled in a worker's machinery. Thus women usually wore kerchiefs to contain their lovely locks. *Boeing*

these massive flotillas of aircraft thunder forth against the nation's enemies.

B-17 Flying Fortress

The B-17 Flying Fortress was without question the most famous American aircraft to serve in WWII. Army Air Force Lt. Gen. Ira Eaker, who served as the first commander of the Eighth Air Force's Bomber Command in Europe, said, "The B-17, I think, was the best combat airplane ever built. It combined in perfect balance the right engine, the right wing, and the right control surfaces." Stories abound concerning the ability of this heavy bomber to absorb incredible damage from hostile forces and still return to base. Even so, forty percent of the B-17s ever built did not survive the war, and this sad statistic was overwhelmingly the result of enemy action.

Boeing budgeted $275,000 to design and build the initial aircraft, known as the Model 299. It first flew

dent Roosevelt entreated each nation to announce "that its armed forces shall in no event, and under no circumstances, undertake the bombardment from the air of civilian populations of unfortified cities." This philosophy was swept away very quickly by the ferocity of the air war over Poland, France, the Low Countries, Great Britain, and Germany. In the Pacific the Japanese bombed enemy cities at will, and terror bombing became a tactic used by every nation that could put its planes on target over an enemy nation. More than two million tons of destruction rained down on cities and industrial centers during WWII. Millions of people, soldiers and civilians alike, died in these devastating raids, and property damage during WWII is beyond calculation. Warfare took on a new dimension, and the United States became the unquestioned leader in its development, building more than 60,000 bombers for WWII.

At the end of the war, most of the bomber fleets finished up on the scrap heap, and never again would

Balanced precariously atop the fuselage of a B-17, a young female "Rosie the Riveter" does her job. The highly polished aluminum aircraft skin reflects her determination. *Boeing*

in 1935 and a Seattle news reporter exclaimed it was a "flying fortress," due to its array of defensive machine guns. Its fuselage was 69ft long, and the wing spread was 103ft. Four 750hp Pratt & Whitney engines equipped with three-blade props, each 11 1/2ft in diameter, provided propulsion. After setting a speed record of 232mph flying the 2,000mi from Seattle to Wright Field in Dayton, Ohio, for Army flight evaluations, the 299 crashed and burned on a test flight and seriously injured the five men on board, two of whom later died from their injuries. The crew had failed to unlock the plane's elevators while on the ground, and once airborne, the 299 went out of control. Although official investigations attributed the crash to pilot error and absolved the plane of any mechanical deficiencies, the Army's initial order was reduced from an expected sixty-five aircraft to only thirteen Y1B-17s. In its place the military

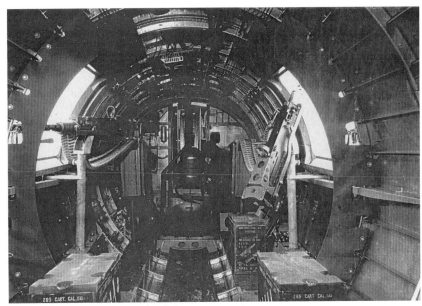

The interior of a B-17 of the 381st Bomb Group in England during the summer of 1943. Most prominent are the single .50cal waist guns, one of the coldest spots in the plane in flight. Gunners wore electrically-heated suits but still suffered a high rate of frostbite due to their exposed positions. Visible forward of the waist guns is an oxygen bottle in place over the top half of the ball turret. *Phil Kaplan Collection*

This pensive worker at Boeing installs a side-firing .50cal machine gun in the nose section of a B-17. The empty links normally held the gun's ammunition. A .50cal bullet is 5 1/2in long. *Boeing*

Four women identified left to right as Lois McFarland, Gladys Roley, Elaine Bradfield, and Goldie Roach installed the Cheyenne tail-gunner compartment in a line of Douglas-built B-17Gs in Long Beach, California. The new rear turret was designed to offer the gunner better visibility as well as increased comfort. Ironically, the compartment actually funneled more cold air into the area, according to gunners who flew both the older F model and the G model. *National Archives*

ordered 133 Douglas B-18s, a two-engined bomber with a top speed of 210mph and a range of 700mi, which was much more conventional at the time. The YB-17s, now upgraded with 850hp Wright R-1820 Cyclone engines, became operational in the late summer of 1937 with the 2nd Bombardment Group under the command of Lt. Col. Robert Olds at Langley Field, Virginia. The group and the YB-17 performed in an exemplary manner, flying more than 1,800,000mi without a significant mishap. In 1938 Lieutenant Colonel Olds set a transcontinental record east to west of 12hr, 50min with a YB-17 and then set a west to east record of 10hr, 46min. The same year six B-17s flew a Goodwill Tour to Buenos Aires, Argentina, a round trip of 12,000mi with no serious difficulties. In 1939 a B-17B set a Seattle–New York record for bomber aircraft of 9hr, 14min, with an average speed of 265mph.

Budget restrictions continued to limit the B-17 program and many War Department officials were not interested in hearing Boeing's side of the story. In addition, turf battles continued between the Army and the Navy and also between advocates of air power and ground forces. However, the USAAC ordered thirty-eight of the improved B-17Cs, which used 1,200hp turbo-supercharged Wright Cyclone engines. The B-17C had a top speed of 323mph at 25,000ft.

With the implementation of LendLease, twenty B-17Cs were transferred to the Royal Air Force (RAF). Despite being officially cautioned by the US military to only use these aircraft as trainers and wait for upgraded B-17s for combat operations, the British employed them in daylight raids over the Continent. In reality, the Americans were extremely interested in observing the B-17's performance under combat conditions against seasoned German aviators. The RAF experienced engine problems, frozen guns and instruments, poor bombing accuracy, and the distinct inability of the B-17s to defend themselves against enemy fighters. After three months of oper-

First Lieutenant Owen G. Cooper, a bombardier in the Eighth Air Force from Baltimore, Maryland, sits at his position in the nose of a B-17G, his top secret Norden bombsight in place in front of him. Note the .50cal machine gun protruding from the side of the aircraft and the chin turret below Cooper. *USAF*

To reduce its vulnerability to head-on attacks by enemy fighters, the B-17G incorporated four .50cal machine guns in its nose, two in the chin turret, and one on each side of the bombardier's compartment. The nose guns are very visible in this April 1944 roll-out of B-17Gs at Boeing's Plant Two in Seattle. Two more .50s could join in from either the top turret or the belly turret, depending on the enemy's angle of attack. *Boeing*

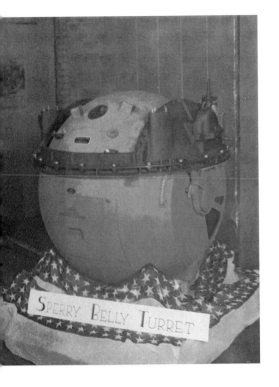

This Sperry ball, or belly, turret was built by Maytag. The turret, weighing 850lb and powered by an electro-hydraulic system, was rotatable through 360deg at a rate of 45deg per second. The turret was armor-plated and carried twin .50cal machine guns. The turret also rotated 90deg vertically, which allowed the gunner access from the fuselage via the hatch door, located in this photograph just below the dark-colored mounting ring. If the unit was damaged, it could be manually cranked into position permitting the gunner to escape back into the aircraft. However, this took time and when a B-17 was going down, it was usually not possible to free the gunner if the mechanism was jammed. In addition, very few gunners could fit their parachutes into the ball turret with them because the diameter of the turret was only 44in, leaving them little choice even if the hatch could open to the outside air. Many a ball-turret gunner fell to his death trapped in his turret. *Maytag Archives*

ations, the twelve surviving C models, now called "Flying Targets" by the British, were turned over to Coastal Command for scouting and reconnaissance duty.

Improved armor plating for crew protection and the addition of self-sealing gas tanks were incorporated into the B-17D, of which forty-two were ordered by the USAAC. However, the B-17D was at best an interim aircraft, soon replaced by the B-17E, an entirely new version of Boeing's bomber. The large dorsal tail fin and a 10ft addition to the elevators introduced on the B-17E vastly improved the Flying Fortress's stability, resulting in more accurate high-altitude bombing. A 6ft addition to the fuselage incorporated a rear gunner's position with twin .50cal machine guns. Just aft of the flight deck was installed a top turret position, also with twin .50cal ma-

Roll-out of the 5,000th B-17 built by Boeing, named *5 Grand*. Employees very proudly painted their names all over the exterior of the G model. By war's end Boeing had built 6,981 (54.8 percent of the total) B-17s and employed 44,700 workers, 34,000 in Seattle and another 8,000 in nearby Renton, Washington. Others were scattered around the state in sub-assembly plants. *Boeing*

The commemorative signings went on throughout the assembly process. This aircraft suffered damage in combat, returned to the States and was scrapped for use in the production of Boeing's B-29 Superfortress. *Boeing*

Four ladies involved in the production of the 5,000th B-17 pose in front of *5 Grand* on the flight line in Seattle. The woman at right wears an inspector's armband. The Boeing work force grew from 641 workers in 1935 to more than 44,000 in 1945. *Boeing*

chine guns. Replacing the remote belly turret with a crew-operated Sperry ball turret improved the aircraft's defensive firepower, and other .50s were added in the nose and in the radio compartment. The B-17E flew at 318mph empty and was a great improvement over the C and D models. In August 1942 Coastal Command took delivery of forty-two B-17Es, and they were also in action in the early days of the Pacific war. A total of 512 were ordered by the War Department, necessitating new methods of mass production by Boeing.

It also resulted in the creation of a construction combine for the B-17F between Boeing (2,300), Douglas Aircraft Company (605), and Lockheed's Vega Aircraft Company subsidiary (500) to meet the total order of 3,405 further-improved B-17Fs. The landing gear was reinforced, additional fuel tanks were installed in the wings, and improved propeller blades were intro-

McDonnell Douglas Aircraft employees in Long Beach, California, also celebrated a special B-17G, their 1,000th. Douglas built 3,000 B-17F and G models (23.56 percent of the total) *Douglas*

The B-17G Flying Fortress, of which 8,680 were manufactured during WWII, was the backbone of the strategic bombing campaign against "Festung Europa." On a short-range mission it could carry 17,600lb of bombs, but normally the load was 5,000–8,000lb. *Boeing*

A close-up of the Hamilton Standard Hydromatic variable-pitch propeller used on all B-17s. The ship is the *Swoose Goose,* a B-17G back in the States to participate in War Bond drives after surviving a combat tour over Europe. *Hamilton Standard Division of United Technologies Corporation*

duced that allowed the B-17F to operate at 37,500ft, about 1,500ft higher than an E model. Even the F model, however, was vulnerable to head-on attacks by enemy fighters. In 1942 and 1943 the Allies did not possess any fighter aircraft capable of long-range escort duty, so the bomber formations had to operate against the enemy without assistance. Vega converted fourteen B-17Fs into "destroyer escorts," designated the B-40, which were equipped with fourteen .50cal machine guns and double the normal ammunition allotment. A "chin turret" was added below the plexiglass bombardier's compartment in the nose of the aircraft which carried twin .50cal machine guns. The experiment was not considered successful. After releasing their bombs, the empty bombers were much faster than the slower escort B-40s (which were still burdened with all the extra guns and ammunition and were further slowed by the aerodynamic drag of the extra turrets) and soon left them behind to face the

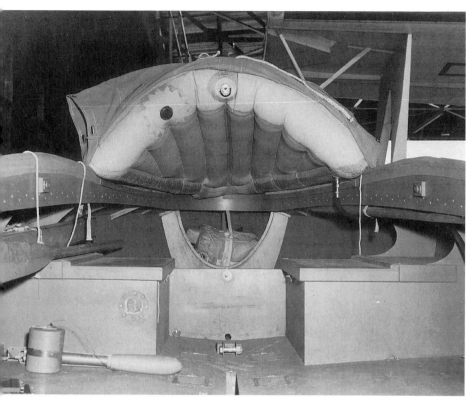

Converted to air-rescue duty was this B-17H, which carried a lifeboat known as the "Flying Dutchman" that could be dropped to survivors in the ocean. Outfitted with survival equipment, food, and water, it was dropped on three parachutes, had a self-righting chamber in case it landed upside-down in the water, and could be sailed to safe shores. *National Archives*

Boeing's Plant Two in Seattle, Washington, still protected by camouflage in June 1945. However, other camouflage, including painted runways, had been removed as the threat of enemy attack faded. *Boeing*

enemy alone as they returned to base.

However, the B-40's chin turret was a major design improvement that was added to the B-17G, of which 8,680 were built. Boeing Aircraft manufactured 4,035 Gs, while Douglas was responsible for 2,395, and Vega built 2,250 of them. Although the additional firepower in the nose of the B-17G was a powerful and welcome deterrent to enemy fighter attacks, some crews felt that it created additional drag leading to a reduction in speed, which was very ominous and possibly fatal if a plane lost an engine over enemy territory or could not operate at full power.

The B-17G was essentially the final version of this legendary heavy bomber. A total of 12,761 B-17s of all models were manufactured. It was the major heavy bomber used in the European Theater of Operations, and in August 1944 there were thirty-three B-17 bomb groups operating 4,574 aircraft around the world.

B-24 Liberator

According to *The Official World War II Guide to the Army Air Forces*, published in 1944, to build one four-engined bomber required "enough aluminum for 55,000 coffee percolators; enough alloy steel to make 6,800 electric irons; enough steel for 160 washing machines; enough rubber to recap 800 automobile tires; enough copper for 550 radio re-

The *Screamin Eagle*, a B-17G of the 385th Bomb Group, Eighth Air Force, dropping containers of incendiary bombs on a German troop concentration in Occupied France, 1944. The smoke contrails indicate the path of marker bombs used to pinpoint the target for the massed B-17s seeking the assigned target. *Jim Dacey Collection*

The B-24E. Consolidated Vultee Corporation built 144 of them at its Fort Worth, Texas, plant, Douglas Aircraft manufactured ninety-four at its Tulsa, Oklahoma, plant, and Ford produced 490 E models at its Willow Run plant near Detroit, Michigan. *Convair–Lockheed Fort Worth Company*

The B-24H was the first of the series to incorporate the electrically operated Emerson nose turret in assembly-line manufacture. Consolidated Vultee produced 738 H models and Douglas contributed another 582. However, Willow Run manufactured 1,780 B-24H aircraft. *Convair–Lockheed Fort Worth Company*

The B-24Es pictured here were the first models of the famous bomber built by the Ford Motor Company at its Willow Run plant. Two workers are finishing installation of the twin .50cal machine guns in the top turret. These aircraft are at the end of the assembly line, only needing propellers fitted to engines before roll-out. At this point the Willow Run B-24s are towed through the line on their own landing gear. *FDR Library*

A bicycle stands in front of the starboard wing of this B-24D nearing completion at Consolidated's Fort Worth, Texas, plant. The bike was almost certainly used for transportation within the facility. Supervisory personnel could easily travel several miles a day overseeing production on the assembly line. In this photo two men working on the tail section are dwarfed by the plane's rudder. By late 1943, there were 30,547 employees at this aircraft factory, mainly recruited from the two surrounding counties, the combined population of which was only 225,000 persons. *Convair–Lockheed Fort Worth Company*

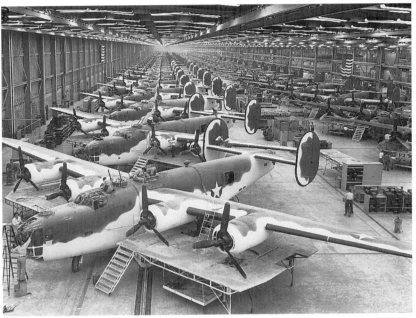

The center wing section of a Willow Run B-24. The wing of a B-24 incorporated fifty-seven different-sized aluminum bulkhead panels, and 85 percent of the aircraft was manufactured from aluminum. Ford engineers viewed the center wing section as the keystone and strongest segment of the aircraft's construction, incorporating the cockpit, bombardier's compartment, landing gear, and basic wing section, which ultimately included the four massive engines. As this heart of the B-24 moved down the assembly line, it was fitted with the nose section, aft fuselage, engines, tail, and outer wings. *Yankee Air Force Museum*

Another group of B-24s at Fort Worth in exactly the same position on the factory floor as those in the previous photograph. However, these are PB4Y-1s as indicated by their US Navy camouflage paint scheme. The white underbelly allegedly made it more difficult for enemy ships and submarines to distinguish these patrol aircraft against a daylight sky background. *Steve Pace Collection*

A B-24 fuselage, with its landing gear already installed and featuring a gaping bomb bay, moves along the overhead monorail at Consolidated's San Diego plant. Bomb-bay doors retracted internally up the sides of the B-24, avoiding the drag created by B-17 bomb-bay doors, which opened out into the slipstream. The dappled sunlight on the nearly finished B-24 in the background indicates that Consolidated was still finishing construction out-of-doors in sunny California, a practice that was appalling to executives at Ford. Consolidated modified this policy later in the war as more of Ford's mass production techniques proved not only profitable but also efficient. *National Archives*

ceivers." Considering that 18,480 B-24 heavy bombers were built before and during WWII, one can appreciate the tremendous amount of raw materials needed to satisfy the demands of aircraft production during the war.

While not as popular with the general public as the B-17 Flying Fortress, the distinctive double tail, four engines, and high wing of the B-24 Liberator made it an easily recognizable aircraft. The B-24 was conceived in 1939 when the USAAC asked Consolidated Aircraft Corporation to design a bomber that was an improvement over the B-17, which at the time was setting and breaking long-range aviation records. The military sought an aircraft that could fly faster than 300mph for more than 3,000mi at an altitude of 35,000ft. The XB-24 first flew twelve months later, in December 1939, resulting in an USAAC order for forty-three planes.

In 1940 the British, who christened the B-24 the Liberator, ordered

A B-24 nose cone assembly at Willow Run. When plexiglass was soaked in solution at 256deg Fahrenheit, it could be easily shaped into patterns, molded, and cut for later aircraft installation. After forming it was dipped in a removable coating solution to prevent scratching during factory handling. *Yankee Air Force Museum*

Female workers at Consolidated's Fort Worth, Texas, plant prepare the stringers in a B-24 fuselage for the plane's aluminum skin. Some shaped stringers were pre-drilled with as many as 312 holes in one function. When the Fort Worth plant opened in the spring of 1942, 11,577 women were on the payroll. *Convair–Lockheed Fort Worth Company*

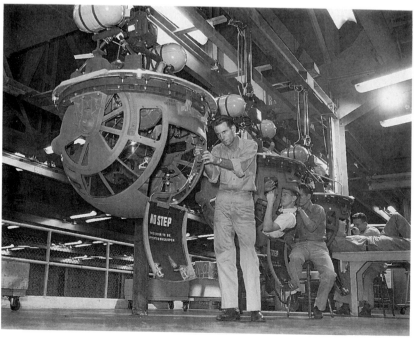

The B-24 ball turret retracted into the fuselage during takeoff and landing. When in combat, it was extremely difficult to fit a parachute into the turret with the gunner. Thus, he had to position the turret so the hatch opened into the fuselage and then climb back inside the aircraft to retrieve his parachute before exiting a mortally wounded plane. While it must have been a strange feeling being suspended beneath the bomber in a glass bowl, the ball turret gunner was actually safer than most of his fellow crewmen from hostile attacking aircraft. Most enemy fighter pilots preferred to attack bombers head-on, where there was less armor and firepower or from above to use their diving speed. *Convair–Lockheed Fort Worth Company*

An overhead crane is operated by a woman employee at Willow Run. Henry Ford was very reluctant to hire women for the assembly line, but was forced to acquiesce due to a severe shortage of male applicants. Due to job opportunities elsewhere, Ford had difficulty with work force turnover throughout the war, and never achieved its employment goals at Willow Run. Southern California was especially attractive to nomadic aircraft workers. *Yankee Air Force Museum*

B-24Es await wing tips, propellers, and installation of the myriad tubes and wires within the wings of the plane. As part of the Ford manufacturing system, clusters incorporating 1,700 different aluminum tubes in twelve control systems were as-sembled prior to installation in the average B-24. These aircraft have just moved off the double production line onto the single line at Willow Run, indicating that they are very close to completion. *National Archives*

Wheels for the B-24 weighed 250lb each. In this image dwarves are seen clambering over the massive tires. According to a Ford Motor Company film made after the war, dwarves climbed into the wing of the B-24 to fasten the outer wing tip to the center wing, which housed the aircraft engines. The film does not mention how the dwarves then extricated themselves from the completed wing! *Yankee Air Force Museum*

Nine-cylinder, air-cooled, 1,200hp, Pratt & Whitney Twin Wasp R-1830 engines await installation on B-24s at an unidentified defense plant. *National Archives*

The outboard engine is installed in the starboard wing of a Willow Run B-24, April 20, 1943. With Ford assembly-line techniques, it only took 15min to install an engine. Each was held in place by four bolts. There were very fundamental B-24 production differences between Consolidated Aircraft and the Ford Motor Company, with the latter viewing traditional aircraft construction by highly skilled workmen as antiquated. Ford used its established automotive assembly-line procedures using semi-skilled employees, while Consolidated essentially built most of the aircraft where they stood on the factory floor. *Yankee Air Force Museum*

164 B-24As and also took over a French order for an additional 120 of the bombers when France was defeated by Germany in June of that year. The new planes were armed with four 20mm cannons and were mainly used as over-water patrol craft. The B-24A was first flown by US personnel in June 1941, followed by the B model with turbosupercharged engines, which increased its speed to 310mph. Self-sealing fuel tanks were also added to the B-24B. Further improvements included an upper gun turret and a tail turret to the C model, of which only nine were built. Major production commenced when Consolidated built 2,718 B-24Ds, and ten more were built by Douglas Aircraft. This model carried ten machine guns for defense, a vast improvement over earlier B-24s. The D model could carry 12,800lb of bombs

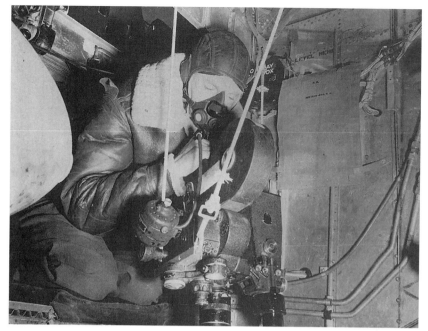

A combat photographer focuses on the enemy below with a USAAF motion picture camera, which is suspended from the B-24's ceiling by three rubber shock cords to provide flexibility and to reduce vibration while filming. Not visible is a shock cord around the photographer's waist securing him to the aircraft as he leans over an open bomb bay. *National Archives*

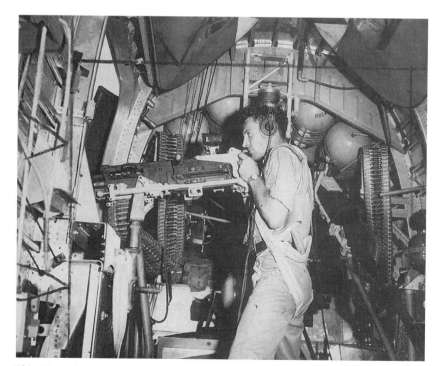

This US Marine Corps combat photographer was interrupted in May 1944 by enemy aircraft as he photographed beach installations on a Japanese-held island in the Southwest Pacific for an upcoming invasion. He is manning a .50cal machine gun positioned in the waist of a B-24 aircraft, most likely a Navy PB4Y-1. Above his head are crew oxygen tanks for use above the altitude of 10,000ft. *National Archives*

Three female employees take shelter in an improvised air-raid shelter at Willow Run on March 4, 1943. It would seem the possibility of enemy aircraft attacking an aircraft plant as far inland as Detroit was rather remote, but apparently the Ford Motor Company was taking precautions anyway. Many women workers like these three became spot welders, a method incorporated pressure with an electrical charge. A worker could perform 300 spot welds a minute. This method replaced 15,000 regular rivets per plane. *Yankee Air Force Museum*

The 5,000th B-24 Liberator built at Ford's Willow Run plant tests its forward firing .50cal machine guns at the facility's gun butt on June 29, 1944. The safety sign above the butt cautions that the aircraft and the guns "must be fixed in immovable position before firing." *Yankee Air Force Museum*

Management representatives supervise B-24 production at the Willow Run plant on January 27, 1943. Both men wear security badges on their jacket breast pockets. Note the siren mounted on the handlebars to warn pedestrian traffic of the scooter's presence. At peak production there were 100 B-24s on the Willow Run assembly line at one time, with an aircraft completed every 55min. *Yankee Air Force Museum*

A partially completed B-24 is broken down by section for trailer transport to another facility for final assembly, December 13, 1943. Ford was forced to subcontract some work to other aircraft manufacturers because it could not fulfill its employee requirement at Willow Run. When completed, each Liberator contained 400,000 rivets in thirteen varieties and 400 different sizes. *Yankee Air Force Museum*

A B-24 fuselage is lowered into a US Army truck on July 8, 1942, at the Willow Run plant for transfer to another location. Ford broke down B-24 production into six sections: center wing, nose, aft fuselage, engines, tail, and outer wings. Tail sections were often manufactured at Ford's Rouge car production plant in Detroit. These immense cargo trucks were enshrouded in tarpaulins to hide the shipment from curious civilians eyes as well as potential enemy agents. *Yankee Air Force Museum*

Shiny, new, recently completed B-24s are parked in rows at the airport at Willow Run, new Detroit International Airport, in March 1944 as they await flight-testing and ultimately fly away to training and combat destinations for the US Army and Navy. *Yankee Air Force Museum*

The 5,000th B-24 manufactured by Consolidated Vultee Aircraft Corporation, covered with the signatures of the employees who built the ship. There were 18,482 B-24s built before and during WWII, making it the most prolific aircraft of WWII. *Convair–Lockheed Fort Worth Company*

and incorporated a ball turret for the first time. It entered combat over Europe in October 1942. Some B-24Ds were converted into a transport known as the C-87, and the US Navy designated its Ds as the PB4Y-1.

The Ford Motor Company entered B-24 production with the 480 E models, and an additional 311 of this model were manufactured by Douglas and Consolidated. North American Aviation built 340 B-24Gs at its Dallas, Texas, plant, many without the ball turret. The F model was experimental with limited production. Its thermal de-icing system, which used hot air ducts along the leading wing edges, was included in the next model of consequence, the B-24J. Ford built 1,587 Js, and Consolidated manufactured 4,350 more. North American built 536 B-24Js, while Douglas Aircraft accounted for an additional 205 aircraft. More Js, 6,678 of them, were manufactured than any other B-24 model. It stood 17ft, 11in high, was 67ft, 2in long and had a 110ft wingspan. The J model cruised at 215mph with a top speed of 290mph. Its ceiling was 28,000ft with a gross weight of

What might be termed the country's largest bedroom was this dormitory for US fliers at Willow Run Airport. Many mattresses are folded in half, indicating vacant cots. However, the full uniform racks scattered about the facility indicate significant occupancy. The airman in the foreground is waving at the camera as his buddy nonchalantly observes this new activity in an obviously boring setting. *National Archives*

The last Ford-built B-24 rolls out of the Willow Run factory on June 28, 1945, headed for the "gas house" before testing and eventual fly-away. The war in Europe was over, and B-29s were the bomber of choice in the continuing strategic bombing campaign against Japan. Ford produced 8,685 Liberators at its famous facility, the largest aircraft factory in the country. One of the most noticeable components on all B-24s was the high Davis wing, which contributed significantly to fuel conservation. It also made the aircraft more difficult to safely "ditch" in the ocean, something B-24 crews in the Pacific knew very well. *Yankee Air Force Museum*

A veteran B-24D of the 450th Bombardment Group, Fifteenth Air Force, the *Swamp Rat*, stationed at Manduria, Italy, in 1944. Each miniature bomb painted on the fuselage represents a completed mission against the enemy. *William "Dick" Cubbins*

Returning from a mission over Eastern Europe, B-24s of the 450th Bombardment Group, known as the "Cottontails," approach their base at Maduria, Italy, for a "buzz job." *William "Dick" Cubbins*

65,000lb. Normal bomb load was 8,800lb and it carried ten .50cal machine guns for defense.

The B-24H, however, was the first model to incorporate the electrically-operated Emerson nose turrets, which were designed by Consolidated and manufactured by both Emerson and Motor Products, on the production line. Consolidated built 738, Ford built 1,780, and Douglas built another 582 H models. The production of 1,500 L models, some of which carried radar, was overshadowed by the features of the newer B-24M. Its replacement tail turret was the last major modification to the B-24, and offered a greater field of fire than previous B-24 tail turrets while also weighing 200lb less than earlier turrets. Consolidated's San Diego plant produced 916 B-24Ms and Ford built 1,677, for a total of 2,593.

The Navy took delivery of 739 single-tailed Liberators designated the PB4Y-2 Privateer for use as patrol bombers, mainly in the Pacific. They were 7ft longer than earlier B-24s and incorporated two Martin top turrets as well as two twin .50cal Erco waist blisters. The USAAF only received nine of these aircraft, known as the B-24N, before the contract was canceled.

Consolidated was sold in 1941 to a holding company that owned The Vultee Aircraft company, resulting in the new name Consolidated Vultee. It had won the initial B-24 contract and remained a major manufacturer of the plane throughout the war. However, the Ford Motor Company introduced automobile-assembly-line techniques to B-24 manufacture at its new Willow Run plant. The company's production chief, Charles E. Sorensen (known as "Cast Iron Charlie" due to his penchant for using castings rather than forgings, which were more expensive), was the father of this L-shaped building. The assembly line was a mile long and a quarter of a mile wide. More than 1,600 precision machines and presses dominated the line, which also required 7,500 manufacturing jigs and 15,000 dies.

A total of 1,619 B-25Cs were built at the Inglewood, California, main plant of North American Aviation. These aircraft await their outboard wings and propellers, but otherwise appear to be complete. The C model was modified to carry an aerial torpedo and was equipped with four external bomb racks. *Rockwell International*

Due to the dry, mild weather in Southern California, final assembly of many aircraft was completed out-of-doors. The last three B-25s in the column to the left in the picture await the painting of the national insignia on their wing tips. *Steve Pace Collection*

There were problems, however, as the plant was more than 30mi from Detroit, where fifty percent of its work force lived. Even though the federal government built a 5,000-bed dormitory, provided 2,000 trailers, and 2,500 temporary family units called Willow Village, Ford never was able to meet its estimated requirement of 58,000 workers. In fact, at the end of 1943 Willow Run peaked at 42,331 employees and faced monthly turnovers that reached fifty percent. Its seventeen percent absentee rate was the highest in the country. With tire, gas, and automobile shortages, many workers had to ride busses that cost seventy cents a day. It was easier to work elsewhere, and plants in every section of the country were hungry for workers.

But even with the problems it faced, Willow Run personified the

North American workers prepare the Wright R-2600 engines for installation in B-25s, which are themselves assembled just behind the half-wall to the left of the photograph. Note the tool box and coat racks built into the wall. Each supercharged Cyclone engine developed 1,700hp from fourteen cylinders. *Steve Pace Collection*

defense production miracles occurring throughout the United States. It was the largest aircraft plant ever built, using 100,000 yards of poured concrete, 38,000 tons of structural steel, and 10 million bricks. Willow Run was both a manufacturing and assembly plant, surrounded by 280 acres of runways and taxiways. Ford spent $500,000 to build a training school adjacent to the plant and 50,000 employees took courses in the intricacies of aircraft manufacturing there during the war. The plant's storage warehouse encompassed eleven acres and stocked 785 different items. The B-24 required 1,225,000 parts as compared to an individual automobile requirement of 15,000 parts. At its peak the factory produced a bomber every 55min. By war's end Willow Run had constructed 8,685 B-24 Liberator bombers. It was quite a place.

B-25 Mitchell

The B-25 Mitchell medium bomber was a remarkably versatile aircraft that served throughout WWII in a variety of roles. B-25Bs were flown off the US aircraft carrier *Hornet* in the first attack against the Japanese homeland in April 1942. This daring raid was led by Lt. Col. Jimmy Doolittle and thoroughly shocked the Japanese, who considered themselves and their Emperor invulnerable to attack after their string of victories in the five months following the outbreak of war in the Pacific. It also boosted the morale of American soldiers and civilians everywhere to know that their country was striking back at the enemy in dramatic fashion. The B-25 was picked for this mission due to its ability to take off within 500ft,

An R-2600 engine being swung into place on the starboard wing of a B-25J. The original B-25 prototype, called the NA-40-1, was equipped with Pratt & Whitney Twin Wasp radial engines that generated 1,100hp each. In order to increase the maximum speed of the B-25, North American switched to the Wright Cyclone engine. Quite visible on the aircraft's fuselage are two pods placed one above the other, each of which will house a fixed, .50cal machine gun. There were two more of these on the port side of the J model. *Rockwell International*

The tail-gunner position on the B-25 was added when the mid-fuselage top turret, which had protected the aircraft's rear, was relocated just behind the cockpit to add to the forward firepower on later models. Initially there was only an observation bubble on the tail of the B-25. *Rockwell International*

A close-up of the tail bubble on an early model B-25 featuring a USAAF combat photographer plying his trade. Cameramen flew a vast array of missions and were expected to capture important information on film regarding attacking aircraft, enemy installations, bombing results, and conditions over the target, as well as good public-relations photographs. It was not an enviable position to be assigned to an aircraft going into combat with no protection except your camera. *National Archives*

rather vital when departing from a carrier deck, and fly 2,000mi with a 2,000lb bomb load. In contrast, the B-26 Marauder needed too much runway, and the B-18 could not haul the fuel and bombs required. Another important consideration was the B-25's 67ft, 7in wingspan, which allowed it to clear the carrier's "island" superstructure on its takeoff roll. The Douglas B-23 Dragon was eliminated from consideration for the Doolittle raid because its wingspan was too great for a carrier deck takeoff. All sixteen of the B-25s successfully flew off the carrier and attacked several Japanese cities, including Tokyo. It was the beginning of a legend.

Manufactured by North American Aviation and powered by two 14-cylinder Wright R-2600 radial engines that generated 1,700hp each, the B-25 normally carried a crew of five and cruised at 230mph, with a top speed of 275mph. Its Hamilton Standard propellers had a 12ft, 7in diameter. The B-25 was flown during the war by the Aus-

This model B-25J retained the traditional bombardier's compartment in the nose, and its not-yet-installed top turret is still positioned far back on the fuselage. However, the rear gun turret has been added as well as side windows for waist guns. The aircraft are mounted on free-moving racks at the Kansas City plant. A row of engine nacelles await installation. *Rockwell International*

Another view of B-25Js on final assembly at North American's Kansas City plant. The aircraft are on trolleys that move forward on tracks in the floor of the plant, maintaining the landing gear in a suspended state above the floor. These Js retained the regular bombardier's compartment in the nose but mounted thirteen .50cal machine guns for extra firepower. The cutout for the top turret, which has been moved forward to just behind the cockpit, and the propellers have not yet been installed. The banner on the plant's back wall says "Make 45 The Victory Drive." *Rockwell International*

tralians, British, Chinese, Dutch, and the Soviets, as well as the US Army, Navy, and Marines. North American's initial contract was awarded in September 1939 and the first aircraft flew eleven months later in August 1940. It had required 8,500 original drawings and 195,000 engineering man-hours. Using a system of forty-eight sub-assembly structures, North American built a total of 9,816 B-25s at its plants in Kansas and California.

Although the B-25 regularly carried out its mission as a medium bomber, later modifications developed an entirely different plane that was very successful in an attack role against enemy ships and ground installations, mainly in the Pacific campaigns. One version of the B-25J mounted eight .50cal machine guns in place of the bombardier's nose compartment, giving the ship fourteen forward firing .50cal machine guns. This arrangement included four fixed firing guns below the cockpit and two additional in the top turret. The B-25G and H models

The bombardier's position in the nose of the B-25J has been replaced by an all-metal nose cone containing eight .50cal machine guns, giving the J model fourteen .50cal machine guns pointing forward, with 500 rounds per gun. Other major modifications include the repositioning of the top turret in order to fire forward and the addition of waist-gunner positions. The B-25J gained a fearsome reputation in the Pacific war, flying low and blasting targets of opportunity on both land and sea. *Rockwell International*

A B-25 suspended above the Inglewood plant floor from an overhead hoist. This appears to be a D model as it is fitted for a single machine gun to fire through the plexiglass nose and has no pods on the fuselage for fixed machine guns. It awaits leading wing edges, landing gear, outboard wing tips, and engine power plants. There was much diversity within the plants of aviation manufacturers regarding the systems best used for mass production. *Rockwell International*

incorporated a 75mm cannon in the nose. In films of this aircraft in combat it appeared to hesitate, nearly stopping in flight, when the cannon was fired. By war's end the latest B-25 models could carry 2,500lb of bombs at 330mph. In the years following WWII the B-25 was used as a two-engined trainer by the Air Force.

B-26 Marauder

Designed and built by the Martin Aircraft Company in Maryland, the short-winged B-26 medium bomber was known to many in the USAAF as the "Baltimore Whore," the result of having no visible means of support. Rumors abounded concerning its negative flying characteristics and led to other such uncomplimentary descriptions as "The Flying Coffin" and "The Widow Maker." "One a Day in Tampa Bay" was another dubious accolade used in describing the B-26 due to the unusually high number of training accidents that occurred early in its career at MacDill Field in Tampa, Florida. Marauder is much more descriptive

The 30,000th plane built by North American Aviation during WWII, a B-25J. The aircraft awaits its top turret, forward-firing machine guns, and propellers. North American also manufactured the AT-6 and SNJ trainer and the famous P-51 Mustang fighter, making it the largest manufacturer of US aircraft during the war years. *Rockwell International*

B-25Hs await installation of their 75mm cannons and propellers in final installation at Inglewood. The 75mm gun was 9ft, 6in long and weighed 900lb. Standard ammunition load for the cannon was twenty-one rounds, which weighed 15lb each. *Rockwell International*

Roll-out of a B-25H minus its outboard wings, top turret, and propellers. The dark circle visible on the lower half of the nose is the tunnel for the 75mm gun. When filmed in combat firing the cannon, the B-25H seemed to stop in midair, the result of the gun's recoil. *Rockwell International*

The exterior of the North American Aviation plant in Kansas City, Kansas. It's a sure bet that all the cars in the photograph were manufactured prior to February 1942, when all civilian automobile production ceased by government decree. *Rockwell International*

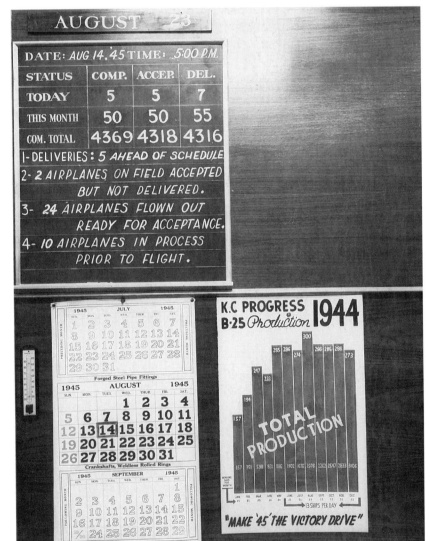

The tally board at North American's Kansas City plant on the last day of the war in the Pacific. The factory was completing five aircraft a day and was ahead of schedule for deliveries. From June to December 1944 the plant in Kansas City produced thirteen B-25s per day. *Rockwell International*

of the B-26, as it certainly did just that in Pacific and European skies during WWII.

In 1939 the USAAC asked aircraft manufacturers to submit designs for a twin-engined medium bomber able to fly 3,000mi carrying a 4,000lb bomb load at 300mph with a ceiling of 20,000 to 30,000ft, specifications rather revolutionary for the time. Peyton Magruder of the Glenn L. Martin Company took on the project and won the contract with 813.6 points out of 1,000 on the government scoring system. The agreement called for 201 aircraft at a cost of $15.8 million. The US government underwrote the cost of a new manufacturing facility at Middle River Airport in Maryland, and the Martin team borrowed workers and equipment from other projects to get started. The production process involved thirty-two major subassemblies which evolved from 650 minor subassemblies. These in turn were constructed from 30,000 parts, exclusive of rivets, bolts, and other fasteners.

In November 1940, seventeen months after receiving the contract, Martin Aircraft submitted the first B-26A for flight acceptance tests. The manufacturer had not built a prototype because of time restraints. Thus the first flight was by the first aircraft off the assembly line. Three months later production models of the B-26 were in the field. Aptly the B-26A had some unusual flying characteristics. Its original wingspan was 65ft, the

Three Martin B-26 Marauders flying in formation somewhere over America. The B-26 incorporated a high wing, that was also short, resulting in the need for high-speed takeoffs and landings, which initially caused many accidents. The B-26 also featured an unusual 8deg dihedral of the horizontal stabilizer, noticeable in this photograph. For some reason the center aircraft does not feature the upper gun turret, visible on the other two planes. It also appears to be unpainted except for the dark-colored registration numbers, while the others are painted in camouflage with light-colored numbers. *Martin Marietta*

A row of B-26 nose sections await the next step in the production process at Martin's Middle River plant. In the second row the nose sections are reversed, pointing in the opposite direction. The hatches above the cockpit open to the side rather than front to back, allowing the pilots to exit the plane against the force of the slipstream in a flight emergency. *Martin Marietta*

Completed B-26 fuselages awaiting wings, tails, and horizontal stabilizers. The circular cutout near the aircraft tail will house the famous Martin gun turret, which was also used on several other aircraft types. Installed 10ft tails on aircraft in the background of this photograph are very prominent, and were one of the B-26's most distinct components. The aircraft move along the assembly line on wheeled dollies, which included an access platform and steps. Empty dollies are visible in the foreground. *Martin Marietta*

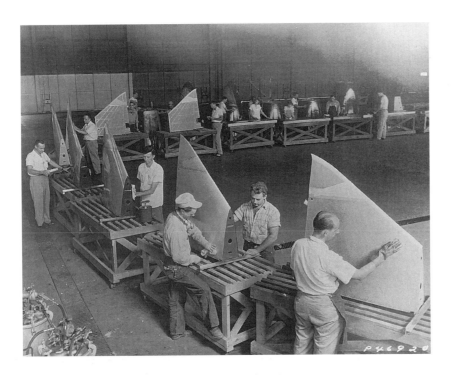

B-26 stabilizer components on a Martin subassembly line. The workers appear to be polishing the sections. In the background, other employees are performing the same task on aircraft nose sections. Glenn Martin was well-known for his benevolence toward employees in need, paying for medical operations and providing interest-free loans for workers with legitimate financial difficulties. The company founder underwrote the development of Aero Acres, less than a mile from the main plant, where Martin employees could purchase two and three bedroom homes for less than $1,500 on streets named Aileron, Fuselage, and Rudder. *Martin Marietta*

A Martin Aircraft plant worker makes adjustments to a B-26's Pratt & Whitney R-2800 radial engine in late 1944. Each engine generated 2,000hp, giving the Marauder a top speed of 285mph with 4,000lb of bombs. In the background, employees are working at the waist window, which housed a .50cal machine gun. The B-26 was the first US bomber to use self-sealing gas tanks known as Mareng Cells. The name is a contraction of the Martin engineers who invented them. *Martin Marietta*

fuselage measured 58 1/2ft and the vertical tail was 10ft high. Powered by two Pratt & Whitney R-2800-39 radial engines that generated 2,000hp each, the B-26 took off at 135mph and landed at 115mph. In order to avoid stalls on landing, the approach was done at 150mph. Pilots fresh out of training were expected to land the B-26A at higher speeds than many of their trainer aircraft could achieve at full throttle. It is certainly understandable that training accidents occurred, especially as these inexperienced fliers were considered B-26 qualified after three takeoffs and landings. As a result, a senate committee headed by Harry Truman of Missouri investigated the Marauder, and at one point ordered a construction halt. However, veteran combat pilots returning from the Pacific Theater praised the B-26's rugged performance in action and helped convince the senators that the B-26 was a vital war machine. The USAAF wanted to keep the B-26 in its inventory and implemented a plan to overcome past difficulties. Included was a recommendation that the wings be lengthened to accommodate less experienced pilots. This was done, and the B-26B wingspan was extended to 71ft. In addition, the tail surfaces were enlarged. Although 1,235 C models built by Martin, while much heavier than their predecessors, returned to the shorter wing, the final F and G models of the B-26 retained the 71ft wingspan.

Jimmy Doolittle also supported the B-26 program, and on occasion would demonstrate one-engine take-offs to reassure the young pilots in the Training Command that the plane was very manageable.

Ultimately, Martin Aircraft manufactured 5,266 B-26 Marauders, and it was necessary to build a second plant in Omaha, Nebraska, to accommodate production. The Maytag Company, which built many a washing machine, became a major contractor of B-26 subassemblies. Although fewer B-26s were built than any of the other major US bombers during WWII, the Marauder held the record for the lowest loss percentage of all US combat aircraft, less than one half a percent. It was rugged, dependable, and usually brought its crew of seven men home.

As more than one B-26 pilot stated, "Once you get her in the air, she's a great airplane."

In 1928, Glenn Martin made a conscious decision to move his company from Cleveland, Ohio, to Maryland because the US Navy's interest in seaplanes made it imperative that the plant have access to open water year-round, and Chesapeake Bay was a perfect fit. Martin also wanted to be closer to the seat of power, Washington, D.C., where procurement decisions would be made. His first plant was located in Canton, Maryland, and this photo records employees leaving work at the end of their shift. While black Americans often faced hiring discrimination in the nation's manufacturing plants, they appear to be in the majority here. *Martin Marietta*

These B-26s are being buttoned up for outdoor storage or transportation. The canvas covers protected the engines and plexiglass canopies from road dirt, wayward projectiles, and the weather. Imperfections or marks on windscreens or gun turrets dangerously interfered with the aviators' ability to discern other aircraft when on a mission. The tarpaulins also discouraged the curious, both the innocent and the subversive. *Martin Marietta*

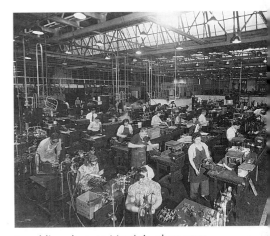

A welding shop at Martin's plant near Baltimore busily preparing minor subassemblies for the B-26. More than 53,000 workers worked at six Maryland locations, with an additional 14,000 employed at the Omaha, Nebraska, facility, where women made up 40 percent of the work force. One supervisor reported that some women employed by Martin could drive 14,000 rivets on an 8hr shift. That translates into approximately twenty rivets per minute with no meal or coffee breaks. *Martin Marietta*

The Maytag Company in Newton, Iowa, was restricted from building washing machines during WWII, so the company turned to manufacturing aircraft sub-assemblies. One of the new wonder products associated with WWII was a plastic derivative called lucite. More than 400 metal parts on the B-26 were replaced with lucite plastic. Featured in this May 1944 photograph is a lucite model of the main landing gear actuating cylinder for the B-26 made by Maytag. Among the dignitaries are, left to right, 2nd Lt. Anne Love of the US Marine Corps, Ens. Lois Swabel of the Women Accepted for Voluntary Emergency Service (WAVES), Lt. Col. Orson Powers of the US Army, Lt. (jg) Alice Terrill of the US Coast Guard (SPAR), Col. F. U. McCoskrie, the commander of the 1st Women's Army Corps (WAC), and Maj. Mary Louise Milligan of the WAC. *Maytag Archives*

Employees make adjustments to an ice-covered, four-bladed Hamilton Standard propeller on a B-26 at a Martin Aircraft facility. Army pilots and mechanics were assigned in groups of 500 to attend Martin's "College of B-26 Knowledge" at the Maryland location to learn proper maintenance procedures. *Martin Marietta*

On July 31, 1943, members of the Maytag War Bond Committee presented a B-26 Marauder to the USAAF, paid for by the employee purchase of US War Bonds. Making the presentation at Omaha, Nebraska, is Committee Chair Cora Shadle. This aircraft was shot down in combat, but employees purchased two more Marauders through payroll deduction purchase of War Bonds. *Maytag Archives*

Mid-fuselages for the B-26 were subcontracted to Chrysler, the automobile manufacturer best known during WWII for B-29 engine production. The employee in the foreground is polishing the aluminum skin of the aircraft. Everyone seems slightly posed! *Chrysler Archives*

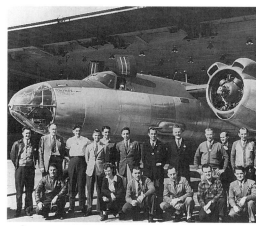

A Martin Aircraft production team proudly poses in front of a B-26G at the Maryland plant. On D-day, June 6, 1944, 269 B-26 Marauders of the Ninth Air Force bombed the Normandy defenses only 10min in advance of the American infantry hitting the beaches. The B-26s were led by six aircraft that had each flown at least 100 missions against the enemy. The attack force dropped 4,404 250lb bombs. *Martin Marietta*

Lockheed Model 14 Hudson

On June 23, 1938, Lockheed signed a contract with the British government to supply 250 military versions of its very successful commercial Model 14 Super Electra, which was faster than any plane then being flown by the RAF. It was the largest single order received by a US aircraft manufacturer up to that time. Working with only a few days' notice, the Lockheed people managed to build a wooden mock-up of the Model 14 at Burbank Airport, configured as a medium bomber. Lockheed's management was able to showcase the plane to British purchasing representatives when they landed there on the way to the nearby Douglas factory. The British, following two months of negotiations, bought the Model 14 and christened it the Hudson, after the explorer, Henry Hudson. A month later Howard Hughes set a world record in the Model 14, flying around the world in three days and 19hr.

Lockheed completed its original contract for the RAF fifty-three days ahead of schedule. The twin-tailed, twin-engined (1,200hp radials) Hud-

B-26s on the factory floor at Middle River, Maryland, await fly-away. By war's end B-26s had flown 110,000 sorties and dropped 150,000 tons of bombs. *Martin Marietta*

51

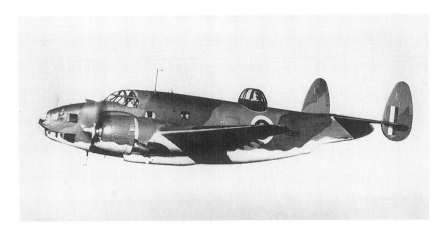

The Model 14 Hudson medium bomber with RAF markings. Had the British not placed an order for 250 of these aircraft in 1938, Lockheed may have gone bankrupt. While not a spectacular military aircraft, it was rugged and reliable. With Great Britain's need as an island nation to defend its sealanes and its coastlines, the Hudson proved to be an important asset. The USAAF purchased the Model 14 as a trainer (AT-18) and also as a medium attack bomber (A-28/A-29). *Lockheed Corporation*

The Lockheed assembly line at the company's Burbank, California, plant. Standing just under 12ft tall, the Hudson fuselage was 44ft, 4in long and its wingspan was 65ft, 6in. The large cutout in the top of the fuselage near the tail houses the upper gun turret. The forward cutout is for an observation bubble. These aircraft already display the RAF roundel on their fuselages. *Lockheed Corporation*

Engine installation on the Lockheed Hudson medium bomber. Supplied with either two Wright Cyclone engines or two Pratt & Whitney Twin Wasps, each generating 1,200hp, the aircraft attained speeds of 250mph in early models and 284mph after modifications later in the war. Weighing in at 18,000lb, the Hudson had a ceiling of 24,000ft and a range of 2,000mi. The Lockheed-Fowler wing flap increased lift, allowing for reduced approach and landing speeds. The Hudson was 20 percent faster than comparable aircraft. These aerodynamic advances were the work of Kelly Johnson, later famous as the driving force behind the Lockheed "Skunk Works." *Lockheed Corporation*

Hudsons in RAF markings outside Lockheed's Burbank factory await transport to the United Kingdom. Engines, propellers, and outer wings are moved separately. When ordered, the Model 14 was faster than any aircraft in the RAF inventory, and the contract was worth $25 million. It also had the distinction of being the first British plane to shoot down an enemy aircraft, specifically a Dornier Do 18 flying boat in October 1939, a month after Hitler invaded Poland. *Lockheed Corporation*

Lockheed Hudsons on the pier at Long Beach, California, awaiting shipment by freighter to Great Britain. Minus engines and outer wings, the planes are sheathed in plastic to prevent corrosion on their sea voyage. As convoys came increasingly under German submarine attack and losses to shipborne Hudsons mounted, the British requested that the aircraft be flown across the Atlantic. Conversely, as the war continued, RAF Hudsons sank more than 200 U-boats and forced one to surrender on the surface in August 1941. Toxic chlorine gas within the damaged submarine's hull forced it to the surface, and the U-boat was not able to withstand the barrage of machine gun fire from the attacking Hudson. It surrendered and was taken into a British port as a prize by surface vessels. *Lockheed Corporation*

A woman worker at Lockheed uses approved safety goggles as she operates a hand drill under the watchful eye of an instructor. The large dark mass below their combined waistlines represents both of them, not just the young woman as it appears from first glance. *Lockheed Corporation*

Cars in the Lockheed employee parking lot at the Burbank plant, roofed over by camouflage netting to screen against enemy air attack. The sunlit netting is reflected in the automobile windshields.

Judging from the open door on the coupe in the front row, someone must have been late for work! *Lockheed Corporation*

purchased twenty more. The USAAF designated the trainer model as the A-18 while the combat versions were the A-28 and A-29. The Navy used the plane for coastal patrol and called it the PBO-1. It was not a significant aircraft for either American service but was very popular with the British.

A-20 Havoc

Douglas experimented with a twin-engined attack aircraft designated the 7A and the 7B in 1936 and 1937. In 1939 the French government bought 270 model DB-7s, the end product of this earlier experimentation. The DB-7 was a 15,000lb, twin-engined bomber capable of 316mph at 15,000ft. The first 100 aircraft were delivered by April 1940, but France fell only two months later, and the remnant of the order was transferred to the British, who also ordered ninety-nine DB-7As. The latter was slightly faster and 2,000lb heavier than the original,

son hauled 1,400lb of bombs at 250mph. It was armed with five to seven machine guns and carried a crew of five. Ultimately the British purchased more than 2,000 of these aircraft, using them mainly as patrol bombers and for over-water reconnaissance.

Unarmed Model 14 Super Electras and Hudson III bombers were the central figures from 1940 to 1942 in a secret airline that flourished between embattled Britain and neutral Sweden. Flown at night from Scottish bases by civilian crews, the planes of Operation Scrutator imported vital steel ball bearings from Sweden for Great Britain's war production. The hazardous flights had to run the gauntlet across the 60mi-wide Skagerrack between German-controlled Denmark and Norway. After the Luftwaffe introduced night-fighters to the contest in 1942, the British replaced the Hudsons with the 400mph wooden Mosquito bomber and continued the service.

During WWII the USAAF also bought 300 Hudsons and the Navy

A British air crew prepares to board its Hudson painted in RAF camouflage, a gift from the employees of Lockheed and Vega, which was a Lockheed subsidiary. Just above their heads is the power-driven top turret from a British Boulton-Paul Defiant. It was equipped with four

.303cal machine guns and poured out a lethal dose of fire when brought to bear on an enemy target. Its height above the fuselage also exposed the gunner to hostile return fire from enemy aircraft. *Lockheed Corporation*

The A-20 Havoc with early-war markings. The distinctive red and white flag on the vertical tail was removed in the spring of 1942, as was the red ball centered in the white star on the fuselage. Allied antiaircraft gunners on several occasions mistook these insignias for the red meatball and Rising Sun insignia on Japanese aircraft and shot down friendly aircraft. *McDonnell Douglas Aircraft*

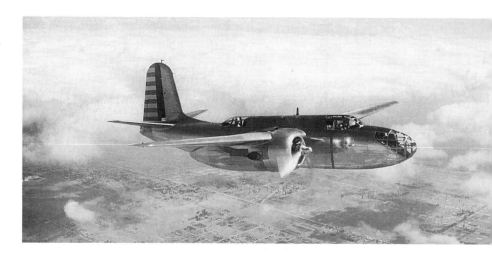

President Franklin D. Roosevelt inspects the Douglas Aircraft plant in Long Beach, California, during a tour of aircraft factories in September 1942. As a result of the poliomyelitis that paralyzed his legs in 1921, FDR could not walk without braces, and was driven through functions such as this one. The aircraft in the background are A-20 Havocs. Specific identifiers on the forward fuselages have been censored for security reasons. The president has an escort of eight Secret Service agents, while the two men following the car appear to be reporters. The Navy photographer standing on the desk in the right foreground discreetly turns his back as he reloads his camera. *FDR Library*

A-20A aircraft populate the ramp area outside the Douglas plant in Santa Monica, California. Due to the mild weather, many manufacturers in southern California completed production in the outdoors to free up needed factory floor space. The sign in the foreground next to the security guard says, "U.S. Army Restricted Area KEEP OUT." In the background are several Douglas DC-3s in the colors of Eastern Airlines, whose motto, "The Great Silver Fleet," is emblazoned along the aircrafts' fuselages. *McDonnell Douglas Aircraft*

A-20 plexiglass nose cones are polished by women defense workers at the Douglas plant in Long Beach, California. Almost all of the women have secured their hair in scarves or snoods. The overhead lights in the factory ceiling are reflected in the rows of shiny nose cones, creating a galaxy of stars. *National Archives*

An employee rivets sheets of alclad (aluminum alloy coated with pure aluminum to prevent corrosion) to the nose section of an A-20 at the Douglas Long Beach plant. *McDonnell Douglas Aircraft*

while incorporating more armor, British .303cal machine guns, and larger engines (Wright GR-2600-A5B), each of which generated 1,600hp.

The A-20A looked very much like the DB-7, but was redesigned as a result of lessons learned early in the war by the RAF in its battles against the Luftwaffe. Labeled the Boston by the British and the Havoc by the USAAF, and carrying a crew of three, the A-20 was slightly longer at 61ft, 4in, and quite a bit heavier at 20,311lb than its predecessor. It was armed with nine .30cal machine guns and carried 1,200–1,600lb of bombs.

Of 7,385 Havocs built by Douglas and Boeing, 3,215 were allocated to the Soviets, and 2,900 were delivered as scheduled. The A-20B, 999 of which were delivered from December 1941 to February 1943, incorporated a 200gal bomb-bay gas tank for extended missions. Its speed was 346mph at 12,400ft, and most of the plane's machine guns were upgraded to .50cal.

As in the case of the B-25, later models of the A-20G eliminated the plexiglass bombardier's nose and replaced it with a "gun nose." These planes were used as anti-shipping weapons and also against ground targets. Some 250 of them destined for the Soviet Union incorporated four 20mm guns and two .50cal machine guns.

The 2,600 A-20C aircraft produced for American forces had six .50cal machine guns in the nose. The A-20J and K models returned to the plexiglass nose, and these later models also added a tail gun position and increased the crew to four men.

Three A-20s were designated F-3s and were used for photo recon missions, two by the USAAF and one by the Navy. The aircraft was also employed as a night fighter in the Pacific, identified as the P-70, until replaced by the P-61 Black Widow in 1944.

The A-20 fought in North Africa, Europe, the Pacific, and the Soviet Union during WWII. Production ceased in September 1944.

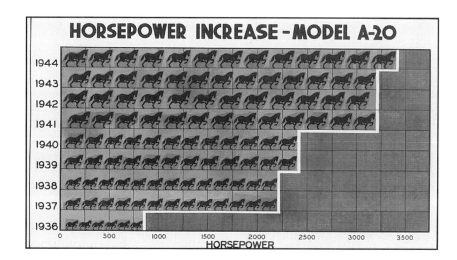

HORSEPOWER INCREASE – MODEL A-20

Left and below

Two A-20 production charts illuminate the prodigious increases in both horsepower and firepower over the production life of the aircraft. Engine horsepower increased from 850hp generated on the 1936 7A model to 3,400hp on the A-20G. Firepower in the same period increased from 100lb of projectiles fired per minute to 1,200lb per minute. *McDonnell Douglas Aircraft*

A-26 Invader

Designed as a replacement for the A-20 Havoc, the Douglas A-26 Invader first flew on July 10, 1942. Delivery of the aircraft began thirteen months later in August 1943. Powered by twin Pratt & Whitney R-2800 engines that generated 2,000hp each, the A-26 entered combat in Europe on November 19, 1944. It cruised at 266mph and had a maximum speed of 359mph. The Invader stood 18ft, 6in high and its wingspan was 70ft, while the fuselage was 51ft, 3in in length. The aircraft weighed 27,000lb loaded.

Armament was highly variable, including a forward firing 75mm cannon on some models. The A-26C carried six forward-firing .50cal machine guns, four of them in twin turrets. With a ceiling of 28,500ft, the Invader was used for level bombing missions as well as strafing and rocket attacks against enemy ground positions. Its internal bomb bay could carry 2,200lb of bombs, and the A-26

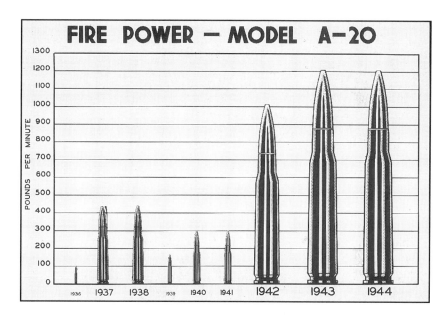

FIRE POWER – MODEL A-20

Douglas workers gather around the last A-20 Havoc to come off the assembly line at Long Beach in September 1944. Nicknamed the *Caboose*, the plane is covered with the signatures of the employees that built it. Interestingly, the great majority of workers pictured here are men. Women defense workers in most plants, including Douglas, usually represented 40 percent of the work force. *McDonnell Douglas Aircraft*

A completed A-20 weighing ten tons is towed by hand from the Douglas production line in Long Beach, ready for flight testing and fly-away in October 1942. *FDR Library*

war in 1940 and the two pioneering four-engined heavy bombers mentioned above were barely into production, the B-29 (originally known as the Model 345) was already on the design board at Boeing to replace them. The Superfortress first flew on September 21, 1942, just nine months after America's entry into WWII.

The B-29 was 99ft long, stood 27ft, 9in high, and had a wingspan of 141ft, 3in. It cruised at 220mph and had a maximum speed of 357mph. Weighing 133,500lb loaded, it was easily more than twice the weight of either the B-17 or the B-24, and the USAAC insisted on designating it a *very* heavy bomber. The B-29's range was 3,700mi, compared to 1,850mi for the Flying Fortress and 2,100mi for the Liberator. Depending on fuel requirements, the B-29 carried from 10,000 to 20,000lb of bombs. Four Wright R-3350 engines generated 2,200hp each, allowing a ceiling of 33,600ft. Armament consisted of eight .50cal machine guns

could hang bombs or rockets externally under its wings. Deployed in Europe for the last six months of the war, the A-26 was especially devastating when used as an attack aircraft against ground positions. In a 120-sortie air strike against the Austrian railroad marshaling yard at Attnanpucheim on April 21, 1945, three groups of A-26s plus one group of A-20s totally destroyed the target without the loss of one aircraft.

Douglas Aircraft built 2,502 A-26 Invaders before the end of the war stopped production. Redesignated the B-26 in 1948, it was used as a night intruder in the Korean War and ultimately was reclassified the A-26A for special operations during the Vietnam War.

B-29 Superfortress

Hard on the heels of the B-17 and the B-24 came the B-29 Superfortress, a high-flying, pressurized, very heavy strategic bomber that dwarfed its predecessors. Even though the United States was not at

Undergoing a final engine check, this A-20G features six .50cal machine guns protruding from the solid nose cone which has replaced the plexiglass nose. Overhead are camouflage nets emplaced to thwart enemy bombers that may be looking for the Douglas plant. The dark, irregular patches are fake foliage. *McDonnell Douglas Aircraft*

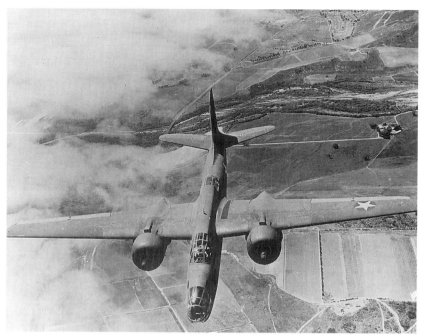

An A-20B Havoc, with late 1942 national insignia on its port wing, in flight over southern California. Note the large engine cowlings that encased the 1,600hp Wright GR-2600 engines. The A-20B carried a crew of three: pilot, bombardier, and gunner. *McDonnell Douglas Aircraft*

The B-29 emerged from the concept of strategic air power; that is, using air power to destroy the enemy's ability to wage war by crippling his manufacturing capability and his will to continue the fight. Nations prefer to fight on other countries' soil or at worst on their own borders, thereby protecting their citizens, their resources, and their internal economic structure. Strategic bombing bypassed direct confrontation with the opponent's military forces and hit instead the enemy's cities, industrial potential, and noncombatant population. Philosophically, this point of view differs dramatically from the tactical use of air power to support ground operations advocated by most US theater commanders during WWII, including Gen. Dwight Eisenhower in the campaign against Germany. The destruction of fortifications, airfields, bridges, harbors, railroads, and personnel concentrations were

in remote-controlled turrets plus two .50cals and a 20mm cannon in the tail. Everything about the B-29 proclaimed *bigger* and *better*.

Even as Boeing developed the B-17, its engineers and designers were seeking the next level in the advancement of four-engined bombers. After designing, modifying, rejecting, and redesigning, the Model 345 was presented to the USAAC Materiel Command at Wright Field in Dayton, Ohio. It was quickly accepted and designated the XB-29. Lockheed and Douglas also submitted designs but these were rejected. Two experimental aircraft were ordered in August 1940 at a cost of $6.3 million. Pleased with the progress exhibited by Boeing, the USAAC ordered fourteen YB-29s for testing and 250 production models in May 1941. Shortly afterwards, on June 20, 1941, the USAAC became the USAAF. This was more than a name change, and set up the Army Air Forces as a separate entity within the Army, finally positioned to initiate procurement, training, and operations free from Army General Staff interference with air priorities.

A line of A-20Gs await final inspection under the nets before fly-away at the Long Beach plant. While the camouflage precautions may seem unnecessary, a Japanese submarine did surface off Santa Barbara, California, and shelled an oil refinery early in the war. In addition, the Japanese possessed a large seaplane bomber that was transported in a special hangar on the deck of a submarine, and could be assembled for flight in less than 30min. One of these was used to drop incendiaries and start forest fires in the Pacific Northwest. *McDonnell Douglas Aircraft*

The A-26D at the Douglas Long Beach plant in July 1945. An upgrade of the A-26B, only one D model was ever built.

Considered a logical continuation of the A-20 Havoc, the Invader was faster and more heavily armed. The A-26 had a

1,400mi range, and its service ceiling was 28,000ft. Each cost the government $172,000. *McDonnell Douglas Aircraft*

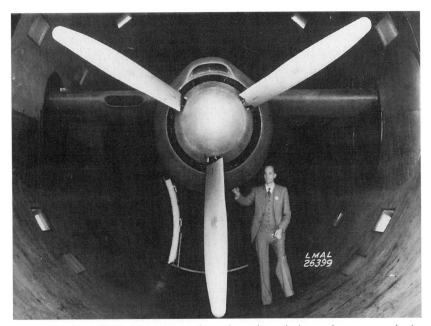

The massive propellers of the A-26 are illustrated in relation to a man's height in a test tunnel. The aircraft was powered by two Pratt & Whitney R-2800 engines producing 2,000hp each and incorporated a thin wing and fuselage. It was the

last plane designated as an attack aircraft in the Air Force inventory, and entered the war in Europe during the last few months of the conflict. During the Korean War the A-26 was used as a night intruder. *National Air & Space Museum*

effective uses of tactical air power, but often, due to finite resources, this usage was a detriment to strategic deployment of air power. With the introduction of the B-29 in the Pacific in 1944, and its direct control by the Joint Chiefs of Staff rather than the theater commander (there were three of them in the Pacific—MacArthur, Nimitz, and Stilwell), the strategic bombing campaign against the Japanese home islands came to fruition.

In order to put the B-29 into production as soon as possible, Gen. "Hap" Arnold, commander of the USAAF, set up the B-29 Liaison Committee consisting of representatives from the civilian companies building the aircraft as well as the involved USAAF personnel. Out of 3,966 B-29s built (including the three XBs) during WWII, Boeing by far manufactured the greatest number, 1,634, at its Wichita, Kansas, plant and 1,120 B-29As at Renton, Washington. Martin Aircraft built

The A-26B was designed with low-level strafing in mind and carried three .50cal machine guns in each wing as well as eight .50cals in the nose. Some versions fired a 75mm cannon through the nose. A total of 1,355 B Models were delivered to the Air Force. *Pete Bowers Collection*

204 Superfortresses in Omaha, Nebraska, while Bell Aircraft built 357 B-29s and 310 B-29As at Marietta, Georgia. An additional 5,000 B-29Cs were scheduled for production by Boeing in Seattle, but the order was canceled as the end of the war became evident. Because the B-29 was rushed into production, most aircraft modifications were in the form of kits and took place in the field.

Slight variations in engines and aircraft weights were the major factory differences between B-29s, B-29As, and B-29Bs. They weighed 137,500lb and cruised at 230mph, with a top speed of 361mph. The B-29As were produced by Boeing at its Renton, Washington, plant. This model was slightly heavier at 140,000lb and cruised at 253mph. Its top speed was a swift 399mph. Bell Aircraft in Marietta, Georgia, manufactured the B-29B. It weighed quite a bit less, 110,000lb, cruised at 228mph, and had a top speed of 364mph. The B-29B's range was 5,725mi, compared

A row of A-26Bs, their engines covered to avoid dirt and debris, await fly-away. The aircraft carried a crew of three, and had an internal bomb bay able to hold 2,200lb of bombs. It could also carry additional bombs or rockets under the wings. It was considered the best attack aircraft in the American arsenal. This version carried eight .50cal machine guns in the nose. *Pete Bowers Collection*

The B-29 Superfortress was the premier bomber of WWII, flying higher and faster with a greater bomb load than any other aircraft. Originally designed as a high-level precision bomber, it gained fame for its low-level attacks on Japan's cities and industries, and destroyed that nation's production base. *Boeing*

Front fuselages for B-29As in production are lined up on the factory floor at Boeing's Renton, Washington, plant. The unusual cross-framed plexiglass cockpit was nicknamed the "bird cage" by Maj. Gen. Curtis LeMay. Initially it caused pilots some difficulty in lining up the big plane with the runway during landing. *Boeing*

The wingspan of the B-29 was 141ft, compared to 104ft for the B-17 and 110ft for the B-24. Pentagon officials feared that the wings carried excessive pounds per square feet of surface, and wanted the wings made even bigger. Boeing countered that this would reduce speed and range. The dilemma was solved with the addition of Fowler flaps, which increased the wing area by 20 percent and reduced takeoff and landing speeds. *Boeing*

Fitting one of five laminated glass panes around the rear gunner's station on a Boeing B-29. Each weighed 65lb, was 2.5in thick, and could deflect .50cal bullets but not the 20mm shells fired by enemy fighters. This gun position was equipped with twin .50cal machine guns and a 20mm cannon. The four other turret machine guns were remote-controlled, fired by a gunner using a periscope and positioned in an observation bubble just forward of the rear top turret. *Boeing*

A Boeing employee wiring the partially pressurized fuselage of a B-29. Faced with significant engineering costs, the Boeing design team only pressurized the aircraft's crew compartments, including a pressurized tunnel over the two bomb bays that connected the cockpit area with the central fuselage. The rear gunner had his own pressurized compartment. Communication between crew members was difficult, especially if the radio system was damaged or inoperative. *Boeing*

to 5,418 for the B-29A and 5,500mi for the B-29. Earlier models of the B-29, which were powered by Wright Cyclone R-3350-23 engines rather than -41 engines, were limited to the 4,700mi range. Later models of the B-29 also incorporated four .50cal machine guns rather than two in the forward top turret.

Due to the unprecedented rush into production of the B-29, there were many performance flaws in the aircraft that had to be corrected before the B-29 could become operational. This resulted in a production effort known as "The Battle of Kansas." Among the B-29's problems were the propeller feathering system, the fire-control system, and the electrical system. In fact, there were fifty-four major modifications necessary on every B-29 produced in 1944. Employees located at four modification centers in Kansas were put on double shifts, and the delivery of spare parts and modification kits increased dramatically from the sub-contractors.

Proud employees of the Curtiss-Wright Corporation pose with an eighteen-cylinder Wright Cyclone R-3350 engine, four of which were matched to every B-29 bomber. Because the aircraft were rushed into production and normal testing procedures were often abridged, there were many refinements necessary before planes and engines operated efficiently and up to specifications. More than 3,000 changes were made to these engines in the first several months of B-29 deployment to India and China. Curtiss-Wright, with a work force of 46,000, built 281,164 aircraft engines and 146,468 propellers during WWII. *Aviation Hall of Fame NJ*

The assembly line at Chrysler's Dodge plant integrating the eighteen cylinders into R-3350 engines for B-29s produced elsewhere. This plant manufactured 18,413 of these engines by the end of the war. Covering eighty-two acres on one floor, the Chicago facility represented 5 percent of all USAAF spending when ground was broken in early 1942. Chrysler met or exceeded all production schedules set by the government and reduced costs more than 50 percent below the original estimates, according to a letter from Gen. "Hap" Arnold to the plant's general manager, L. L. Colbert. *Chrysler Archives*

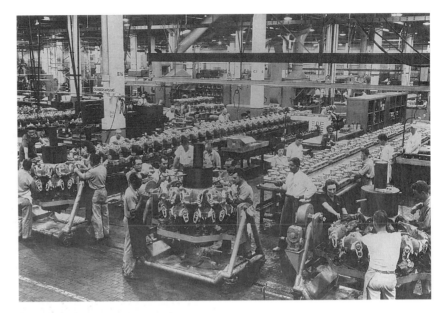

Aviator Eddie Rickenbacker, who had been an American flying hero in WWI, talks to a group of women workers at an undisclosed B-29 plant. Several of the ladies seem focused on something or someone else out of the picture. As a civilian advisor to Secretary of War Henry L. Stimson, Rickenbacker was a passenger on a B-17D that ran out of fuel and was forced down in the South Pacific in October 1942. Along with seven crewmen, Rickenbacker at age fifty-two spent twenty-four agonizing days in a rubber raft before being rescued. One of the crewmen died during the ordeal. *Chrysler Archives*

Using an electric hoist capable of lifting 4,000lb, Chrysler employees position a massive R-3350 engine for testing in the wind tunnel at the Dodge plant in Chicago. Different models of this engine generated from 2,200hp to 2,500hp. *Chrysler Archives*

In this view of the Dodge plant wind tunnel in Chicago, a massive, four-bladed propeller has been attached to the engine. One employee climbs a ladder on the side of the tunnel while another makes final adjustments to the engine prior to testing. *Chrysler Archives*

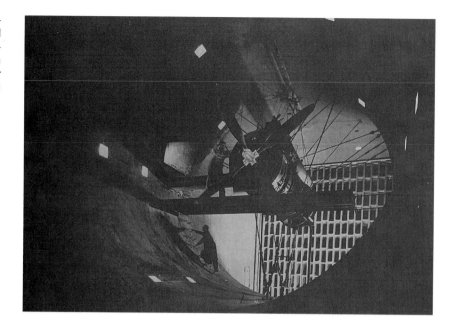

Looking northwest toward Kennesaw Mountain from the site soon to become Rickenbacker Field in Marietta, Georgia. The Defense Plant Corporation, a subsidiary of the Reconstruction Finance Corporation, built this Bell Aircraft plant in Marietta, in which Bell would build B-29s. Ground was broken in March 1942, and construction was completed thirteen months later. Even before it was finished, however, B-29s were rolling off the assembly lines here. *Lockheed-Marietta*

Partially completed Bell Plant Six at Marietta. The finished B-29s exited through the large doors on the left of the building after the dirt area in front was paved to accommodate them. Bell Aircraft employed 28,000 workers here. *Lockheed-Marietta*

Workers at Bell Aircraft's Plant Six in Marietta, Georgia, attach stringers to the frame of a B-29 fuselage. One veteran newsman alluded to many of the employees as "woolies," a reference to their previous experience as textile workers in rural Georgia. *Lockheed-Marietta*

range of the B-29 made it a practical weapon to be implemented over the vast distances in the Pacific.

First deployed in China and India, the B-29s initial efforts against the Japanese were not very successful. Incredible but true, it was necessary to fly two B-29 supply missions from India to bases in China in order to provide the fuel and munitions needed for one combat strike against the enemy. It was a difficult arrangement. Crews had been hastily and poorly trained before leaving the States. Fuel was in short supply. The first mission was flown against Japan on June 15, 1944. Coupled with aircraft maintenance problems and the heretofore unknown jet stream over Japan, the results were unimpressive. The USAAF looked to the capture of the Marianna Islands in the mid-Pacific as the solution to their base and supply problem. Complicating these difficulties was a Japanese offensive in November 1944 that resulted in the loss of several B-29 airfields in China.

In September, due in part to dissatisfaction in Washington with the efforts of the commanding general of the Twentieth Air Force in China, Maj. Gen. Curtis LeMay was sent to replace him. LeMay introduced major changes to training, opera-

The crisis was met and overcome, and B-29s went on line in India in mid-April 1944.

Army Air Forces planners had decided that the B-29 would not be employed in Europe, as much of the strategic bombing campaign against Germany would be concluded before the B-29 was operational. The Japanese home islands had not been bombed since the Doolittle Raid in April 1942. In addition, the great

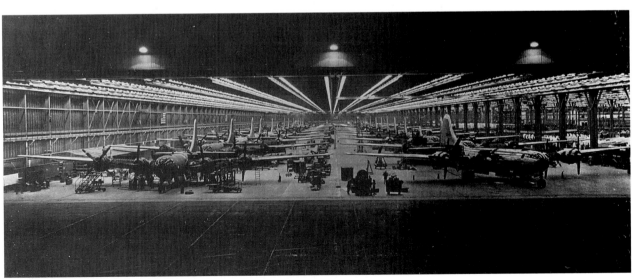

Finished B-29Bs reach the end of Bell's twin production lines at Marietta, where 667 such aircraft were built from 1943 to 1945. The building, today known as B-1, encompassed 3.5 million square feet of manufacturing space. *Lockheed-Marietta*

tional, and administrative procedures. Although definite improvements resulted, it became clear that supporting an independent command in China was not the solution required for the defeat of Japan.

Shortly thereafter, the Mariannas were liberated, and B-29s of the XXVI Bomber Command began flying missions from the islands of Guam, Saipan, and Tinian against Japan. The first such attack was launched on November 24, 1944, and for the next nine months the B-29s devastated the enemy, burning his cities and factories out of existence. On March 9, 1945, an incendiary attack on Tokyo destroyed 267,000 buildings and burned 16.8sq-mi of the enemy's capital, killing 83,000 civilians. Millions were left homeless and government services were unable to cope with the catastrophe. In ten days 1,505 B-29 sorties were flown against the Japanese homeland, bringing warfare to Japan with dreadful results. The carnage did not stop—on August 1, 784 B-29s bombed Japan as part of a single mission. On August 6 the first atomic bomb was dropped on Hiroshima, followed by a second atomic bomb on Nagasaki three days later.

When WWII ended on September 3, 1945, there were 2,242 B-29s in the USAAF inventory. One year previously only 647 B-29s were operational. The great majority of the survivors were placed in desert storage just in case there was another war in the near future. There was.

When first deployed against the Japanese homeland, the B-29s dropped their bombs from altitudes of 25,000–30,000ft. Enemy fighter performance was poor at these altitudes, and on frequent occasions the fighters would deliberately ram the massive B-29s. If the American crew was able to bail out of a crippled airplane, the members were usually killed by the Japanese on the ground, often by decapitation. Many were tortured. Very few of the 2,400 US airmen missing on B-29 missions over Japan survived the war. *Boeing*

B-29s at Renton, Washington, await deployment to the Pacific. The Superfortresses flew 380 combat missions against Japan and dropped 147,000 tons of bombs during 1944 and 1945. Losses were 512 aircraft, plus another 260 in training accidents, mainly in the States. It is estimated that 602 significant Japanese war factories were destroyed, and that 40 percent of sixty-six major cities was devastated by B-29 raids. Civilian casualties totaled 330,000 killed and 476,000 injured. More than 2,000,000 homes were obliterated. Japanese civilians suffered more casualties by far than the military in the bombing campaign against the Home Islands. *Boeing*

Chapter III

The Fighters

During WWI on the Western Front great aerial battles known as "dogfights" took place between the pilots of the Imperial German Air Force and those of the major Allied participants: France, Great Britain, and the United States. Romantic and exciting as these struggles were to the observer, they had very little to do with the outcome of the war, which was decided by economics and the infantry, aided by tanks and artillery. Air supremacy was certainly important, as it permitted observation of the enemy's daylight movements as long as the weather cooperated, but in itself air activity was not decisive. After the

Armistice of November 1918, it became the mission of the various national air staffs to define the role of the airplane in future conflicts. Dogfights were not enough—an aviation strategy was needed.

The emerging consensus among military professionals in the 1920s and 1930s was that heavily armed bombers would be able to fight their way through to objectives behind the enemy's lines or even into his heartland and return without suffering undue casualties. To counter this offensive weapon, it was necessary to develop antiaircraft systems, which included both guns on the ground and pursuit aircraft. Government

funding in the democracies was meager and air forces remained small. The American people had suffered an isolationist backlash as a result of the essentially failed peace negotiations at the end of WWI, and defense spending was not a priority. The depressed economy of the 1930s was centered on the loss of jobs in the civilian sector, and there really was no defense industry in place. The combination resulted in stagnation. In addition, competition between the various air services was at times acrimonious, not to mention the visible friction that existed between military aviators and the traditional land and sea forces of the US Army and Navy.

Thus, the peacetime development of the single-seat pursuit plane was perniciously slow, and it wasn't until the advent of the Boeing P-26A in 1933 that the USAAC was able to include a monoplane in its inventory, albeit one with fixed landing gear and an open cockpit. While this procurement was a start, it was a very sluggish one. Slowly the Army realized that the *P* for pursuit needed to become an *F* for fighter, and that these aircraft were needed to play a major offensive role in battle, not being organized just for defense. It must be said that most of the US fighter aircraft that ultimately performed so successfully during WWII were in fact being developed before America's entry into the conflict. However, in December 1941 the two operational fighters available to the USAAC were the P-39 and P-40, and neither was able to compete successfully in combat with the Axis' frontline aircraft at that time.

In general, US fighters were heavier than their opponents and conveyed more firepower. They also

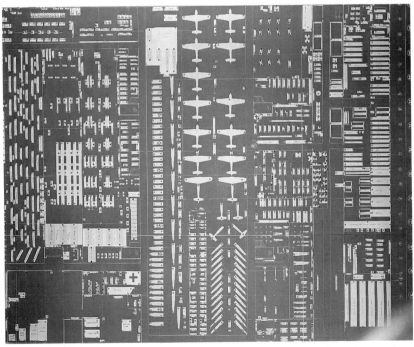

North American Aviation's production layout for the P-51. Most recognizable to the non-engineer is the center of the scheme, where the rear fuselage and tail section are mated to the center wing and then to the nose and engine section. Prominently marked with a large cross in the lower left of the photograph is the medical facility for workers injured on the job. *Rockwell International*

Early production models of the P-51 featured four 20mm cannons protruding from the wings and a three-bladed propeller. The USAAF accepted 150 of these aircraft, using fifty-five of them for photo-reconnaissance and most of the rest as A-36 Apache dive bombers. *Rockwell International*

P-51Bs, recognizable by the pre-bubble cockpit, nearing final production on the North American assembly line at the Inglewood, California, plant. Powered by the Allison engine, the P-51B cruised at 307mph and had a maximum speed of 390mph at 20,000ft, considerably lower and slower than the later D model. Its bomb load was limited to 1,000lb. *Steve Pace Collection*

An opposite view of the P-51B assembly line at Inglewood. Visible in the leading wing edges are the cutouts for the two .50cal machine guns mounted in each wing. The P-51D increased wing armament from four to six .50cal machine guns. *Pete Bowers Collection*

69

A P-51B in RAF markings. This aircraft appears fitted for photo-reconnaissance as there are no machine guns in the wings and a camera pod is visible protruding from the lower rear fuselage. *Rockwell International*

The North American assembly line at its Dallas, Texas, plant. Although 1,750 P-51Cs were produced in Dallas, these aircraft are the later P-51D models, which introduced the bubble, or teardrop, cockpit seen in this photograph. *Rockwell International*

incorporated more armor around the cockpit and carried self-sealing gas tanks, saving many a pilot from an unpleasant ordeal by fire. The price paid was usually maneuverability and early in the war, speed. However, as aircraft continued to evolve during the war years, these deficits were overcome by US engineering and productivity. In fact, productivity was the key as the Axis could never match the output of America's factories. The lack of opponents in the air allowed the expansion of the role of US fighters to that of fighter-bombers, and created an entire new dimension in the air war. Used in a support role for Allied infantry and armor and in the interdiction of the enemy's transportation and communications systems, the fighter-bomber became an important adjunct to the role of ground forces in WWII.

In the air the P-47 and P-51 reigned supreme, especially the lat-

Center wing sections for the P-51D at the Inglewood plant. The open trap in the port wing is receptacle for the three .50cal machine guns located in each wing. A group of military officers is gathered in the center of the photograph. The fuselage in front of the wing is being fitted with its completed wing section. *Rockwell International*

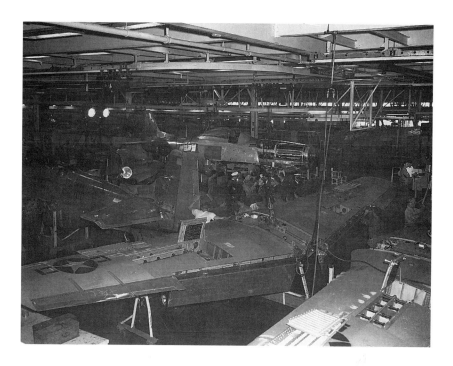

A close view of the Hamilton Standard propeller used on the P-51Ds. *Hamilton Standard Division of United Technologies Corporation*

ter. No other fighter in any air force came close, and the Mustang's presence as an escort fighter on long-range bombing missions over both Germany and Japan ensured the devastation of Axis defense production, thus ending any hope of victory or even an armistice for these aggressor nations. American fighter aircraft were instrumental to the successful prosecution of the Allied air war, and much of that success was due to the production and engineering miracles carried out on the Home Front.

P-51 Mustang

Considered the best piston-engined fighter aircraft of WWII, the P-51 was designed and manufactured by North American Aviation, a firm well-known for its military training aircraft, but a neophyte in fighter production prior to 1940. The British, fighting alone against Germany and Italy, sought a follow-on aircraft to the American-built Curtiss P-40. While Curtiss was developing a next-generation fighter called the XP-46 in 1939–40, it did not have the capacity to maintain P-40 production and at the same time manufacture a significant number of this new aircraft, which was only slightly superior to the P-40. Thus, the British turned to North American, located in Inglewood, California.

The legend persists that North American designed and built the initial version of the P-51, known as NA-73X, in slightly more than four months with no previous experience in fighter design. However, it appears that engineers from North American worked with their counterparts at Curtiss and had access to information about the XP-46 that aided significantly in planning the NA-73X. In fact, North American bought the experimental aircraft's wind tunnel data from Curtiss for $56,000, according to Jeffrey Ethell's 1981 book, *Mustang: A Documentary History*. Be that as it may, the NA-73X first flew on October 26, 1940, achieving 382mph while carrying nearly twice as much fuel as contemporary fighters on active service at the time.

Engine run-up for three P-51Ds on the factory ramp at the Inglewood plant. The famous Merlin engine was built by the Packard Automobile Company for North American. The V-1650-7 engine's normal rating was 1,490hp, with a maximum of 1,720hp. Service ceiling for the P-51D was 41,900ft and its rate of climb was 20,000ft in 7.3sec. *Rockwell International*

Propeller spinners were produced by the Hamilton Standard Company by the thousands to be used on the P-51 as well as several other fighter aircraft. By covering the propeller hub with this streamlined fairing, airflow into the engine inlet was improved and drag was reduced. *Hamilton Standard Division of United Technologies Corporation*

Mustang fighters being painted at the North American Inglewood plant. Early models consigned to the British were usually painted in camouflage, which reduced their speed by 8mph. Starting with the D models, the P-51s were left unpainted to save time on the assembly line and to save weight. By mid-1944, the Allies had complete air superiority, so camouflage was thought to be unnecessary. The Mustang is instantly recognizable by the radiator intake scoop set in the lower fuselage behind the pilot. *Steve Pace Collection*

An Inglewood P-51D, minus wings, tail, and propeller, is crated for shipment to Great Britain. The message stenciled on the wooden sign in front of the cockpit says, "IMPORTANT HAND TURN ENGINE BEFORE INSTALLING SPARK PLUGS TO CHECK POSSIBILITY OF EXCESS COMPOUND IN CYLINDERS." *Steve Pace Collection*

In Dallas, a North American T-6 trainer with Soviet markings heads a line of P-51Ds with French, British, and US markings. The second row of aircraft features more Soviet T-6s and another French P-51D. The United States provided the Soviet Union with many American-made fighter aircraft through LendLease, but the P-51 was not one of them. *Rockwell International*

The P-51H did not fly until February 1945 and never did become operational with the USAAF. It had a water-injected V-1650-9A Merlin engine that generated 1,380hp, and the P-51H attained the speed of 491mph. Although 2,400 P-51Hs were ordered from North American, only 550 were delivered before contract cancellation. *Rockwell International*

A P-47N Thunderbolt fighter featuring "zero-length" rocket launchers, as well as eight .50cal machine guns. The N model was equipped with a larger Pratt & Whitney engine (R-2800-77) and incorporated "wet" wings, which increased internal fuel capacity to 1,266gals and range to 2,350mi. Republic's Farmingdale plant built 1,667 N models, and an additional 149 were produced at the Evansville plant. *Cradle of Aviation Museum*

Republic Airport at Farmingdale on New York's Long Island in 1944. The hangar is still in use today for private aircraft. While Curtiss built P-47Gs at its Buffalo, New York, plant and Republic used a second plant in Evansville, Indiana, the greatest number of P-47s were manufactured at this location. These are P-47D-28 models. Farmingdale ranked fourteenth in total airframe pounds produced by plant location in the war years. *Cradle of Aviation Museum*

This skinless P-47N-25 was used for employee training at the Farmingdale plant. The complexity of aircraft production is quite apparent from this photo, which magnifies the intricacies of merging airframe, engine, internal systems, and armament, not to mention that 13ft propeller. Such models were also used for company publicity directed at the general public. *Cradle of Aviation Museum*

Republic employees attaching transverse bulkheads to the stringers, which run the length of the upper fuselage of a P-47. The upper and lower halves of the aircraft's fuselage were fabricated separately and then bolted together. The two women working on this 1943 plane in the foreground are using compressed air guns to facilitate construction. *Cradle of Aviation Museum*

Although the program was delayed for a time due to a test flight crash, the P-51A went into production in September 1940 with 620 machines slated for the RAF and two for the USAAF. The Americans experimented with a dive bomber model known as the A-36 Apache, which was designed to carry two 500lb bombs, and also with the F-6A, a photo-reconnaissance aircraft, both of which saw excellent service for the USAAF during the war. The P-51A was powered by a liquid-cooled Allison V-1710-81 engine generating 1,200hp and armed with four .50cal machine guns in the wings. Of the 1,570 P-51As finally produced, the USAAF acquired 806 of them and the RAF received 764 aircraft.

The Mustang did not perform as well as expected at high altitude, so the British replaced the Allison engine with a Rolls-Royce Merlin 61 engine, increasing the aircraft's speed to 432mph, 50mph faster than the original NA-73X. The United States was impressed with this modification and gave the Packard Automobile Company a contract to build an American version of the Merlin engine known as the V-1650, which

Sheets of alclad are attached to the upper fuselage of a P-47C or early D model. The protruding pins are "cleco" clips, used to hold the panels in place while some of the 79,000 rivets used in P-47 construction affixed the panel to the frame. With little more than her head in evidence, a female employee is working in the cockpit, which was considerably larger than the standard fighter aircraft cockpit during WWII. *Cradle of Aviation Museum*

Some manufacturing work was subcontracted. In Moline, Illinois, a John Deere Company employee assembles a P-47 tail wheel. Note the row of completed tail wheels on the shelf behind her. The woman is using a floor pad to alleviate the lower leg and foot stress associated with standing on a hard surface for long periods of time. John Deere contracts for various aircraft parts totaled $36 million during WWII. *Deere & Company*

The upper halves of P-47D center fuselages moving through the assembly line from bare frame to aluminum skin. Engine installation is next, after which tail sections and wings will be attached. The banner in the center rear under the American flag reads, "Fuselage Department." *Cradle of Aviation Museum*

generated 1,595hp at 17,000ft. North American Aviation built 1,988 of this aircraft designated the P-51B. Another 1,750 P-51Cs were manufactured by North American at its new Dallas, Texas, plant beginning in August 1943. They were essentially the same as the B model, only differing in the letter designator to distinguish their place of manufacture.

The major production model Mustang was the P-51D, which introduced the new bubble canopy for better pilot visibility and upgraded the aircraft's armament to six .50cal machine guns in the wings. The Inglewood plant produced 6,502 P-51Ds and the Dallas plant produced another 1,454.

The increased range of the P-51D, which incorporated wing-mounted drop tanks and an 85gal gas fuel tank behind the pilot's compartment, allowed it to escort Allied bombers all the way from England to Berlin and back, a benefit not available to the heavy bombers of the Eighth Air Force prior to early 1944. In fact, German fighter aircraft as well as antiaircraft batteries had caused unacceptable losses to long-range daylight penetrations by US B-17s and B-24s in 1943, virtually bringing the strategic bombing campaign to a halt. After the P-51D became operational, the Germans had to either come up and dogfight with them or allow the American bombers to attack German targets unmolested. Ultimately this led to the destruction of the Luftwaffe as a tactical air force.

As the war progressed, North American designers attempted to produce a lighter weight, and therefore faster, aircraft. While there was no P-51E, five F and G experimental models with three-bladed and five-bladed propellers were produced, and resulted in 555 P-51Hs being manufactured before V-J Day, after which the contract was canceled. The P-51H, which retained the four-bladed prop, weighed 540lb less than the D model and had a maximum speed of 487mph at 25,000ft. Two XP-51Js, which never entered production, achieved 491mph at 27,400ft.

The P-51, redesignated the F-51 in 1948, stayed in the Air Force Reserve inventory after WWII, and three wings were activated for service in the early days of the Korean War. While it could not absorb as much battle damage as its famed counterpart, the P-47 Thunderbolt, the F-51D proved itself in the role of fighter-bomber over the fiercely contested Korean peninsula.

P-47 Thunderbolt

Known to thousands of Air Force personnel as the "Jug" because its fuselage was reminiscent of a 1940s bottle (the National Air & Space Museum asserts milk bottle—various aviation historians contend moonshine whiskey bottle), the P-47 was the largest and heaviest standard US fighter plane of WWII, weighing 13,500 to 14,500lb loaded. Its wingspan was 40ft, 9in and the P-47's fuselage was 36ft, 1in long. Standing 14ft, 2in tall, it was armed with eight .50cal machine guns and could carry 1,500lb of bombs and rockets. Later models accommodated an additional 1,000lb of weaponry. It was also the most numerous American fighter, with 15,683 P-47s built by Republic Aviation of Farmingdale, New York, in three years of wartime production. Previously Republic had been known as Seversky Aircraft, but had changed its name when Alexander P. de Seversky left the firm in October 1939.

While most US fighters had V-12 engines, the P-47 used the 2,300hp Pratt & Whitney R-2800 eighteen-cylinder radial engine called the Double Wasp. The "Jug" cruised at 260mph with a maximum speed of 433mph. It had a range of 1,100mi and a service ceiling of 40,000ft. The P-47 could out-dive anything in the Luftwaffe inventory, and in July 1943 an auxiliary fuel tank was added, allowing deeper penetrations of enemy airspace as a bomber escort. It was flown by the Americans, British, Brazilians, Free French, Mexicans, and the Soviets during WWII.

In the development years before the war, designer Alexander Kartveli

Prominent RAF roundels and their camouflage paint schemes indicate that the early P-47Ds in the foreground of this photo are destined for Great Britain. The first aircraft in line is an early bubble-canopy model, differing from the rest of the row. The stainless steel firewall between the engine compartment and the cockpit is visible on these planes. The British received 240 B models and 590 D models through LendLease, operating sixteen P-47 squadrons in Burma and Southeast Asia. American aircraft in the background are only lacking landing gear, engine cowlings, and propellers before roll-out. *Cradle of Aviation Museum*

Fitting a completed tail section to the center fuselage of a P-47, where it will be bolted and the skin riveted to the last frame. The cut-out on the bottom of this section will house the tail wheel. The upper opening will accommodate the tail fin and ailerons. *Cradle of Aviation Museum*

Installation of the four-bladed, 12ft controllable-pitch propeller on a Pratt & Whitney R-2800 radial engine. The air-cooled Double Wasp generated 2,000hp through eighteen cylinders and was equipped with a 28gal oil tank mounted at the rear of the engine. Later D model Thunderbolts incorporated a 13ft Curtiss Electric propeller. The size of both these propellers required adjustable landing gear, which extended 9in in order to allow landing clearance for the propeller and retracted for gear storage within the bottom wing compartment. *Cradle of Aviation Museum*

of Republic worked on the P-43 and P-44 fighters. These in turn became the XP-47 and XP-47A. None of them achieved production except for the P-43, and most of those were shipped to China under LendLease. In June 1940 Republic submitted to the USAAC the design for the XP-47B known as the Thunderbolt. Three months later the US government ordered one aircraft, and followed up with an order for 171 P-47Bs before the first model even flew in April 1941. The B model incorporated a side-opening cockpit door (difficult to exit in an in-flight emergency) and a turbo-supercharger on the Pratt & Whitney engine. It also featured a flush pilot canopy and a sharp-spined fuselage, giving rise to the appellation, "Razorback." The C model (602 produced) replaced the side door with a sliding canopy. First ordered in October 1941, D models were originally built at Republic's

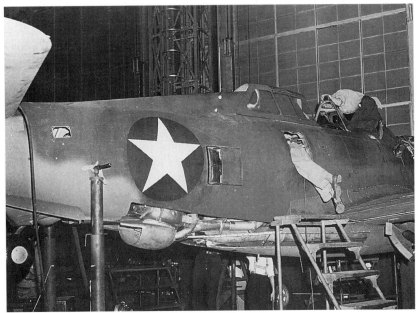

The prominent aft vent under the US star on this early D model is the engine exhaust outlet. The turbo-supercharger on the P-47 was located behind the pilot compartment, 21ft from the engine. The employee whose legs are dangling from the side hatch is probably making adjustments to this complicated equipment before the installation of the main self-sealing fuel tank into the large opening in the lower fuselage. Slightly-built men and women were a necessity in reaching otherwise inaccessible areas during the production process on all types of aircraft. *Cradle of Aviation Museum*

Evansville, Indiana, plant, but ultimately included the ships built at Farmingdale. Those P-47s built by Curtiss Aircraft in Buffalo, New York, were designated G models.

In July 1943 the D model was redesigned, replacing the flush sliding canopy with a bubble canopy, and smoothing out the sharp-spined rear fuselage. This latest P-47 also used a 13ft Curtiss Electric propeller. The D model had the largest production run, with 12,602 of them constructed during the war. Other experimental models followed, with the XP-47J reaching 504mph in level flight in August 1944. The P-47M, of which 133 were manufactured, was slightly faster than the D model. The last major production model was the P-47N, which had square wing tips and larger ailerons, and was designed for the war in the Pacific. Only 1,800 were built due to the cessation of hostilities, at which time an order for 5,934 additional P-47s was canceled.

The P-47 first achieved prominence in the European Theater as an escort to American B-17 and B-24 daylight bombing raids against targets in Europe. As the strength of the US Bomber Command grew and missions were targeted deep inside Germany, a drop tank was attached to the P-47's underbelly to increase its escort range. While valiant, the P-47 could not offer sufficient range to escort the bombers to Berlin and back, and this role was taken over by the P-51 Mustang in early 1944. The massive Thunderbolt was an effective fighter, however, and could both inflict terrible punishment with its eight .50cal machine guns and absorb damage from enemy fire. In fact, every P-47 ace survived the war, even though several of them were shot down by the enemy. Their aircraft, though heavily damaged, saved their lives. After the invasion of the Continent in June 1944 the P-47 gained a fierce reputation as a fighter-bomber, both in support of ground troops and in destroying targets of opportunity. The Luftwaffe had to conserve its meager air resources, and American fighters were

In July 1943, Republic designers borrowed a bubble canopy from a British Hawker Typhoon and fitted it to a P-47D. Even though the D model was in production, it was decided to incorporate this new canopy into the remaining Ds as well as subsequent models of the P-47. Fitted to a sliding track, the bubble canopy significantly improved pilot visibility, especially to the rear, much as it did for the P-51 fighter. The canopy was one-piece, molded plexiglass. *Cradle of Aviation Museum*

Final P-47 assembly was completed in two parallel rows in the Farmingdale plant in March 1944. These early D models are ready to receive engine cowlings and propellers, while the aircraft on the right are awaiting tail assembly installation. Production peaked in late 1943 at 600 aircraft per month, and in 1944 Republic averaged more than twenty planes per day. *Cradle of Aviation Museum*

A P-47 test-fires its eight wing-mounted .50cal machine guns and empty cartridges tumble to the ground. The national insignia on the fuselage indicates that the photo was made in 1942 or 1943. Each of the plane's machine guns was supplied with 450 rounds of ammunition. The P-47 was one of the most heavily armed fighter aircraft of WWII. *Cradle of Aviation Museum*

Two XP-47H aircraft were built by Republic Aircraft incorporating a sixteen-cylinder liquid-cooled Chrysler 2,500hp inverted-V engine, and creating a very streamlined, different looking P-47. In the fifty-six–month study begun in 1940 to research this program, which involved more than 300 designers, technicians, and engineers, Chrysler invested 25,000 hours of testing and wrote more than 1,000 engineering reports comprising 15 million words. To reduce engine vibration, Chrysler incorporated three rubber isolation mounts, comparable to those in the company's automobiles. The aircraft never went into production. *Chrysler Archives*

Late-model P-47Ds await fly-away at the Republic plant and airport in Farmingdale in October 1944. Those painted in camouflage colors are destined for the RAF. While Republic Aviation no longer exists, the airport is still in operation today. During WWII the company's work force increased from 176 in 1939 to 5,900 in 1941 and ultimately to 24,450 in 1944. *Cradle of Aviation Museum*

The clean lines of the P-47D-27 are apparent in this November 1944 publicity photo featuring aircraft of the RAF, USAAF, and the Brazilian Air Force.

Brazil provided a squadron of P-47Ds to the Allied cause in Europe. *Cradle of Aviation Museum*

essentially free to operate as attack aircraft, blasting railroads, shipping, airfields, supply centers, and enemy troop concentrations. Existing records indicate P-47s destroyed 9,000 locomotives, 86,000 railroad cars, 68,000 trucks, and 6,000 enemy tanks. When challenged, the P-47s were a formidable opponent, incorporating an excellent rate of climb, superior diving ability, powerful armament, and the ability to absorb significant damage and still return to base. They were equally comfortable at altitude or ground level. American Thunderbolts accounted for 3,916 enemy planes in air-to-air combat.

The P-47 stayed in the Air Force inventory for several years after the war, and into the 1950s with National Guard units. It was also the mainstay of several foreign air forces for many years following WWII, especially in South America.

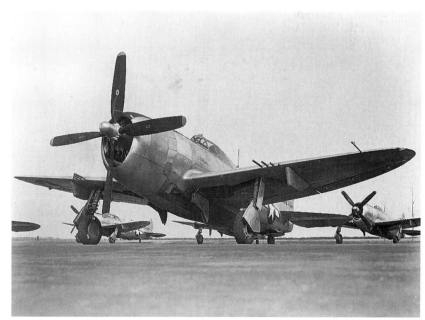

Early-model P-47D-22s in March 1944 are easily recognizable by their razorback fuselages, soon to be replaced on the bubble-canopy D models. The metal pieces extending from the bottom of the wing are wheel covers that cover the landing gear when retracted in flight. *Cradle of Aviation Museum*

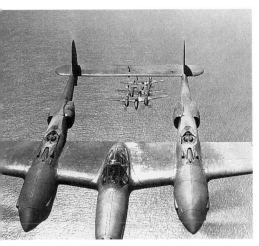

The P-38 was America's first twin-engined interceptor, designed as a defense against enemy bombers. This photograph offers an unusual view of the aircraft's exhaust-driven turbo-superchargers, positioned behind and on top of each engine. These areas used significant stainless steel construction. The protuberances on each side of the tail booms are the coolant radiator scoops and shrouds. Each P-38 Lightning cost the US government $125,000. *Lockheed Corporation*

The P-38 assembly line at Lockheed's Burbank, California, plant during the engine-installation phase of production. Spare engines are positioned in the center row between the aircraft. While the planes' machine guns and cannons have not yet been installed, the open panels on each side of the forward fuselage indicate the armament procedure is next. The P-38 carried four .50cal machine guns and a 20mm cannon in the nose. *Lockheed Corporation*

P-38 Lightning

The Germans called it *Der Gabelschwanz Teufel*, the fork-tailed devil, and the Japanese were not fond of it either. In the Pacific Theater the P-38 shot down more enemy planes than any other Allied aircraft. The twin-engined, twin-boomed Lightning gained fame and honors during WWII as a front-line fighter plane. Yet it was not even designed to be a fighter, but rather as a pursuit aircraft, whose role would be the interception and destruction of enemy bombers.

In 1936 the US government asked six aviation companies—Boeing, Consolidated, Curtiss, Douglas, Lockheed, and Vultee—to bid on a contract for an interceptor capable of 360mph at 20,000ft and 290mph at sea level, with the added ability to reach optimum altitude within 6min. Lockheed engineers under the leadership of H. L. Hibbard and Clarence "Kelly" Johnson responded that they could surpass those requirements and were awarded a pro-

The first two aircraft in line have received their three-bladed Curtiss Electric propellers, while those behind still await this production step. Barely visible just forward of the coolant radiator scoops on these two P-38s are the roundels of the RAF. At the far end of the plant between the hanging American flags are two Hudson bomber fuselages, also destined for Great Britain. Lockheed's main assembly line was 820ft long and contained thirty assembly stations. *Lockheed Corporation*

As wartime production soared, Lockheed did not have sufficient factory floor space to meet its manufacturing requirements, even though the company had purchased and converted a liquor distillery in 1939 to sustain production. The solution pictured here took advantage of the pleasant southern California weather and moved a major segment of the P-38 production out-of-doors. *Lockheed Corporation*

A woman worker put the finishing touches on the rear section of the P-38's bullet-proof plexiglass canopy. The US national insignia visible behind the worker is the early-war variety. The red ball in the middle of the white star was removed in mid-1942, as some American and Allied antiaircraft gunners mistook it for the famous red "meatball" used to mark Japanese aircraft. *Lockheed Corporation*

Another view of the P-38 outdoor assembly line at Lockheed's Burbank plant. The aircraft in the foreground is undergoing cockpit installation as well as engine completion. Guns and propellers will be added later. The whole factory area was camouflaged in case of an air attack by the Japanese. The P-38 was a large airplane, with a 52ft wingspan and a tail span of 26ft. The fuselage was nearly 38ft long, and the aircraft stood 11ft, 6in high. Its size alone created a space dilemma for the manufacturer. *Lockheed Corporation*

totype contract. The XP-38 first flew on January 27, 1939, and two weeks later, February 11, 1939, it set a transcontinental speed record. The XP-38 departed March Field, California, and arrived at Mitchel Field, New York, 7hr, 2min later, with two fuel stops along the way. Unfortunately, the pilot, US Army Lt. Benjamin Kelsey, lost an engine on his final approach and crash-landed, but the point had been made most emphatically. The contract was awarded.

Powered by twin 960hp Allison V-1710 engines, thirteen YP-38s were ordered by the USAAC and delivered between September 1940 and June 1941. In order to prevent engine torque that could pull the aircraft to one side, Lockheed used counter-rotating propellers. The plane's arma-

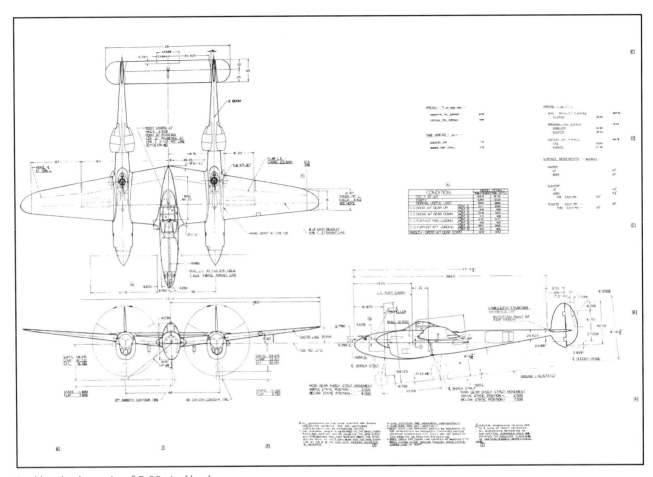

Lockheed schematic of P-38. *Lockheed Corporation*

Complete with external fuel tanks slung under their wings, these P-38Ls await final roll-out and fly-away. The national insignia featured on the wings and fuselage was standard after August 1943. At the top of this photograph is a Lockheed C-69 Constellation, a four-engined transport that first flew on January 9, 1943. It had been designed as a civilian aircraft before the war for TWA. Only twenty-two Constellations became operational during WWII with the USAAF. *Lockheed Corporation*

ment was formidable, consisting of a 37mm cannon, plus two .50cal and two .30cal machine guns. The weapons were all concentrated in the nose, where they could be fired unsynchronized because there was no propeller in the way. The XP-38 was 37ft, 10in long and stood 12ft, 10in high, later reduced to 9ft, 10in. Its wingspan was 52ft and loaded weight was 13,500lb.

The P-38, of which thirty were ordered, differed only slightly from the XP-38 (the two .30cal machine guns were upgraded to .50cal). One XP-38A was built incorporating a pressurized cockpit. The B and C designations were not used. Replacing the 20mm cannon with a 23mm Madsen gun and adding self-sealing fuel tanks were the major refinements to the P-38D, of which thirty-six were delivered to the USAAF. Of the 210 P-38Es manufactured, ninety-nine became F-4 photo-reconnaissance aircraft. The P-38F was the first model accepted for combat, and 527 of them, including 150 planes originally destined for the RAF, were delivered to US forces. Another 1,082 G models were built, again with only minor variations, and 601 H models, which had improved turbo-superchargers and could handle a larger payload, before the arrival of 2,970 P-38Js.

The J model was a major departure from previous P-38s. Capable of carrying a 4,000lb bomb load and armed with a 20mm cannon and four .50cal machine guns, it could operate at 44,000ft, and its range was increased to 2,600mi. The relocation of turbo-supercharger intercoolers from the leading edge of the inner wings to under the propellers permitted an increase in internal fuel capacity to 410gals, up from 300gals. The curved windscreen was replaced with a flat, bullet-proof one, and war emergency power was increased from 1,240hp to 1,425hp by modifying and improving the cooling system while retaining the V-1710-89/91 engines. Some P-38Js were outfitted with retractable dive brakes and others incorporated a bombardier's compartment in a plexiglass nose.

A slightly different view of the same production line features P-38s undergoing engine modification and gun installation prior to final assembly. Note the scooters and bicycles visible on the right side of the photograph. They provided swift transportation along the assembly line without adding to the noise level on the plant floor. The sign on the center bike says "U.S. Army Air Forces." In this picture, three Constellation fuselages are visible in the background. *Lockheed Corporation*

Thousands of employees at Lockheed's Burbank plant gather under camouflage netting to observe the raising of a government "E" banner. Ceremonies such as this were staged to support employee morale, especially as the war dragged on and the zeal exhibited in 1942 and 1943 flagged to a certain extent. A P-38 is visible in the center of the crowd. *Lockheed Corporation*

The K designator was used for one experimental aircraft, followed by 3,810 P-38Ls from Lockheed and another 113 Ls from Consolidated-Vultee in Nashville, Tennessee. This aircraft could fire rockets from under-wing launchers and increased war emergency power of each engine to 1,600hp at 28,700ft, using Allison V-1710-111 engines.

The last P-38 was the M model, used as a two-seater night fighter. The radar was positioned forward of the nose landing gear, and the radar operator was seated just behind and slightly above the pilot.

The P-38 enjoyed a successful career as a photo-reconnaissance aircraft designated F-4 and F-4A, followed by F-5A through F-5G. Total production, which ended with the Japanese surrender, totaled 9,923 P-38s.

Operationally, the P-38's greatest assets were its long range and ability to operate above 35,000ft. Although not combat ready at the time

Nearly as big as the B-25 medium bomber, the P-61 Black Widow was the only true American night-fighter developed during WWII. It operated in an atmosphere quite free of predators, and could unleash a fearsome amount of firepower with four .50cal machine guns and four 20mm cannons in the B model. The P-61 carried three crewmen, including a radar operator. *Northrop*

Looking much like the caricature of an absent-minded professor, an instructor explains the complexities of proper riveting procedures to a group of women employees. The wall chart diagrams examples of improper technique. All of the women in this picture wear kerchiefs to prevent their hair from being caught in moving machinery. Early in the war, movie actress Veronica Lake publicly snipped off her dangling hair curl as a patriotic gesture and an example to her fans working in factories who had copied her famous hair style. *Northrop*

In the foreground stands a row of rear center fuselage sections that will house the P-61B's gunner. A clear plexiglass observation bubble will be attached to complete the crew station. The upper turret's four .50cal machine guns and the four 20mm cannon mounted in the belly were fired by remote control. The circular cutout on top of the fuselage delineates the upper turret, which was usually locked in the front-firing position, but could be rotated rearward by the gunner. *Northrop*

of Pearl Harbor, it was operational in Europe by August 1942, and three P-38 groups were active in the North African campaign in late 1942–43 as well as in the later campaigns in Sicily and Italy. In the spring of 1942, P-38s sank three midget Japanese submarines, probably scheduled to land undercover agents on the California coast, only 20mi at sea from San Francisco, and in August 1942 P-38s shot down two Japanese flying boats near Adak, Alaska. The Lightning was used as a bomber escort in the European Theater, and in the Pacific the P-38 could undertake the long over-water flights necessary to strike back against the Japanese. It also could carry a respectable bomb load, with F models able to haul 2,000lb.

A worker using a pneumatic rivet gun attaches an aluminum panel to the frame of a P-61. The second woman holds a "bucking bar," which flattened the rivet end to complete the operation. Northrop, which had been in existence only two years when America entered the war, employed 10,000 workers, 3,600 of them women. *Northrop*

Looking north along the final P-61B assembly line at Northrop Aircraft's plant in Hawthorne, California. These aircraft await top turrets, cockpits, and propellers, as well as the glossy-black paint finish that was the trademark of the Black Widow. The P-61 was the most expensive US fighter built during WWII, costing $170,000 each. *Northrop*

In fact, one P-38 fighter group was used in a dive-bombing attack against the famous and heavily defended German synthetic fuel plant at Ploesti, Romania, in June 1944. These later J and L models were capable of delivering a 4,000lb bomb load.

The P-38's most famous episode took place on April 18, 1943, when eighteen Lightnings departed Guadalcanal in the Solomon Islands and made a perfect 435mi interception of an aircraft carrying Adm. Isoroku Yamamoto, commander-in-chief of Japan's combined fleet, the man who had planned the attack on Pearl Harbor. The P-38s shot down Yamamoto's aircraft, killing him and all those on board. They also shot down several enemy escort planes. All the P-38s but one returned safely to base.

American intelligence experts had broken Japanese military codes long before Pearl Harbor, which led directly to the knowledge of the Japanese leader's flight schedule exactly to the minute, essential for such a perfect long-range intercept. However, US military leaders first considered Yamamoto's probable successors before deciding to elimi-

Checking the control connections for the starboard rudder inside the starboard vertical stabilizer. The horizontal stabilizer between the two verticals was also anchored in the twin tails of the P-61, and the entire empennage was connected to the rear of the two engine nacelles with a double boom construction. *Northrop*

Backed by a row of rear center fuselages still lacking their plexiglass gunner enclosures, an imposing row of inner wing sections with engines and landing gear already in place await the next step in Northrop's assembly-line attachment to the completed fuselage. The P-61 featured two Pratt & Whitney Double Wasp engines that generated 2,000hp each (ultimately increased to 2,800hp each) and four-bladed props. *Northrop*

Exhibiting physical beauty suggestive of nearby Hollywood, this blond Californian (probably transplanted) rivets bulkhead rims to the fuselage frame of a Vengeance dive bomber. Northrop built 400 Vengeance dive bombers, which were designed by Vultee, as well as engine nacelles and cowlings for both the PBY5 and the B-17. Northrop's wartime contracts and subcontracts were valued at $65 million by war's end. *Northrop*

nate him and reached the conclusion that there was no superior military strategist available to the enemy who would be more difficult to deal with in the future. While acknowledging Yamamoto's brilliance, the American leadership felt that they understood him and could counter his efforts, which would not necessarily be true of his successor. Thus, the admiral's fate was sealed because his subordinates in the Japanese military did not possess his skills and abilities.

Aviation historian Robert F. Dorr tells of another unusual P-38 episode when photographer David Douglas Duncan was crammed into a fuel drop-tank with a plexiglass nose to take novel photographs of the air war in the Pacific. The tank was suspended from the belly of a P-38. While it is assumed that the pilot would not have released the tank under any imaginable circumstances, serious damage to the aircraft, such as loss of landing gear, or if the pilot was forced to bail out of a burning plane, would have left the famous

photographer in a rather untenable position!

The role of the P-38 changed as faster, more powerful and fuel efficient US fighters became available to the American war effort. The change in mission resulted in opportunities as a photo-reconnaissance aircraft and also as a ground strafer, concentrating the fire power of a 20mm cannon and four .50cal machine guns in its nose against enemy shipping and installations. Various other P-38 experiments included medevac duty utilizing converted drop tanks and also as a tow aircraft for combat gliders. After the war the P-38 was considered too difficult to maintain by emerging smaller air forces around the world, and it quickly disappeared from active status.

P-61 Black Widow

While only 706 P-61s were built during WWII by Northrop Aircraft in Hawthorne, California, it was the first American plane to be designed strictly for nighttime operations, and

There is a saying in the military that there are no atheists in a foxhole, and the same seems to be true of this employee luncheon scene atop a Northrop plant. Flanked by an invitation to play volleyball and a War Bond poster, the man on the podium in the rear of the picture appears to be praying, and without exception the workers have bowed their heads. Thermos jugs, brown bags, and black lunch boxes are much in evidence on the newly-constructed picnic tables. *Northrop*

Prominent in this frontal view of a P-61 under construction is the fiberglass nose housing the SCR-720 radar. Airborne Interception (AI) radar resulted from a joint British and American scientific effort at the Massachusetts Institute of Technology (MIT), near Boston, Massachusetts. The radar included components from Bell Telephone, Sperry, and Westinghouse. The glossy post extending downward from the bottom of the nose is the antenna, which spun continually, searching for enemy aircraft with a radar beam. Also prominent is the P-61's nose wheel. In early models, the gear on occasion accidentally extended in flight when the four 20mm cannons were fired. *Northrop*

A row of early-model P-61Bs (no dorsal turret) are ready for fly-away at Northrop's Hawthorne plant. While awaiting construction of the company's first building in 1939, founder Jack Northrop maintained his office in the Hawthorne Hotel, which in earlier times had been a house of ill repute known as the "Yellow Peril" due to its garish appearance. Before starting his own company, Northrop had been an aircraft designer with both Lockheed and Douglas Aircraft. *Northrop*

also to possess design-integrated airborne radar.

In the years prior to WWII, most nations were technically unable to pursue the complexities of night operations, or their military budgets would not support the effort. Early in the conflict, however, the British and the Germans, as a result of nighttime bombing campaigns against their homelands, seriously but haphazardly deployed night interceptors for defense. Much of the Blitz against London took place at night, and after suffering prohibitive daytime bombing losses, the RAF

A silver-painted P-40N awaits fly-away, October 20, 1944. Standing 12ft, 4in off the ground, with a 37ft, 4in wingspan, the N model was 33ft, 4in long and had a wing area of 236sq-ft. Its maximum speed was 343mph at 15,000ft. It was armed with six .50cal machine guns and could carry 1,500lb of bombs. *Pete Bowers Collection*

In this January 1943 ceremony at an airport in North Africa, a dozen P-40F Warhawks are formally transferred by the United States to the Free French Air Forces. The USAAF ordered 1,311 F models, which were powered by Merlin V-1650-1 engine, built in America by Packard. A C-47 stands guard over the proceedings at the far end of the apron. *Pete Bowers Collection*

Bomber Command concentrated its efforts against Germany in the dark. However, airborne radar was rather crude and susceptible to failure, so night-fighter pilots still needed to search the surrounding air for the blacker silhouette of an aircraft against a black sky, or the exhaust flames from its engines. Then they had to stalk the enemy and bring it down, all in all a rather difficult program. The United States experimented not very successfully with the A-20 Havoc medium bomber configured as the P-70 night interceptor against the Japanese. It also converted several P-38Hs for night-time duties with measurably better results, but the P-38M, designed specifically as a night-fighter, was barely operational (four aircraft) when the war ended in the Pacific.

In the fall of 1940 the USAAC had asked Northrop Aircraft to design a plane capable of carrying an airborne radar unit, which was eventually known as the SCR-720 and was under development at Massachusetts Institute of Technology by American and British scientists.

Amid some rapid design changes, a price quote for two prototype airplanes was presented, and a contract signed in early January 1941. Two XP-61s and thirteen YP-61s were ordered in January and March 1941, followed by a production contract for 150 P-61s in September 1941 and another contract for 410 P-61s in February 1942, after the outbreak of war increased the urgency for all war production.

The P-61A (200 produced) was a massive airplane for a fighter, powered by two eighteen-cylinder Pratt & Whitney R-2800-10 radial engines. It could fly at 366mph at 20,900ft and had a 41,000ft ceiling, with a range of 1,350mi. With its twin-boom fuselage it was superficially similar to the P-38, but the comparison ended quickly. The P-61A weighed 25,150lb loaded and carried a crew of three: pilot, radar operator, and rear gunner. Radar was contained in the elongated nose. The P-61A was 48ft, 11in long with a wingspan of 66ft. It stood 14ft, 8in off the ground. Initially it was designed to carry a dorsal (top) turret and a ventral (bottom) turret, both of which were remote-controlled; each was equipped with four .50cal machine guns. The ven-

A line of P-40N Kittyhawks in British camouflage await tail sections on the floor of the Curtiss plant in Buffalo, New York. The P-40 was not used as a first-line fighter by the British because the RAF possessed its own Spitfires and Hurricanes for that capacity early in the war.

However, the P-40 was very popular within the British forces as a ground-support aircraft, and its rugged construction was capable of absorbing significant punishment while fulfilling this role. *Pete Bowers Collection*

A row of P-40B forward fuselages with twelve-cylinder Allison V-1710 engines already installed at the Curtiss Buffalo plant. These aircraft were not equipped with turbo-superchargers and were not

very effective above 15,000ft. The B models were armed with two .50cal machine guns in the nose and two .30cals in each wing. Only 131 B models were manufactured. *Pete Bowers Collection*

tral turret was replaced while still on the drawing board with four 20mm cannons in the wings. The cannons were repositioned on a lower fuselage platform while the aircraft was still in the experimental stage. After the P-61A became operational the upper turret was removed due to excessive tail buffeting. Later A models had slightly larger engines and could carry under-wing two 1,600lb bombs or two 300gal drop tanks.

The main production model of this unique aircraft was the P-61B, of which 450 were built. The last 250 aircraft in this version were refitted with the dorsal gun turret as the tail buffeting problem was corrected. Many B models were also fitted with two additional external racks for bombs or drop tanks. Engines were upgraded to Pratt & Whitney R-2800-65 radials, loaded weight to

Subcontracting came into its own during WWII, mainly due to the enormous strain placed on the facilities of the primary manufacturers of major defense systems. The Maytag Corporation, famous for its washing machines, was a major sub-contractor in the aviation industry, building the Allison V-1710 engine used in the P-38 and P-40, and in the early P-51 Mustangs. The engine pictured here was on display at a Maytag product show in Newton, Iowa, open to employees as well as the general public in December 1943. Maytag provided parts for sixteen different Allied aircraft. *Maytag Archives*

P-40Es in early-war markings. This model was equipped to carry a drop tank or 500lb bomb under the fuselage. Still powered by the Allison engine, the E model was flown by many Commonwealth air forces, including those of Australia, Canada, New Zealand, and South Africa. In the background at Plant Two in Buffalo are O-52 Owl observation planes under construction. Curtiss built 203 O-52s but they were not used under combat conditions. *Pete Bowers Collection*

29,700lb, and range to 1,900mi. The final forty-one P-61Cs were much the same as the end of the B model production run. However, the CH-5 turbo-supercharged R-2800-73 engines increased the maximum speed to 430mph at 30,000ft. Another order for 476 C models was canceled at war's end.

As part of the P-61's flight testing, three planes were flown through searchlight patterns at night to ascertain the best nocturnal camouflage color scheme. The olive-drab model and the unpainted model were both seen rather quickly by ground observers, but the aircraft painted glossy black was not seen at all, even though it flew directly through a searchlight beam. Glossy black was immediately adopted as the color for this night-fighter. As its registration numbers were painted in red, assembly line employees nicknamed the P-61 the Black Widow, after the poisonous spider that possessed the same color markings (black with red underside).

The combat role of the Black Widow varied as the offensive abilities of Germany and Japan decreased. As a defensive aircraft, the P-61 was used to shoot down invading V-1 rockets ("buzz bombs") fired from the Continent against Great Britain. On the other side of the world, the Japanese by mid-1944 were forced to use their dwindling air resources at night due to American air superiority during daylight hours. In this theater the P-61s patrolled assigned sectors to disrupt enemy attacks and harassment missions with deadly effect. Due to many friendly aircraft in the vicinity of US bases and forces, it was necessary for the P-61 crew to make a visual identification before firing. With the Black Widow's fire power, this close-range procedure usually resulted in a kill or at least serious damage to the enemy aircraft. The P-61 was also used to protect the B-29 bases on Saipan and Tinian from night attacks by Japanese aircraft. The presence of these night-fighters was well-known to the opposition, creating a very uncomfortable operational atmosphere for them as they realized they could be stalked at any time by a superior aircraft, and that the darkness would no longer protect them. Army Air Force night-fighters had 158 confirmed kills during WWII, along with an unknown number of probables that disappeared into the darkness, often badly damaged. There were eight night-fighter aces, six of them in the 422nd NFS in Europe. By war's end, there were fifteen P-61 squadrons operating in all theaters.

As Axis offensive capabilities waned, the Black Widows went hunting over enemy territory at night, putting at risk various enemy aircraft carrying out internal missions, such as troop transports, cargo flights, and courier missions that heretofore could carry out their assignments behind their own lines untroubled by US aircraft. Dropping flares for visibility, the P-61s attacked enemy airfields, troop concentrations, and rail facilities at night, causing significant damage while depriving the Germans of any respite from Allied attacks. The P-61s were also used as night and even day intruders in the Pacific, once again due to their awesome firepower and the meager opposition from Japanese fighters. Until 1950 it was the only night-fighter available to the US Air Force. As several aviation historians have noted, the P-61 Black Widow fighter was the forerunner of the all-weather fighter-bombers that are the mainstay of the tactical US Air Force to this day.

P-40 Warhawk

The P-40 was the only combat-ready fighter in the USAAF arsenal when war became a reality in December 1941. It was soon very recognizable to the public due to the ferocious shark's mouth painted on the engine cowlings of P-40B Warhawks flown by the "Flying Tigers," who were operating against the Japanese in Burma and China. This public relations gimmick was not an American creation, but originated in a British P-40 fighter squadron based in North Africa in 1940.

Although the P-40 was inferior in performance to many enemy aircraft early in the war, it was America's front-line fighter and the only one produced in significant numbers. During 1941 2,246 of them were built, and this figure increased to 4,453 in 1942. The superior American fighter aircraft needed to win the war would not become operational until 1943 and 1944. In the meantime, the venerable P-40 bore the brunt of the USAAF's battle against the Axis. *Pete Bowers Collection*

The P-40C was a transitional aircraft (only 193 became operational) that first incorporated self-sealing fuel tanks. These planes feature the early-war national insignia, a red ball inside a white star inside a blue ball. In an effort to reduce weight and increase maneuverability, armament was reduced from three machine guns to two in each wing, as evidenced by the two gun ports in the forward wing edge of the plane in the foreground. *Pete Bowers Collection*

P-40s share the factory floor with C-46 Commandos at the Buffalo plant of Curtiss-Wright in April 1942. The next step in P-40 manufacture is the mating of fuselage and wings. Although plant construction went forward at a great rate during the war years, it could not keep pace with the outpouring of defense products required for victory. *National Archives*

This two seat training version was known as the TP-40N, some of which carried the Allison V-1710 engine due a shortage of Merlin (Packard) engines. Two C-46 transports stand outside the Buffalo hangar in August 1944. *Pete Bowers Collection*

This early P-40 in pre-war markings (note red-and-white striped tail) is taking off from a US Navy carrier in the North Atlantic. P-40s were not designed as carrier aircraft, but wartime conditions create unusual circumstances. The plane's destination was Iceland, occupied by American forces in 1940 and used as a weather station. Throughout the war Germany was denied this vital information, and the Allies capitalized on this advantage on many occasions, most notably with precise weather data prior to the Normandy invasion in June 1944. *Pete Bowers Collection*

A new P-40B prepared for over-the-road shipment, with the complete wing section in place over the fuselage. Large aircraft were usually flown to their destinations, but the reduced fuel capacity of most fighters required truck shipment from the factory, especially if the ultimate destination was overseas. *Pete Bowers Collection*

A P-40D at the Buffalo plant in early 1942 undergoes compass calibration on a painted "Compass Rose." Other P-40s and O-52s await their turn on the ramp in front of the hangar. *National Air & Space Museum*

Three P-40Es with centerline drop tanks visible are parked prior to flight testing, while inside the hangar other P-40s are in various stages of construction. Note the company logo emblazoned on the wall over the massive hangar doors. *Pete Bowers Collection*

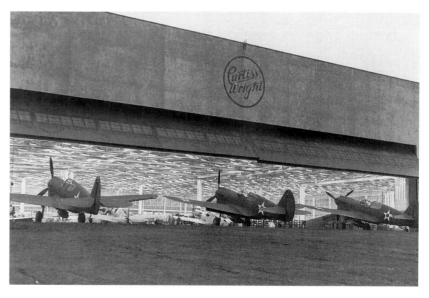

Although it was not the aerodynamic equal of its German and Japanese adversaries, the P-40 could compete against them (most notably the Japanese for American pilots early in the war) when combat tactics were modified to enhance the P-40's strengths and minimize its weaknesses. As the "Flying Tigers," whose real name was the American Volunteer Group (AVG), were under contract to China and were not part of the US military, their leaders, specifically retired USAAC Col. Claire Chennault, were free to design their own tactics, and the AVG had a tremendously successful kill ratio against the Japanese, losing only four pilots in combat while destroying 286 enemy planes in the skies over Burma and China. The same could not be said of American P-40 pilots in the Philippines who were required to follow USAAF air combat procedures, most of which were not only obsolete but actually suicidal when facing experienced opponents flying

Buffalo, New York, is well-known for its annual snowfall, as this photograph of the Curtiss-Wright ramp area attests. Three P-40Fs and a British Lendlease Kittyhawk III in company with several C-46 await disposition. The national insignia seen here was in use in late 1942 and the first half of 1943. *Pete Bowers Collection*

A P-40N known as *Flung Dung* parked on the airfield at Dinjan, India. The N model reached the greatest production numbers of any P-40, with 5,219 of them built at three different Curtiss plants. Even so, the United States exported more of them than it used in its own forces. The P-40 was flown by twenty-eight different Allied air forces during WWII, and gained a reputation for durability, if not for speed and maneuverability. More than 14,000 of them were manufactured during WWII. *Pete Bowers Collection*

"Wings Over America" was a famous USAAC recruiting poster by Tom Woodburn, first displayed in 1939. As war clouds gathered, many young men responded to the call. The aircraft featured appear to be P-36A Hawks, developed in 1938 by Curtiss Aircraft. Although obsolete by 1941, two Hawks fought against the attacking Japanese at Pearl Harbor, after which the plane was relegated to trainer status. *National Archives*

Below

A B-25B in early-war markings. The red ball in the center of the aircraft's national insignia was removed in mid-1942 to avoid confusion with the red "meatball" vividly displayed on Japanese aircraft. Sixteen B-25Bs were used by the Doolittle Raiders in their attack on Tokyo, Yokohama, Nagoya, Kobe, and Osaka on April 18, 1942. Each carried 2,000lb of bombs. Because the attacking fleet was detected by enemy picket boats, the aircraft were launched more than 600mi from Japan and did not have enough fuel to reach their destination airfields in China. Fifteen crews either parachuted from their planes or crash-landed in China. Three aviators were killed in landing accidents and eight were taken prisoner by the Japanese. The captured fliers were incarcerated as war criminals, and three of them were executed during the war. Another died in captivity. One crew landed in the Soviet Union and was interned for thirteen months. The rest of the Doolittle Raiders were assisted to safety by Chinese soldiers and civilians. In retaliation, the Japanese killed 250,000 Chinese villagers. *Rockwell International*

An operational B-25H with four .50cal machine guns in the nose protruding above the mouth of the 75mm cannon. Also visible are the port-side, fixed .50cal guns, as well as the top turret, waist guns, and rear gunner turret. *Rockwell International*

An A-26C, of which 1,091 were manufactured, featuring postwar national insignia. The red bar in the white field became official in January 1947. The C model was designed as a conventional bomber with a plexiglass nose and less armament than the B models. *McDonnell Douglas Aircraft*

The P-51D was the major production model of the famed Mustang fighter in WWII. Standing 13ft, 8in off the ground, it had a wingspan of 37ft and was 32ft long. The aircraft weighed 10,100lb loaded and cruised at 362mph. Its maximum speed at 25,000ft was 439mph. With a 2,000lb bomb load the P-51D had a range of 2,300mi. *Rockwell International*

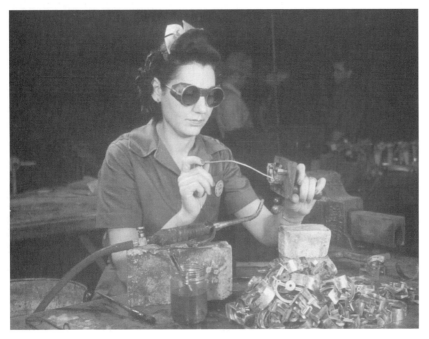

Pages 100 -103
American women joined men on assembly lines all over the nation during WWII. They were often referred to as "Rosie the Riveter," an appellation that became a proud badge to these women who proved their ability to perform many of the tasks previously reserved for male laborers. These six ladies, some wearing company blouses, were employed at North American's Inglewood plant and are observed performing a number of machine tool and assembly-line tasks.
Author's Collection

First flown in 1941, the Curtiss AT-9 Fledgling, later known as the "Jeep," entered production in 1942. A total of 791 AT-9s and AT-9As were built at a cost of $34,900 each before production ceased in February 1943. It was the major multi-engined trainer employed by the USAAC, and was later replaced by the plywood and aluminum AT-10 manufactured by Beech Aircraft. *Author's Collection*

A "Rosie the Riveter" tightens an aluminum panel just aft of the ammunition storage panel on a P-38 Lightning. While many women war workers, especially in southern California, were indeed glamorous, they were also very proficient and won legitimate praise for the high quality of work performed in aircraft manufacture. *Lockheed Corporation*

A C-47B on a test run over southern California in July 1944. The size of the air crew on board varied according to mission, but there were usually two pilots. While C-47s were not combat aircraft they were often used in combat situations, whether carrying ammunition and supplies to front-line areas or dropping paratroopers and glider troops behind enemy lines. As they were neither armed nor armored and did not have seal-sealing fuel tanks, they were often in precarious positions when attacked by enemy planes or antiaircraft guns. Throughout the war the C-47 retained windows or portholes on the fuselage, as it was thought that riflemen could defend the plane from enemy attack by firing through these openings. *McDonnell Douglas Aircraft*

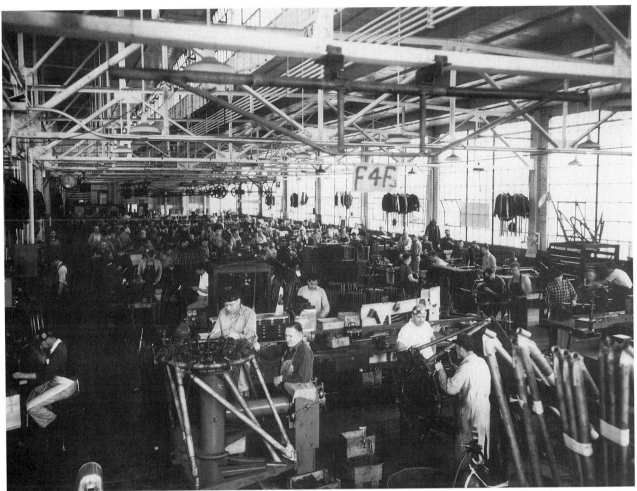

Grumman workers welding engine mounts for the F4F at Plant Thirteen in Lindenhurst, Long Island, not to be confused with Linden, New Jersey. The company had four plants at its Bethpage locale, and during the first five months of 1942 opened five auxiliary plants on Long Island employing 3,000 workers. By war's end Grumman had converted twenty alternate sites, including a shooting gallery, a wheelbarrow factory, and the Pan American World Airways base at Port Washington. *Northrop Grumman Archives*

Men and women of Grumman in Plant Three in Bethpage building leading wing edges for the F4F during 1942. The folding wings of the Wildcat pivoted and stored parallel to the aircraft's fuselage. They were hand-cranked into position and secured with internal locking pins. It was estimated that this innovation increased carrier aircraft storage capability by 150 percent. It also increased the cost of the plane to the government by $5,000 to $31,000 a copy. *Northrop Grumman Archives*

The Grumman F6F-5 fighter was 33ft, 7in long and stood 13ft, 1in off the ground. Its wingspan was 42ft, 10in, and the total wing area was 334sq-ft. The F6F was powered by Pratt & Whitney's R-2800 Double Wasp engine, which generated 2,000hp. Although contracted for by the Navy as a backup to the F4U Corsair, the Hellcat became operational before its competitor did, and finished the war as the best all-around carrier-based fighter in the service of any of the participants. *United Technologies Archives*

In Bethpage's Plant Three, multiple rows of F6F fuselages, recently sprayed with yellow zinc chromate to retard corrosion, await the next step in the manufacturing process, which will be the fitting of tail surfaces and wing stubs. As the Hellcat operated almost exclusively in a saltwater environment and was most often stored on the open deck of an aircraft carrier, corrosion was a factor not to be overlooked. Any structural weakening of the aircraft could lead to unnecessary losses of valuable planes and pilots. *Northrop Grumman Archives*

One of Grumman's 8,000 female production workers sets rivets in the bottom side of an F6F fuselage, approximately midway between the cockpit and tail surfaces. The two big holes are on the centerline and will hold two recognition lights. The third recognition light is located in the next panel, and is not visible in this photograph. The other holes are fuselage drains, and the small protruding posts are temporary fasteners. *Northrop Grumman Archives*

The F4U Corsair Navy and Marine Corps fighter was 33ft, 4in long and stood 16ft, 1in off the ground. Its wingspan was 41ft, and its wing area was 314sq-ft. The F4U's loaded weight was approximately 14,000lb. Powered by a Pratt & Whitney R-2800-10 water-injected Double Wasp engine, its rate of climb was 2,890 feet per minute and its service ceiling was 36,900ft. Depending on the model, the F4U's range was 1,015 to 1,300mi, which was increased by 300mi at cruising speed with the addition of external fuel drop tanks. Early Corsairs had a top speed of 417mph. Late-war F4U-4s reached 448mph. The plane stayed in production for more than ten years and operational until 1965, with a total of 12,571 manufactured. *Loral—Goodyear Aircraft Archives*

Grumman expanded its plant facilities as rapidly as possible even before the war began, but with shortages of skilled workers to build the plants and lack of materials due to defense production demands, the company turned to "dispersal," buying or renting existing plants in the area for parts production. In this photograph, Grumman employees are manufacturing TBF wings at Plant Fifteen in Port Washington on Long Island. Turrets and cowlings were also produced at this location, which had before the war hangared Pan American World Airways' giant trans-Atlantic Clippers. *Northrop Grumman Archives*

First ordered by the Marines, the Douglas SBD was 31ft, 9in long; stood 13ft, 7in tall; had a wingspan of 39ft; and a wing area of 325sq-ft. This weary SBD-1 is missing its rear gunner and his twin .30cal machine guns, but does have a yellow practice bomb in place. Upon release, the 500lb bomb would swing down on the yoke that connected it to the fuselage, thereby missing the propeller as it fell free toward the target. The long tube attached horizontally to the fuselage in front of the pilot is the bombsight, which would sometimes fog over due to the dramatic change in temperature from cold to hot during the attack dive, especially over the Pacific Ocean. *McDonnell Douglas Aircraft*

An SBD-5 Dauntless with 500lb bomb in place and the rear gunner, armed with twin .30cal machine guns, on alert. The SBD's top speed in level flight was 250mph and its range was 1,115mi at 138mph. The Wright R-1820-60 engine created 1,200hp. The plane's initial rate of climb was 1,400 feet per minute and its service ceiling was 25,100ft. The SBD-5 weighed 6,675lb empty and 10,855lb loaded. A total of 2,409 of this model were built, while the sum total for all models of the SBD were 5,936 planes. *McDonnell Douglas Aircraft*

Judging from the tail numbers on this row of SBDs, these are the -3 version, of which 584 were manufactured. The SBD-3 incorporated a much larger engine than its predecessors, a Wright R-1820 that generated 1,000hp. The Dauntless was fitted with a three-bladed Hamilton Standard hydromatic propeller. Outlining the national insignia on the wing and fuselage in red was only standard practice for a few months, June through August, in 1943. *Northrop*

Let me tell you of my heroes...
braver men I never knew,
They came into my boyhood world -
in the fighter planes they flew.
For I lived just south of Mitchel Field,
and from fond memories I yield
my story of the things I saw...
of those fighter pilots bound for war.

Dream back with me to that airbase,
and watch them down the runway race,
just distant specks, but coming fast -
in seconds, they would roar on past
and rise from Mitchel's concrete slabs -
their props, just discs of whirling jabs
that lift them onward, toward the sky,
my heroes—in the planes they fly!

Airborne, and barely off the ground,
they streak in front of me...
and as each Thunderbolt flies by,
its pilot I could see,

all harnessed in their flight machines;
their silhouettes still stir my dreams!

With goggles on and parachutes,
hunched forward in those chunky brutes...
each flyer, now formation bound,
full throttled engines shook the ground...
swept by so low, you'd feel the breeze,
some barely cleared the roofs and trees!

They climbed with power, heading west,
each banking sharp to catch the rest.
Up over Hempstead they would ride,
their presence filled us all with pride!
In massive waves, they'd circle high...
I stared in awe as they flew by!

Those pilots and their Thunderbolts,
have long since flown away...
but their deeds honored
in that World War,
we remember, to this day.

Deep over Europe, as escorts,
through flak-filled skies, with Flying Forts;
they battled bravely, that we know,
and earned respect from every foe
who felt the blows, the jarring jolts -
from brave men in their Thunderbolts!

They're older now, some turning gray...
and Mitchel's closed, I'm sad to say.
Along its runways slowly rise
new buildings now to fill the skies
where once upon a bygone day,
those planes and pilots came my way.

Yes, I was there, I saw it all...
for you, their daring, I recall!
Though nothing stays the same, it seems,
their silhouettes still stir my dreams!

—Wendell S. Storms
April 1984

The P-39D-1 Airacobra in 1941, featuring a 20mm cannon fired through the propeller hub and two .30cal machine guns in each wing. Powered by an Allison V-1710-35 engine and incorporating self-sealing fuel tanks, the D model was ordered by the British through LendLease as the Airacobra I, but failed to live up to expectations. Without the turbo-supercharged engine that was part of the original specifications, the P-39 performed poorly above 17,000ft and was relegated mainly to trainer status in the United States, although it was very popular as a tank buster and low-altitude fighter in service with the Soviet air forces. *Pete Bowers Collection*

The first major production model of Bell Aircraft's unique fighter was the P-39N, with 2,095 manufactured. The P-39N-5 featured here reduced armor weight from 231 to 193lb and replaced the armor in the rear of the cockpit with bullet-resistant glass. Most of this production went to the Soviets, who enjoyed great success with the P-39 in a ground-support capacity. The shackles visible under the fuselage could support a 500lb bomb or a 75gal fuel tank. *Pete Bowers Collection*

faster and more maneuverable aircraft. However, until it was replaced by superior American fighters such as the P-38, P-47, and P-51, the P-40 acquitted itself satisfactorily for its time and place. By the summer of 1945, there was only one P-40 group still operational in the USAAF.

Curtiss Aircraft initially planned to upgrade its P-36 Mohawk fighter in 1938 by replacing the plane's radial engine with the Allison V-1710 V-12 liquid-cooled engine. It was known as the XP-40 and mounted six .30cal machine guns. When the US government offered Curtiss a $12.8 million mass-production contract for 524 of the altered aircraft in April 1939, the P-40 was born. At this time the plane's radiator was moved from the rear of the fuselage to the nose, giving the P-40 a distinctive barrel front end which lent itself to the shark teeth artistry. Most initial production was sold to the French and British, and the latter designated the P-40 as the Tomahawk. The P-40B incorporated armor protection for the pilot and self-sealing gas tanks, which spared many an aviator the terror of a fuel fire at altitude and speed. With President Roosevelt's approval, 100 B models were sent to the AVG before America entered the war.

The C model offered improved self-sealing tanks, and the United States ordered 193 of this model in 1941. Almost all of the 582 D models produced were shipped to the RAF, which named them Kittyhawk I. Mass production became a reality when the United States procured 2,320 P-40Es, and the British, calling it the Kittyhawk II, also purchased several hundred E models. Increased

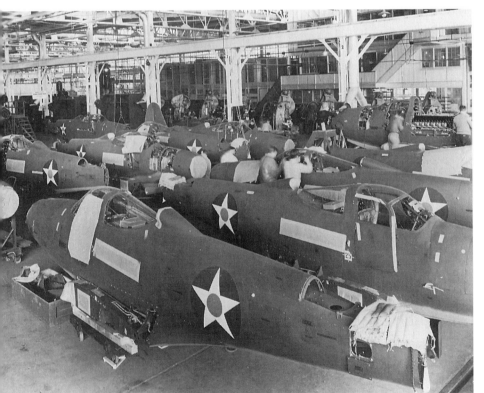

P-39Ds in early-war markings on the assembly line at Bell's Buffalo, New York, facility. At this point the forward and rear fuselages have been joined and await the center wing section. The window on the P-39's automobile-style door actually rolled up and down as it would on a car. *Pete Bowers Collection*

Close-up of the 37mm cannon that was fired through the propeller spinner on the P-39N. In this instance the propeller is a three-bladed Curtiss Electric. This cannon was effective in the ground-support role assigned to the P-39 by virtually all the Allied services that operated this aircraft in combat. A continuous circular magazine located in the forward compartment contained thirty rounds of 37mm ammunition for the cannon. *National Air & Space Museum*

Unique to the P-39 was the installation of the Allison V-1710 engine behind the cockpit, visible on these N models under construction. The 8ft propeller shaft ran under the pilot's seat. A 37mm cannon, upgraded from 20mm on the D model, was positioned forward of the cockpit and is discernible in this photograph. C-46 transports built under license by Bell share the factory floor. *Pete Bowers Collection*

fuel capacity to 200gals and a weight increase to 8,840lb were significant changes incorporated in the E model. It could also carry an external fuel tank under the belly or a 500lb bomb, and the six wing-mounted machine guns were upgraded to .50cal.

The P-40F was a vastly improved version of this rugged aircraft and was equipped with Packard V-1650 engine, which was the US version of the Rolls-Royce Merlin engine used in the P-51 Mustang. Its speed increased to 373mph and its gross weight rose to 10,000lb. Even though newer aircraft rolling off assembly lines all over America could outperform the P-40, the US government ordered 1,311 F models. Design experiments continued with the J model, which had a a turbo-supercharger fitted on its Allison V-1710 engine, but this model did not go into production. The P-40K used the

This drawing illustrates the engine and cannon placement that was unique to the P-39 Airacobra. The engine is located behind the cockpit and attached to the propeller by a shaft that runs under the cockpit. A 37mm cannon and two .50cal machine guns are positioned in the nose and fire through the propeller hub, while two .30cal machine guns are located in each wing. *National Air & Space Museum*

Allison V-1710-73 engine rated at 1,200hp. This aircraft also introduced a longer fuselage and taller tail for the P-40. Although priority for the limited supply of Merlin/Packard engines was given to P-51 Mustang production, a version of this power plant was used in the P-40L. The USAAF ordered 700 L models, which only carried two .50cal machine guns as part of a weight-saving program designed to improve performance. It was soon followed by the M model, which incorporated an improved Allison 1,200hp engine.

The largest number of P-40s manufactured was the N model, of which 5,219 were built. It was powered by the Allison V-1710-99 engine and had a maximum speed of 243mph at 15,000ft, weighing 8,850lb loaded. It could carry 1,500lb of bombs. The N model had a ceiling of 31,000ft and its range was 1,100mi. This final mass production model was 33ft long and stood 12ft,

Many Hollywood actors and actresses gave wholehearted support to the war effort by participating in War Bond and defense-plant rallies to foster civilian employee morale and to raise money. In this instance, popular movie star Dorothy Lamour appeared at an Allison engine plant rally in Indianapolis, Indiana. Allison built the V-1710 engine that powered the P-39, in addition to the P-38 and P-40. At peak production in 1943 Allison built 3,000 engines per month and employed 23,019 workers, of which 31 percent were female. *Allison Gas Turbine Division, General Motors*

The port wing is being fitted to this P-39D in early-war markings at the Bell plant in Buffalo, New York. The center wing section was incorporated into the forward fuselage and each outer wing was attached with thirty bolts to the center section. The wingspan of the P-39 was 34ft. *Pete Bowers Collection*

4in off the ground. Its wingspan was 37ft, 4in. When a shortage of Packard/Merlin engines for 300 F and L models occurred, these aircraft were fitted with Allison engines and designated the P-40R, the last of the P-40s.

While the P-40 was the third most numerous fighter produced with 13,753 aircraft built at three Curtiss plants, it was superseded early in the war by the P-47 and P-51. Thereafter, it was most often used by American forces in an air-to-ground strafing role, and it proved a rugged, durable aircraft able to absorb heavy damage. In air combat it was not maneuverable enough to stay with front-line enemy aircraft in climbs and turns. However, if the P-40 held an altitude advantage and attacked enemy aircraft from above, its weight allowed it to dive away from opponents after inflicting damage with its six .50cal machine guns. When flown in Burma and China by the AVG, the P-40B's cockpit armor and self-sealing fuel tanks were distinct advantages not enjoyed by Japanese pilots flying aircraft that were aerodynamically superior, but offered little protection from enemy guns.

Many Allied nations flew the P-40 during WWII, including Great Britain, Australia, Canada, South Africa, and New Zealand. It was also supplied in great numbers to the Soviet Union and served from North Africa to the South Pacific, and everywhere in between.

P-39 Airacobra

While the P-39 was considered at best a mediocre fighter aircraft during WWII, in truth it had the potential to be much more. Designed by Robert Wood of the Bell Aircraft Company in 1937 in response to a US government request for bids, the most unusual feature of the P-39 was its engine location in the middle of the fuselage, connected to the propeller by an 8ft shaft. In the Model 3 the liquid-cooled engine was in front of the cockpit, which in turn was placed far back on the fuse-

Called the P-400 by its American manufacturers because it was scheduled for export, it was known to the British as the Airacobra I. This aircraft has been packaged at the factory for shipment across the Atlantic Ocean and is already painted with RAF roundels on the wings. *Pete Bowers Collection*

Reconfigured as a trainer aircraft at a stateside air base, this TP-39Q is equipped with two seats in tandem for the student and the instructor. Painted with post-August 1943 markings and featuring a teepee on the squadron insignia, this plane carries no armament. *Pete Bowers Collection*

The Bell P-39Q Airacobra, of which 4,905 were built. This aircraft was armed with the 37mm cannon, two .50cal machine guns in the forward fuselage that fired through the propeller, and one externally-mounted .50cal machine gun under each wing, noticeable in this photograph. *Pete Bowers Collection*

While the British were not overly pleased with the performance of the P-39D (Airacobra I) as a pursuit aircraft, they did in fact equip RAF 601 Squadron with approximately sixty-five planes, several of which are shown here at Duxford Air Base on October 19, 1941. Two months later the United States entered the war and requisitioned the remaining RAF P-39D order for use by American forces. *Pete Bowers Collection*

lage. The result was inadequate visibility for the pilot and led to the model's rejection. In the Model 4, which was accepted, the Allison-1710 engine was located behind the cockpit and positioned amidships. Bell hoped to enhance the P-39's maneuverability by positioning the weight of cockpit, pilot, and engine at the aircraft's center of gravity. The manufacturer also installed a 20mm cannon forward of the cockpit in what would normally be the engine compartment, and this weapon fired through the propeller hub. Among the Airacobra's other unique features was a cockpit door that swung open like a car door and, for the first time on a US fighter, retractable tricycle landing gear.

The P-39 was powered by the twelve-cylinder Allison V-1710-37 engine, which generated 1,200hp. The initial design called for a rear-mounted booster engine to improve the aircraft's rate of climb, but this was rejected in favor of the B-5 turbo-supercharger.

A year and a half later, in April 1939, the XP-39 was test flown by pilot James Taylor at Wright Field, Ohio, attaining 390mph at 20,000ft. Although some cooling problems had to be corrected, the aircraft had performed well, and one dozen YP-39s were ordered by the US government. In addition, one YP-39A was ordered, which used a more powerful Allison engine that did not incorporate the turbo-supercharger. This model became the standard, and the P-39 never lived up to its high expectations after this modification.

Only one B model was built with minor changes including the installation of two .30cal machine guns in the nose. The USAAC then ordered twenty P-39Cs which added self-sealing gas tanks and a bullet-resistant windshield. Due to the many planning changes since the original government contract had been signed, the twenty aircraft had been designated P-45s. However, for bureaucratic and budgetary reasons, they were redesignated P-39Cs.

In August of 1941 the RAF ordered 675 D models armed with a 20mm cannon manufactured by Hispano Suiza and six .303cal machine guns. The remaining 248 P-39Ds built for the USAAF carried different armament: a 37mm cannon and two .50cal machine guns in the nose and two .30cal machine guns in each wing. The D model's internal fuel tank capacity was reduced from 170 to 120 US gallons, but a 75gal center line external fuel tank was added. The external-fuel-tank mounts could also carry a 500lb bomb. The British were not pleased with the performance of the P-39, and quickly phased them out as front-line fighters. These export versions were designated P-400s and were assigned to American units in the early months of the war and were also shipped in quantity to the Soviet Union. They were used as trainers but also for air-

In July 1943 these P-39s were ready for delivery to the Soviet Union. The great majority of the 4,773 P-39s destined for the Soviets via LendLease were flown across Canada to Alaska and then across the Bering Sea to the Soviet Union. According to the engine manufacturer, the Allison Division of GM, all the P-39s were delivered in this fashion without a single engine failure. *Pete Bowers Collection*

to-ground support, a role for which they were better suited than for air-to-air combat.

The next several variations of the P-39—E, F, G, H, and J—were either experimental or "paper" models. There were 210 Ks manufactured, 250 L models with the Curtiss Electric propeller, and 240 Ms, also with the Curtiss propeller. It wasn't until 2,095 N models were built that the P-39 went into major production. This model returned to the Aeroproducts propeller and reduced internal fuel capacity to 87gals. Later variations replaced armor at the rear of the cockpit with bullet-resistant glass and reduced total armor weight by 38lb. The final model P-39 was the Q, and 4,905 of these were built, the

last few series incorporating a four-bladed propeller. P-39 production ended in August 1944, with a total of 9,584 Airacobras manufactured. The Soviets received 4,773 P-39s through LendLease, including most of the N and Q models, and used them exclusively in ground attack and "tank-buster" roles. Because American aircraft production during WWII was so overwhelming, planes such as the P-39 that failed to operate at levels originally expected were able to find a niche in the vast American offensive system, thus allowing them to contribute rather than be cast aside, or worse, be used in a role that wasted not only the equipment but the lives of the men that flew them.

Chapter IV

Transports and Trainers

Civil air transport made great strides worldwide during the 1930s, and in the United States Boeing Aircraft and Douglas Aircraft were among the industry leaders. Passenger service became a reality, but aircraft capacity was limited and the trip was expensive and usually uncomfortable. While airmail service had been established by the government and there was some movement of small cargo by air, until the advent of planes like the Douglas DC-3 in 1935, the possibility of routine movements of significant numbers of people, large objects, or great weights could not become an actuality. The DC-3 introduced air conditioning and heating, hot food served from an on-board galley, cabin soundproofing, and airborne lavatories. It also had an autopilot, wing flaps, constant-speed propellers, and power brakes. By 1938 the very modern DC-3 was carrying ninety-five percent of the civilian passengers in the United States.

The US military had depended on railroads since the Civil War and trucks since WWI. Pack horses and mules were still integral methods of both civil and military transportation, especially in rugged terrain. To cross an ocean required the assistance of the US Navy and the country's merchant marine. Time and distance were the twin dictators of any system of transportation. As airliners increased their load capabilities, their usefulness in moving men and materials became apparent to the military. Invasion by air with paratroopers and gliders was pioneered in the late 1930s although it had been discussed twenty years earlier during WWI.

The Army ordered fifty military versions of the DC-2 in 1935. The DC-2 was the predecessor of the famed DC-3, the plane that would revolutionize air travel. These Army versions had several different designations, including C-33, C-34, C-35, and C-39. In 1940 the USAAC or-

Known, colloquially, to American servicemen as the "Gooney Bird" and called the Dakota by the British, the C-47 Skytrain had a 95ft wingspan and was 64ft, 9in long, while standing 16ft, 11in tall. It weighed 33,000lb loaded and often carried loads far in excess of that weight. The C-47 was powered by two 1,200hp Pratt & Whitney R-1830 engines, and cruised at 175mph. Its top speed was 232mph, its service ceiling was 24,450ft, and its range was 1,513mi. This photo was taken in October 1942. *McDonnell Douglas Aircraft*

A C-47 production line in November 1942. Center wing sections are on the left, cockpits in the center and fuselages on the right. After this initial assembly the two engines, tail sections, and outer wings would be added on a moving production line. The Douglas plant at Long Beach employed 30,000 workers at its peak. *National Archives*

dered 2,000 military versions of the DC-3—the C-47 Skytrain—from Douglas. The introduction of mass production in the aircraft industry led to fleets of powerful transports being built during WWII. They were used to carry all manner of cargo, as troop carriers, as couriers and, as mentioned above, for dropping paratroopers and towing gliders. Transports became military hospitals in the air and were used to evacuate the wounded. They were modified to land on snow, ice, and water and were capable of crossing an ocean, cutting days from the delivery time for important people or goods. Allied air superiority allowed free movement to these unarmed planes, and they added an element of modernity to the battlefield that could not be matched by the Axis powers.

The workhorse of the US transport fleet during WWII was the renowned C-47 Skytrain, with more than 9,000 of them produced for the US military. This was followed by the Curtiss C-46 (3,182) and the Douglas C-54 (1,200). Several other smaller aircraft were built as transports or couriers, but none matched the performance or the sheer production volume of these three major aircraft. Lockheed's C-69 Constellation was an excellent troop carrier, but only twenty-two of them were delivered to the USAAF before the war ended.

It is axiomatic that warfare was revolutionized by the development of the airplane, specifically combat airplanes. But production and supply, logistics, if you will, are vital in winning wars, and the development of passenger and cargo-carrying aircraft by the United States as well as her Allies contributed directly and significantly to victory in WWII.

The Long Beach production line early in the war. The national insignia used from May 1942 until June 1943 (white star on blue circle) is barely visible behind the open cargo door. Aircraft rudders and tails have been attached to the other main components but engines and outer wings are still missing. The white blocks on various planes are censors' marks obscuring the aircraft identification numbers. *McDonnell Douglas Aircraft*

Nearly completed C-47s that still lack propellers are marked with the national insignia adopted in August 1943. The censors no longer considered it necessary to obliterate aircraft numbers. The huge banner at center was hopefully an incentive for greater productivity. At peak production Douglas workers built nearly two C-47s per hour. *McDonnell Douglas Aircraft*

C-47 Skytrain

Certainly the most famous non-combat aircraft to come out of WWII, the C-47, was described by Gen. Dwight Eisenhower as one of the five items of hardware most important to winning the war. The other four were the bulldozer, the 2 1/2 ton truck, the jeep, and the amphibious "duck" used to get troops and equipment ashore. Interesting that they are all support systems, rather than front-line combat equipment.

The twin-engined transport was known in civilian aviation as the DC-3 and the DST (Douglas Sleeper Transport), and before war broke out it was undoubtedly the most important and impressive airliner in the sky. It was flown by US airlines such as American, Eastern, TWA, and United as well as thirty foreign airlines around the globe, and built under license in Japan, the Soviet Union, and Holland. Initially the USAAC commandeered 149 DC-3s on order for commercial airlines as part of an order for 545 C-47s. The kidnapped aircraft were used for a number of purposes and were designated as C-48s, C-49s, C-50s, C-51s, C-52s, and C-68s. The various model classifications were based on differ-

Typical overhead camouflage netting at a Douglas Aircraft plant in southern California. Directly above the pie delivery truck in the center of the photo is the outline of a house and several bushes silhouetted against the sky. The Blue Star sign on the right, which replaced individual flags, indicates that 8,363 Douglas employees are in military service. The lettering at the top of the sign says, "They Are Fighting For You—Let's Work For Them." *McDonnell Douglas Aircraft*

The EDO Corporation of College Point on New York's Long Island was the major manufacturer of floats for US aircraft during WWII. Featured here is the Model 78 Amphibious Float Gear used by C-47's that have been modified for water takeoffs and landings. EDO employed 2,440 men and women during the war years. *EDO Corporation*

ent interior configurations for seating and cargo storage and different engine types, both Pratt & Whitney and Curtiss Wright.

The aircraft ordered to military specifications incorporated several different features, including a reinforced cabin floor, a large cargo door on the port side of the plane, and more powerful engines. A slightly different model of the C-47, the C-53 Skytroop glider tow plane, was part of this order. In addition, the US Navy ordered more than 600 C-47s during WWII. They were known as the R4D and ultimately included seven different configurations.

The C-47 pioneered the trans-Atlantic ferry route to Great Britain that was such an important link between the United States and its major ally. Starting in Presque Isle, Maine, the air route created major terminals in Gander and Goose Bay, Newfoundland, as well as Bluie West 1 in Greenland and Reykjavik, Iceland, and terminated in Prestwick, Scotland. All types of aircraft were transported over this route, and during the height of wartime flight activity an aircraft was traversing the trans-Atlantic air bridge every 4min.

Douglas Aircraft produced 10,629 DC-3–type aircraft, of which

A C-47 using the Model 78 Float on the sea. *EDO Corporation*

A C-47 using the Model 78 Float on land. *EDO Corporation*

The undercarriage of a Douglas C-47 fitted with skids for landing on ice and snow. The Skytrain was ubiquitous, serving with distinction in every theater of the war. *McDonnell Douglas Aircraft*

A C-47 being loaded with wounded American soldiers beginning their trips to rear area or stateside hospitals. Reliable estimates indicate that 750,000 wounded and sick personnel were transported in C-47s during WWII. The cargo door, which was wide enough to accommodate a Jeep or a small field-artillery piece, made loading and unloading a little less onerous. *McDonnell Douglas Aircraft*

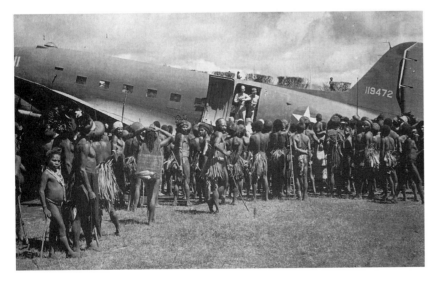

The war took Americans to some strange and mystifying places around the world, and their presence was often an even bigger surprise to the natives of those far-off lands. The crew of this C-47 has only opened one side of the plane's cargo door while surveying these New Guinea tribesmen and women who have gathered to view the "Big Bird." *McDonnell Douglas Aircraft*

A C-46 in early-war markings takes flight near the Curtiss-Wright plant in Buffalo, New York. The aircraft's serial number on the tail has been obliterated by government censors. The P-40 also featured in the photograph reflects the newer national insignia, on which the red ball was deleted from the center of the white star. *Pete Bowers Collection*

This view of a C-46 on the factory floor illustrates the size differential between the transport and Curtiss-Wright's other major military aircraft, the P-40 fighter shown at left. Engine nacelles were riveted to the center wing section on the C-46. The positioning of floodlights to the left of the aircraft indicate this was a major photo opportunity. Visible to the right are wing sections for the P-40, painted in camouflage for export to Great Britain. *Pete Bowers Collection*

The first production C-46A awaits roll-out in Buffalo. The Commando was 76ft, 4in long and stood 22ft off the ground. Its wingspan was 108ft. Powered by twin Pratt & Whitney R-2800 engines that generated 2,000hp each, it cruised at 175mph and had a top speed of 245mph. The C-46's range was 1,200mi and its ceiling was 27,600ft. *Pete Bowers Collection*

Kittyhawks and Commandos crowd the factory floor at the Curtiss-Wright plant in Buffalo, New York. The P-40 fuselages are on wheeled dollies, while the C-46 aircraft are static. The cost to the USAAF for each C-46 was $233,000. *Pete Bowers Collection*

Army personnel oversee the loading of a Jeep into a C-46 at a US Army base as part of a 1942 training exercise. While the nearly eight tons cargo capacity of the C-46 was legendary, it was also used as a troop transport and a drop aircraft for paratroopers, carrying forty men and their equipment. In addition, the C-46 was used for medical evacuations and towing gliders into combat areas. *Pete Bowers Collection*

An impressive display of C-46D and P-40N aircraft in late-war markings await fly-away at a domestic air base. The individuals in the photograph appear to be civilians, indicating another public relations opportunity for Curtiss-Wright and the USAAF. *Pete Bowers Collection*

Starting in late 1943, the USAAF deleted the requirement for camouflage painting of the C-46. Both variants are pictured here. The Commando normally carried five crewmen. Its rounded fuselage was the result of initial plans to partially pressurize the aircraft in its civilian version, and the cockpit windshield was contoured to meet the fuselage. *Pete Bowers Collection*

A C-46A carries vital war materiel to China from India, using its excellent high-altitude performance to surmount the hazards of crossing the Himalayan Mountains in its path. After the closing of the Burma Road in 1942, "Flying the Hump" was the only method available to supply China in its war with Japan. The C-46 entered this phase of its service in May 1943. *Pete Bowers Collection*

9,660 were C-47s and derivative models, at company plants in Long Beach, California, and Oklahoma City, Oklahoma. This truly unique aircraft served in every imaginable capacity during and after WWII, and is still in service around the world today.

C-46 Commando

The CW-20, an American civilian airliner designed by Curtiss Aircraft to carry thirty-six passengers and widely viewed as a replacement for the DC-3, was the forerunner of the C-46 Commando. Designed in 1937 with a pressurized fuselage, the C-46 did not fly until March 1940. However, due to its high-altitude performance and load capabilities, the USAAF ordered twenty-five planes without delay.

Initial deliveries were scheduled for July 1942. Unfortunately, due to production difficulties, the C-46 did

This is the original CW-20, which was the prototype for the Douglas civilian airliner that was planned in 1937 as a replacement for the DC-3. As the United States began its military build-up prior to the country's entry into WWII, the CW-20 became the prototype for the C-46. Finally, it was produced as the C-55 and later sold in small quantities to Great Britain. *Pete Bowers Collection*

The second production model of the C-54 Skymaster in early-war markings. Designed by Douglas Aircraft in 1938 as the fifty-two passenger DC-4, it was the first four-engined transport in US service. Airline orders were taken over by the USAAF, and ultimately 1,200 of these 60,000lb behemoths became operational. The US Navy version was designated the R5D. President Franklin D. Roosevelt's private airplane during the war was a C-54 nicknamed the *Sacred Cow*. The wingspan of the C-54 was 117ft, 6in, and its length was 93ft, 10in, nearly 30ft longer than the workhorse C-47. *Pete Bowers Collection*

The C-54 was powered by four Pratt & Whitney 1,350hp (later R-2000 Twin Wasps), fourteen-cylinder, air-cooled radial engines. With a crew of six, it could operate at more than 20,000ft of altitude and had a top speed of 275mph. Its range was 6,700mi. Normally configured for twenty-six passengers plus cargo, the C-54 was heavily used by the Air Transport Command for trans-Atlantic service. Subcontracting of aircraft and engine components became standard procedure during WWII. In this photograph predominantly female employees at a John Deere plant in the Midwest assemble C-54 engine nacelles with propeller mounts and cylinder heads for transshipment to final production. *Deere & Company*

Due to a worldwide shortage of aluminum, Curtiss Aircraft in early 1943 built the twin-engined C-76 Caravan from wood, covered by fabric. It was a short-lived experiment, and only five of them were manufactured. *Pete Bowers Collection*

Although only twenty-two C-69s became operational, this Lockheed product went on to great fame as the civilian Constellation immediately after the war as fifty-one additional aircraft on order became available to the commercial airlines. Designed by Lockheed for TWA in 1939 and first flown on January 9, 1943, the "Connie" could transported sixty-five fully-equipped soldiers and had a top speed of 329mph. Its range was 2,400mi and its ceiling was 25,000ft. Powered by four 2,200hp Wright Cyclone eighteen-cylinder air-cooled radial engines, the C-69 entered active military service in 1944. *Lockheed Corporation*

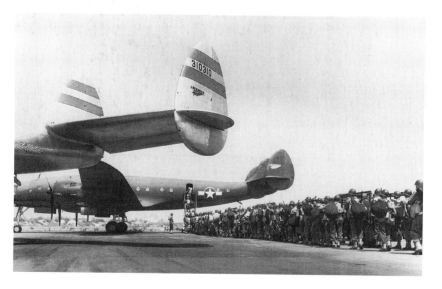

North American Aviation was an early leader in building military trainers, winning a 1934 competition with its NA-16 design against Seversky Aircraft. This aircraft was the prototype BT-9 Yale trainer, of which hundreds were ordered by the US Navy and USAAC. Featured in this photograph is the first offering of the fabric-covered BT-9 in 1935, manufactured at North American's Inglewood, California, plant. *Steve Pace Collection*

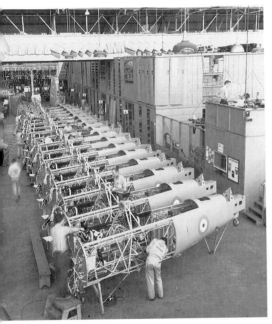

Other nations contracted with North American for the BT-14. They were exported as NA-64s. These fuselages on a primary assembly line are destined for France. However, many of them were redirected to the Royal Canadian Air Force (where they were designated Yale I radio trainers) after France was defeated in 1940 by Germany. *Steve Pace Collection*

The BT-14 was the aluminum-covered version of the BT-9. There were also differences in cowlings, wings, and the shape of the tail. The assembly-line construction displayed here was primitive compared to mass production standards introduced a few years later as America prepared to enter WWII. The Inglewood plant incorporated 159,00sq-ft of factory floor space and employed 150 workers. In addition to the BT-14s and BT-9s (Navy version SNJ), the factory also produced O-47 observation planes for the Army, of which 278 were manufactured by North American. *Steve Pace Collection*

This export model NA-64 had a most unusual career, being shipped to the France as part of a prewar aircraft order, and subsequently captured by the German Luftwaffe. Pictured in its enemy color scheme and national insignia, the aircraft was ultimately returned to American control in the winter of 1944–45. *Pete Bowers Collection*

The Stearman Company, pictured here in 1940 after having been purchased by the Boeing Company in 1938, was a major manufacturer of trainers for both the Army and the Navy. Lines of PT-13 Kaydets, which were the first trainers developed jointly for the two services, with interchangeable components, appear ready for fly-away. *Pete Bowers Collection*

A long line of PT-13s await their student aviators at Randolph Field, Texas, in prewar markings. The Kaydet had a 32ft wingspan and was 24ft, 10in long. Its range was 450mi, and its ceiling was 14,000ft. They were powered by a 220hp Lycoming R-680 engine and cost the US government $11,000 each. *Pete Bowers Collection*

Stearman's P-17 was the same plane as the P-13, except it was powered by a Continental engine, also 220hp (if powered by a Jacobs engine it was a PT-18).

When painted in Navy yellow and blue, the fabric-covered Kaydet, while designated the N2S, was known to students as the "Yellow Peril." Weighing 2,700lb

loaded, its top speed was 125mph and its cruising speed was 104mph. *Pete Bowers Collection*

On March 27, 1941, Stearman rolled out its 1,000th Kaydet. The company built 10,346 of these famous trainers for the

Allied cause before and during WWII. Production ended in February 1945. *Pete Bowers Collection*

not become operational until 1943. However, by the end of the war, 3,144 C-46s at a cost of $233,000 each were produced, and 1,410 of these were D models mounting the powerful twin Pratt & Whitney R-2800 radial engines of 2,000hp each.

The C-46 was used for many of the same service missions as the C-47, but performed them higher and faster. The Commando was more of a maintenance problem than the C-47, and this often created major difficulties on the primitive airstrips used in many inaccessible areas in the Far East. It was also the biggest and heaviest twin-engined transport in US Army service during WWII. The C-46 owed much of its fame to its role in flying supplies over the "Hump," the Himalayan Mountain range between India and China, and was mainly operational in the China-Burma-India (CBI) Theater and in the Pacific. In Europe, C-46s

This promotional photograph features the PT-17 in the colors of five different services. Front to back they are the US Army, US Navy, China, Great Britain, and Peru. *Pete Bowers Collection*

were instrumental in the airborne attack across the Rhine River at Wesel, Germany, in March 1945, shortly before V-E Day. The C-46 stayed in the USAAF inventory after WWII and saw active service in the Korean War.

Other Transports

There were several additional US aircraft designed as military transports before and during WWII, and still other planes converted to this category for wartime purposes. Among the former were the C-54 Skymaster and the C-69 Constellation, the C-55 (CW-20) and the C-76 Caravan. Others of lesser prominence were the twin-engined Beech C-45 Expeditor (powered by two nine-cylinder radial engines and carrying six to eight passengers plus a crew of two) and the Lockheed C-56 Lodestar, also equipped with two air-cooled radial engines and able to transport seventeen passengers.

The air transport systems developed during WWII laid the basis for the incredible passenger and cargo aviation transportation systems available worldwide in this generation, and a debt is owed to those men and women of vision who brought it to fruition.

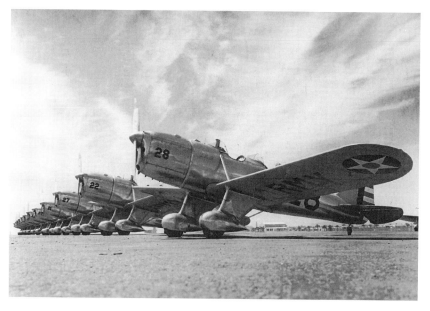

The Ryan Aeronautical Company of San Diego, California, had been in the forefront of civilian pilot training during the 1930s. The company graduated its first military class in 1939, and by the end of the war had trained 14,000 air cadets. The YPT-16 was the military version of Ryan's civilian STA. First ordered in 1940, it was of mixed wood and metal construction. The initial aircraft order of fifteen planes was equipped with 125hp inline Menasco L-365 engines, but later versions used the Kinner R-440 radial engine. *Pete Bowers Collection*

The YPT-16 was the first monoplane purchased by the Army for use as a primary trainer, and its success led to additional Ryan trainers, all of which featured exterior wing struts and fixed landing gear. The PT-20As pictured here retained the covered landing gear, but were essentially the same aircraft as the YPT-16. *Pete Bowers Collection*

The PT-21 Ryan. Once again the same aircraft but in this version featuring uncovered, or open, landing gear. The PT-21 also allows some additional fuselage area between the student and the instructor, and the windshield was changed. *Pete Bowers Collection*

The PT-22 Recruit was the last open cockpit Ryan trainer in the series that started with the YPT-16. When production ceased in 1942, 1,023 PT-22s had been sold to the government for $10,000 each, and twenty-five additional aircraft ordered by the Dutch military had been diverted to the USAAF as PT-22As in 1942. The 160hp Kinner R-540 engine powered the PT-22 at a maximum speed of 125mph, a range of 205mi, and a ceiling 15,400ft. *Pete Bowers Collection*

The Trainers

In order to use the vast number of aircraft produced by the United States during the war years, it was necessary to instruct sufficient pilots to fly them. Most student pilots had no prior experience, but even if they had previously flown aircraft as civilians, everybody went through the same military training programs, either for the Navy or the USAAF. There was a myriad of training aircraft produced in the United States both before and during WWII. Among the famous names are Ryan, Stearman, North American, Vultee, and Beech. The aircraft used to instill the necessary skills were categorized as primary, basic, and advanced trainers. Often the primary trainers were bi-winged machines and flew low and slow. Later the students graduated to single-wing aircraft capable of greater speed and specialization, including bombardier training and air-to-air gunnery. Some trainers were very forgiving aircraft; others less so. American manufacturers built more than 30,000 training aircraft for the Army

Aeronca Aircraft Corporation built 620 PT-19 (above) and 375 PT-23 (below) trainers at its plant in Middletown, Ohio. The PT-19, shown here being rolled out of the hangar on wooden boards due to the muddy field, featured an inline engine, while the PT-23 incorporated a radial engine. Both trainers are equipped with wooden, two-bladed propellers. *Aeronca Archives*

A rather unusual trainer manufactured by Aeronca in Middletown, Ohio, was the TG-5 glider trainer. The company built 253 of them to train Army glider pilots. Gliders were used to resupply troops having no ground access to friendly forces. They were also used to carry soldiers into combat, towed by transports such as the C-46 and C-47. When released from their tows, the gliders were flown to designated landing areas by two pilots and essentially crash-landed, hopefully placing the soldiers in a tactically-superior situation. *Aeronca Archives*

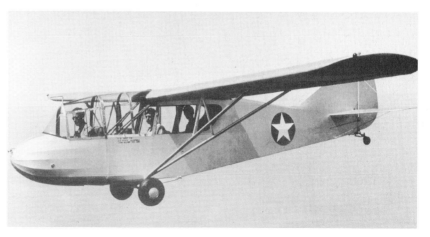

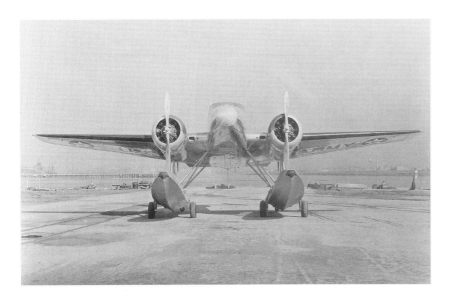

Aviation cadets needed training aircraft to learn how to fly, and they also needed specialized planes to assist in acquiring navigation, gunnery, and bombing skills. The twin-engined AT-7 Navigator manufactured by Beech Aircraft was designed to fulfill the navigational role, as its name suggests. It was the military version of the Beechcraft Model 18 commercial transport. The Model 18 was also used as the C-45 (transport) and the AT-11 (bombing trainer). Incorporating a celestial dome and space for five to six personnel, the AT-7 was powered by two Pratt & Whitney 450hp engines, had a cruising speed of 190mph, and a service ceiling of 24,000ft. In this photograph the Navigator is equipped with floats for water landings and takeoffs. The wheels on the bottom of the floats were only for ground-handling and could not be used for regular runway landings. Beechcraft manufactured 718 AT-7s during the war. *EDO Corporation*

The best known training aircraft during WWII was the AT-6, manufactured by North American Aviation and operated by thirty-four different countries. It was designed as a combat trainer, and a total of 15,495 of them were built between 1939 and 1945, at a cost of $24,952 each. This an AT-6A, which featured improved fuel tanks and engine, and entered production in 1941. Known as the Texan in the USAAF and as the SNJ to the Navy, the AT-6 was called the Harvard in the RAF and used to train British pilots, many of them in Canada. *Pete Bowers Collection*

Incorporating retractable landing gear and a controllable-pitch propeller, the AT-6 was powered by a 550hp air-cooled Pratt & Whitney Wasp R-1340 engine, which pulled the Texan to a maximum speed of 205mph at 5,000ft of altitude. The AT-6C, featured here with the national insignia of China prominently displayed, was structurally modified in order to save aluminum. The plane's side panels were made of plywood, saving 1,246lb of aluminum in each aircraft. Production total for this model was 2,970. *Pete Bowers Collection*

The Navy version of the AT-6 was the SNJ, in this photograph flaunting yellow-painted inner wing panels, with the remainder of the aircraft displaying blue and silver paint. Because they operated on or near the ocean, the frame and most metal components of Navy aircraft were coated with zinc-chromate paint to prevent corrosion. *Pete Bowers Collection*

As a result of its creation as a combat trainer, the AT-6 often found itself used in combat situations by many of the nations that procured this sturdy aircraft. It could be fitted with bomb racks, machine guns, and rockets, and often fulfilled ground-support missions. The AT-6, redesignated the T-6, stayed in the US inventory until 1959, and was used as a spotter aircraft during the Korean War as well as continuing its role as an advanced trainer. *Pete Bowers Collection*

and Navy during WWII. Very few of the older ones survived, and their legacy is often neglected.

Thousands of young Americans volunteered for pilot training, and although many failed to complete the flight programs of the Army and Navy, the United States had a surplus of pilots by mid-1944, and 10,000 air cadets were assigned to other duties, which often included the infantry. Ironically, this phenomenon was the direct result of fewer casualties being incurred in the air war than expected, resulting in an excess of aviators.

Chapter V

People, Places, and Planes

During WWII, the American civilian population was mobilized by a combination of outrage over the Japanese attack on Pearl Harbor, sympathy for the victims of German aggression in Europe, and some clever propaganda emanating from the various wartime commissions and governmental agencies in Washington that were charged with the successful prosecution of the war.

There were certainly other factors to consider. Many segments of the economy were flourishing as a result of the profitable contracts for war materiel that were pouring into factories all across the land, especially in California, from both foreign governments desperate to increase their armaments and from US military departments that were gearing up for what appeared to many professional soldiers and politicians to be an inevitable war in both Europe and the Pacific. President Roosevelt's signature on the LendLease Bill in

This bucolic suburban landscape is actually the camouflaged canopy over a Boeing plant building in the Seattle area. Utilizing wire and wood framing, burlap and ingenuity, American manufacturers attempted to conceal their vital facilities from airborne prying eyes. Fear of enemy attack was very real during the early days of the war, especially on the West Coast, as the Japanese possessed the delivery systems, namely aircraft carriers, large submarines, and a victorious surface fleet, necessary to bring the war to America's shores. *Boeing*

The new Pratt & Whitney plant in East Hartford, Connecticut, is bare of any camouflage attempt. While residents of the East Coast often observed attacks on merchant ships off their shore by German U-boats, the Kreigsmarine had no aircraft carriers, and the Luftwaffe did not possess any long-range bombers capable of crossing the Atlantic to bomb the United States. When the war ended in Europe, however, Germany, already employing the dreaded V-2 rocket against Allied targets in Great Britain and on the Continent, was developing a multi-staged rocket known as the A9/A10, which would be capable of hitting the United States. *United Technologies Archives*

Employees of the Champion Spark Plug Company in Toledo, Ohio, are congratulated on their wartime production efforts by an American military officer. The ladies assembled in the front rows are exhibiting a variety of hair styles. They are also wearing their winter coats, and appear to be meeting in an unheated warehouse. *Cooper Industries Champion Spark Plug*

Employees of Pratt & Whitney building Twin Wasp engines on the assembly line in East Hartford, Connecticut, in 1943. It is rather unusual to see no women represented in the work force after two years of war. The R-1830 Twin Wasp, standard power plant on the B-24, was a two-row radial engine that generated 1,350hp. Pratt & Whitney built 173,618 of them. *United Technologies Archives*

Prior to the war, women had little or no factory work experience, but they acquitted themselves very well on the nation's assembly lines and became an extremely important segment of the work force during WWII. Pratt & Whitney saluted its female employees in this static display promoting the opening of the company's Kansas City, Missouri, plant. *United Technologies Archives*

139

1941 was an especially major inducement for manufacturers who could convert assembly lines idled by a decade of Depression to current military production.

This vast increase in industrialism demanded a corresponding increase in the work force. Men and women from all walks of life, usually unskilled, were hired by the thousands and trained to meet production goals. Due to its nearly year-round mild weather, Southern California was a favorite destination for many of these mobile workers, and it was no accident that a large part of the aircraft industry was located there. Significant final production could be undertaken out-of-

An O-47A observation plane in US Army markings. Carrying a crew of three seated one behind the other, the O-47 was designed by North American Aviation as a replacement for the O-19 and O-38, both biplanes. Armed with one forward-firing .30cal machine gun and a flexible .30cal pointing rearward, this aircraft had windows on the bottom of plane for unrestricted observation. However, the O-47 was not very maneuverable and could not perform as well as other aircraft available for the role it was designed to play. The Army purchased 248 O-47s for $38,000 each. They were powered by the Wright R-1820 engine, which generated 1,060hp and powered the plane to a top speed of 227mph. This O-47 is rigged with floats for water takeoffs and landings. The O-47's range was 840mi and service ceiling was 24,100ft. *EDO Corporation*

On April 22, 1942, production of radios for civilian use was discontinued by government decree. In this photograph Zenith Company president and founder E. F. McDonald, Jr., accepts the last civilian radio manufactured by the company at its Glenview, Illinois, facility from W. E. Fullerton, plant manager, in front of several dozen enthusiastic and cheering employees, mainly female. The first four women on the left in this rather posed photo are wearing exactly the same dress. *Zenith Electronics Corporation*

A Vultee L-1A Vigilant, originally the Stinson O-49, on EDO Corporation amphibious floats. The USAAC purchased 324 L-1s and L-1As in 1939 and 1941 at a cost of $21,000 each. Powered by a 295hp Lycoming engine, the Vigilant had a top speed of 122mph, and a cruising speed of 109mph. The aircraft incorporated full-span, automatic slots on the leading edges of the wings and slotted flaps activated by the pilot on the trailing edges, and operated as a general-purpose spotter and liaison aircraft. *EDO Corporation*

A Big Mouth to Feed!

Throughout WWII government agencies and civilian organizations organized scrap drives to gather scarce materials such as rubber and steel needed for the war effort. This newspaper cartoon illustrates Uncle Sam feeding the voracious appetite of a steam-blowing warrior furnace. Among the scrap awaiting salvage is a wood-burning cook stove, an integral part of most American households in the early 1940s. *Brown Foreman*

A naval aviator models a prewar life vest and proudly displays the newest inflatable life raft for single-seat fighters manufactured by the US Rubber Company. It weighs only 11lb. As the war progressed the air services provided aviators with the "Mae West" life vest, which allowed the wearer more freedom of movement while on operations and inflated as two separate balloons, one on each side of the wearer's chest. The actress heartily accepted the accolade. *National Archives*

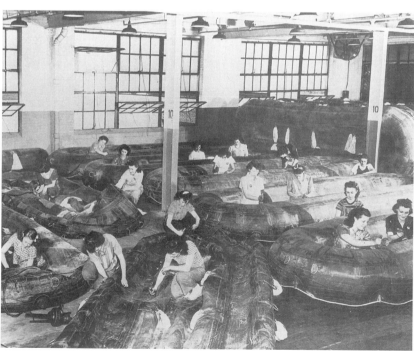

In the spirit of the times, a wartime caption for this photograph might have read, "Damsels' derrieres dedicated to defense!" Actually, these two female workers are partially inside the forward hatch of a PV-2 Harpoon reconnaissance aircraft built by Lockheed. This hatch contained five to eight (depending on model) forward firing machine guns. Powered by two Pratt & Whitney R-2800-31 Double Wasp eighteen-cylinder air-cooled radial engines generating 2,000hp each, the PV-2 had a top speed of 282mph. Its range was 2,930mi and ceiling was 23,900ft. Lockheed delivered 533 PV-2s to the US Navy in various models during the war. *National Archives*

Employees of General Tire Corporation in Akron, Ohio, are shown gluing and sealing the seams on multi-man life rafts for the US Navy. This type of raft was standard issue for large aircraft carrying several crew members. Because this task required flexible and sensitive finger work, many companies used women exclusively for such specialization. *General Tire Archives*

141

In December 1944 this array of equipment represented the state of the art in survival-at-sea situations, and was packed with a Navy flier's inflatable raft. Included is a supply of emergency drinking water, kits for converting sea water, fishing tackle, food for two weeks, a flare pistol and supply of flares, medical kit, and a manual of instruction for those in peril on the sea. *National Archives*

Citizens and companies all over America were acutely aware of the blessings of freedom provided by a free country and also mindful of the sacrifices being made on their behalf by neighbors, relatives, friends, and millions of Americans who would never know each other. This was the company Christmas card of the Great Northern Railroad in December 1942. "V" For Victory. *Burlington Northern Railroad Archives*

doors, and lessened the need for additional plant buildings. There was also less weather-related absenteeism (unless it was for a day off in the sun!), and the transportation of both incoming raw materials and finished goods was not negatively affected for the same reason.

The US aircraft industry was transformed by WWII into the biggest industry in the world. Dozens of new plants were constructed, often in the nation's interior, far away from coastal areas so they were less vulnerable to potential enemy air attacks. Aircraft design was brilliant and imaginative for its time. The subcontracting of major assemblies became standard practice, and efficient assembly line produc-

These two workers were part of a ship-yard safety exhibition in the Los Angeles area in 1942. Their unidentified company apparently employed a large work force, based on the astronomical number of employees with eye injuries in just one month, according to the upper poster in the photograph. The woman on the left is very efficiently attired for the assembly line, with work gloves, coveralls, safety goggles, and a large cap to enclose her hair. The other woman appears a little more whimsical, and was picked to display a feminine chest protector. Her right arm has obscured the final word of the admonition on the poster, "Protect your priceless...." *National Archives*

A nighttime view of Vultee A-31 Vengeance dive bombers in the final stages of assembly in Nashville, Tennessee. More than 1,900 of them were built, with 1,205 destined for the RAF. The British designated this aircraft the V-72 and used it mainly in Burma. The United States used the Vengeance as a trainer. It was initially armed with six .30cal machine guns, but later models were equipped with .50cal weapons. This aircraft incorporated an internal bomb bay with a 1,000lb capacity, later increased to 2,000lb. Its Wright Cyclone R-2600-19 engine generated 1,600hp and drove the Vengeance to a top speed of 275mph. Northrop also built 400 A-31s under license. Production ceased in May 1944. *National Archives*

Northrop Aircraft was in dire financial straits when, in the summer of 1940, the British Purchasing Commission asked the company to build 200 Vultee Vengeance dive bombers for the RAF. The price was $17 million, and this infusion of capital allowed Northrop to double its manufacturing capacity. A few months later Boeing gave Northrop a subcontract to build engine nacelles and cowlings for the B-17E bomber. The rough forms for these engine accessories are visible to the right in this photograph. *Northrop*

The PV-1 Ventura was a US Navy land-based reconnaissance bomber derived from Lockheed's commercial Model 18 Lodestar, and first flew on July 31, 1941. It was initially ordered by the British, but part of the order was taken over by the USAAF, which designated the aircraft the B-34. It was armed with six machine guns and could be used as a level bomber or even carry a torpedo. Top speed was 312mph, with a maximum range of 1,600mi and a ceiling of 26,300ft. The PV-1 carried four or five crewmen. While the aircraft in this photo appears to be in the final construction stage at the Lockheed plant, the three men working on it are all clad in navy dungarees and "dixie cup" hats, indicating this picture was probably taken at a US Navy installation. *National Archives*

Two Stinson L-5 observation planes over Burma in 1944. This was the military version of the Stinson 105 Voyager, and cost the government $10,000 per copy. Weighing 2,050lb maximum and powered by a 190hp Lycoming O-435-1, the Sentinel was the second most heavily procured observation-liaison plane for the Army during the war, with 3,590 of this versatile aircraft ordered between 1942 and 1945. It was often used for medical evacuations from primitive, small air strips. Its range was 360mi, its top speed was 130mph, its cruising speed was 90mph, and its ceiling was 15,600ft. *National Archives*

Employees of defense firms during the war years came from all walks of life, and many of them were nomadic, changing jobs for a variety of reasons, with compensation and climate leading the list of desirable working conditions. Most companies accepted the fact that they would never fill all their employment needs. Thus overtime was always available to the workers who sought it, and the pressure to complete contracts on time was intense. The workers featured in this photograph are new employees at one of Douglas Aircraft's plants in California. As the war progressed, Douglas reported it was hiring three times as many women as men. *National Archives*

In a midwestern defense plant, row upon row of 2,000lb bombs await transshipment to battlefronts around the world. The logistics required in moving military supplies and munitions during WWII are staggering to contemplate. Trains, trucks, ships, airplanes, and personnel were all needed and vital components of a transportation system that, while always overstressed, managed to complete its mission successfully. These bombs are inert, and would not be fused and armed until they were prepared for a combat mission. *National Archives*

tion was the industry norm. Aircraft production had become a highly-sophisticated and profitable business.

This availability of high-paying jobs for a generation that had been without work for several years resulted in massive relocations, all of which placed great strains on the services provided by the local communities. Housing, schools, utilities, transportation, and social institutions were all affected. Minorities were offered job opportunities not available a few years earlier, and tensions between ethnic groups not only smoldered, but often broke into major conflagrations. A significant increase in juvenile delinquency resulted from children left unattended while parents reaped the rewards of a wartime economy, and there were disturbing increases in prostitution and social disease. While there was serious concern on the part of many citizens as a result of these social dislocations, the great majority of the

Aeronca's versatile L-3 "Grasshopper" observation plane carried a crew of two at a top speed of 80mph. It was powered by a 65hp Continental engine, and was famous for its short takeoff and landing requirements. Used for spotting, courier service, and general liaison duties, the L-3 was also employed as an air ambulance, carrying one or two stretchers at a time. In Burma, the L-3 was credited with evacuating more than 500 casualties. By the end of the war the US Army had received 701 L-3Bs and 499 L-3Cs from the manufacturer's plant in Middletown,

A view of the Douglas Aircraft "cold room" laboratory, where aviation equipment was tested at temperatures as low as 90deg below zero, Fahrenheit. As design and efficiency increased, American aircraft flew at altitudes thought inconceivable a few years earlier, and both crews and equipment had to be prepared to operate at exceedingly low temperatures. During WWII Douglas opened its "cold room" to the members of the Aircraft War Production Council and also shared the results of previous research with the other aircraft manufacturers. *National Archives*

Maj. Ralph Slater, operations officer, instructs Ms. Mildred McLelland, a Women's Airforce Service Pilots (WASP) pilot from Tulsa, Oklahoma, in aerial navigation at the USAAF Navigation School at San Marcos, Texas. The WASPs were civilian women who ferried aircraft from factories and air bases throughout the continental United States to other domestic destinations, thereby freeing military pilots for combat and other priority missions. The WASPs had an enviable safety record, although thirty-eight of them were killed in training and operational accidents, and they flew every type of aircraft in the USAAF inventory. *USAF*

Thousands of cylinders for Pratt & Whitney R-1830 Twin Wasp engines await installation in the company's East Hartford, Connecticut, plant. The Twin Wasp powered the B-24 bomber and the F4F fighter, and was a two-row radial engine with fourteen cylinders. Pratt & Whitney built 173,618 of these engines during the war years. *United Technologies Archives*

Two women workers complete the wiring on an engine mount for a P-61 Black Widow night-fighter at Northrop in Hawthorne, California, and appear to be enjoying their work. Their attire is rather casual, with none of the attendant hats, hair nets, gloves, and coveralls usually identified with assembly line work, and thus the photograph is probably posed. *Northrop*

Aircraft workers take their lunch break out-of-doors in sunny southern California. Camouflage netting is visible overhead. These men all appear relatively fit and young, and probably had critical-skills deferments from military service. Some men who quit deferred jobs to join the service were dragged back to their civilian employment by the FBI, as they could not be spared from crucial defense production. *National Archives*

The band plays, and John Deere employees at the Waterloo Tractor Works applaud as the cherished Army-Navy "E" flag for production excellence is awarded at the Iowa plant in August 1942. By war's end this facility added five "E" stars to the flag. Note the V for Victory symbols and the statue of the stag on the speaker's platform. Also visible behind the platform is a section of the company baseball field. *Deere & Company*

147

The USAAF Training Command maintained this hangar location at Yale University in New Haven, Connecticut. Identifiable aircraft in the photograph, taken June 5, 1944, are a P-38, P-39, P-40, P-47, B-25, B-26, and what is probably a Vultee Vengeance in British colors in the center rear of the picture. *National Archives*

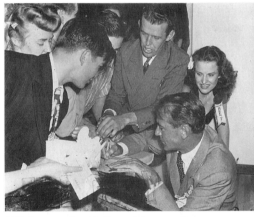

Wildly popular Hollywood actor Gary Cooper signs autographs for employees at Northrop in Hawthorne, California. The young woman behind Cooper is wearing a ribbon imprinted with "Mardi Gras Queen?" Hundreds of theatrical and motion picture performers traveled around the country and the world entertaining America's military men and women, and they also participated in War Bond rallies and defense plant rallies at home. Actors Tyrone Power, Jimmy Stewart, and David Niven served honorably in the military throughout the war. In a reversal after the war, two of America's most heavily decorated combat soldiers, Audie Murphy and Neville Brand, became Hollywood actors. *Northrop*

Russian émigré Igor Sikorsky was a brilliant aeronautical engineer who had designed many commercial aircraft, including the flying boats that preceded the famous Boeing Clippers in trans-ocean travel. He was also successful with helicopter design. Shown here in the air is the R-4, which first flew in January 1942 and became operational in the same month of 1944. On the ground is an R-5, a heavier version of the R-4 that used a 450hp Pratt & Whitney Wasp Junior engine. It flew its first test in August 1943 at the company's Bridgeport, Connecticut, location. Including the R-6, Sikorsky delivered 400 helicopters to the Army and Navy during WWII. *United Technologies Archives*

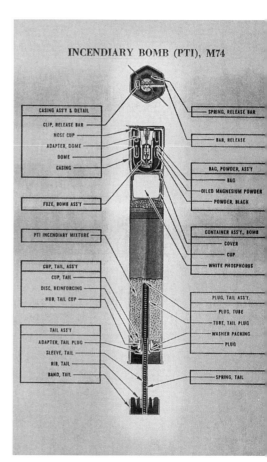

INCENDIARY BOMB (PTI), M74

Several very powerful and destructive conventional bombs were developed during WWII that caused extensive damage when dropped on targeted enemy facilities. Chrysler Corporation built 7,500,000 M-74 bombs at its Evansville, Indiana, plant. These 10lb incendiaries were packed in clusters of thirty-eight inside the shell of a 500lb bomb. Upon release the container broke open and spilled the incendiaries over a broad area of enemy territory. The M-74s were used with great effectiveness against Japanese cities, which contained thousands of highly combustible wood and paper dwellings and businesses. *Chrysler Archives*

Recently lacquered bomb casings pass between banks of infrared drying lamps at the Thermador Company plant in Los Angeles in February 1943. The company had recently won an Army-Navy "E." *National Archives*

population continued its economic and personal activities at a feverish pace, and did not stop to count the cost until the war was over. At that point what was done could not be undone.

Still, Americans had put away more than $140 billion in savings and defense bonds during the war. This investment in the postwar economy, coupled with the GI Bill, which allowed millions of ex-servicemen (7.8 million) to attend college, resulted in the creation of a middle class that has been the backbone of America since WWII ended in 1945. These civilian workers worried about their family members in the armed services, worked hard at both defense and non-defense jobs, put up with rationing and restrictions, earned their overtime, and played hard with the money and time the war had brought to their generation, while building the greatest economic power the world had ever known. They could be proud that they were a major force in winning the war.

By war's end the jet aircraft upon which the future of international and military aviation rested were a reality in manufacturing plants and on airfields all over Amer-

Maytag produced vital components for sixteen different Allied aircraft during WWII, including seven US bombers and five US fighters. On May 12, 1944, the Office of Civil Defense presented the Security Award flag to Maytag, and individual awards to 112 employees in the plant fire, police, safety, and maintenance departments. As part of the ceremony a WAC band from Fort Des Moines entertained the crowd of employees gathered to witness the awards. The ladder in the center of the picture is for the photographer. Although many of the employees are enjoying their shirtsleeves, the leafless trees indicate a late spring in Iowa that year. *Maytag Archives*

A December 1, 1944, War Bond Rally at the US Steel Federal Shipyard at Port Newark, New Jersey, during lunch time was attended by more than 3,000 employees even though the wind was blowing at 30mph and the temperature was near freezing. The mood is obviously festive, as men and women jitterbug to the music of the Navy Armed Guard Center Band from Brooklyn, New York, on the other side of New York Harbor. Babushkas seem to be the preferred headwear for the affair. The speaker at the rally was Lt. John F. Mueller, US Navy Reserve, and the response to his appeal was very good, according to a company press release. *National Archives*

Hamilton Standard was a major manufacturer of controllable-pitch aircraft propellers during WWII, supplying 75 percent of the Allied requirement. The pitch control operated on a counterweight principle and was altered by forcing oil through a hydraulic cylinder in the propeller hub, which moved the blades from standard high pitch to low pitch. The other major producers were Curtiss-Electric and Hydromatic. These dural blade forgings await machining at the company's East Hartford, Connecticut plant. *United Technologies Archives*

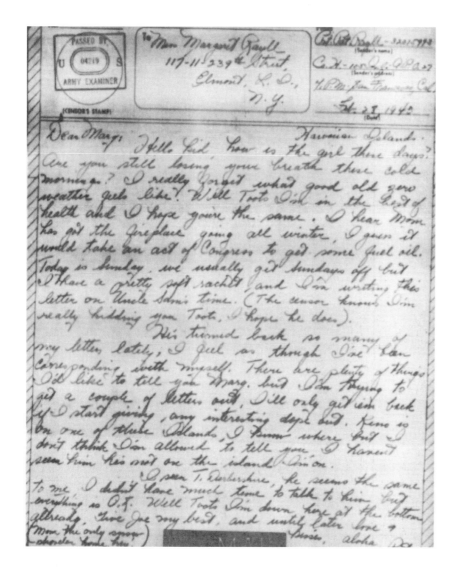

A V-Mail letter from Army private Patrick Ryall in the Hawaiian Islands to his sister Margy at home in Elmont, New York. It is dated a little less than three months after the attack on Pearl Harbor. The censor's stamp is in the upper left-hand corner. Patrick survived the war. *Margy McVey Archives*

V-Mail was developed to save space and weight in the shipment of mail for millions of American servicemen and women. Letters were written on a special form that was in turn photographed onto a film strip, shipped to an overseas post office and transferred back into the letter format. The government advertised that 1,700 letters could fit into a cigarette package. *The Ad Council*

Civilians were faced with all types of rationing, including gasoline, shoes, cigarettes, and liquor. However, food rationing created the shortages most acute to the majority of Americans. Families pooled their ration points and even attempted to trade for favored items. Hoarding was frowned upon, but black markets flourished across the land. Curiously, restaurants were not rationed so if money was no object, and for many defense workers it wasn't, a citizen could eat practically anything and in any quantities. *National Archives*

ica. The postwar leadership role thrust upon the United States was the result of the nation's dominance, not only in men and in military proficiency, something certainly matched by the Soviet Union, but by technology, in which the United States was unsurpassed. Much of it could be attributed to the men and women of the aviation industry.

A Chrysler employee test-monitors a Wright Cyclone R-3350BA engine built by the auto manufacturer for the B-29 bomber. By the end of the war Chrysler had built 18,413 of these eighteen-cylinder radial engines at its Dodge plant in Chicago. Each engine produced 2,200hp. The B-29 was used exclusively in the Pacific Theater during WWII. *Chrysler Archives*

New York City's Times Square is the site of this rally for the government-sponsored 5th War Loan during the summer of 1944. A giant cash register recorded the sales of War Bonds to patriotic citizens. During the war Americans purchased $157 billion in War Bonds. *Invisible Man's Revenge* was playing at the Rialto Theater and the *Times* Building supported the bond efforts with a major sign, as did two other buildings in this photograph. *National Archives*

The fighting in Europe was over, but recruiting to aid the war effort against Japan continued. This car was part of the Minneapolis Aquatennial Parade on July 21, 1945. Featured are Lieutenant Reynolds of the US Army, Eleanor Krousey, and Audrey Brink. The railroads played the major role in the transportation of raw materials, equipment, and personnel throughout the United States. *Burlington Northern Railroad Archives*

On November 1, 1941, Northrop was awarded $2.91 million to build an experimental flying wing. Designated the XB-35, this tailless bomber weighed 155,000lb and was powered by four 3,000hp engines. Its wingspan was 172ft. Engineering difficulties delayed its first flight until June 1946, and the results, especially regarding stability, were disappointing. It was also propeller-driven, and the attempted conversion to jet propulsion lowered its range dramatically. *Steve Pace Collection*

Willys-Overland manufactured the famous Jeep during WWII, and like many other automobile manufacturers, also built aircraft or aircraft sub assemblies. This August 19, 1942, employee rally in Toledo, Ohio, was typical of the government and corporate-generated programs designed to improve workers' morale, although the faces visible seem less than enthusiastic. Many of the workers in this photograph are wearing identical small white paper hats with a broad dark stripe around the crown. *National Archives*

Early in the war General Electric had built the GE-IA turbo-jet engine at its Lynn River, Massachusetts, facility. In this 1943 photograph, jet engine experts from Great Britain examine the "Eye-A" under the gaze of the engine's designer, Donald F. "Truley" Warner, smoking a cigar in the center of the picture. An interested pilot on the right also observes the engine of the future. *Steve Pace Collection*

Four P-59 Airacomets, America's first jet-propelled aircraft, await fly-away by the USAAF, while a fifth takes to the air in the distance. The P-59 first flew at Muroc Dry Lake in California on October 1, 1942. Production models were powered by two GE engines, either the I-14 or the I-16 engine, which were improved versions of the IA. Bell Aircraft built 66 P-59s, but they never flew in combat, having a maximum speed of 450mph and range of 440mi. *Steve Pace Collection*

In 1943, a Lockheed engineering team led by Kelly Johnson designed and built the prototype P-80 in only 143 days. Known as the Shooting Star, it first flew on January 8, 1944, but never achieved combat status during WWII. It was, nevertheless, the first American aircraft to sustain in excess of 500mph in level flight. These P-80As are parked on the ramp at Lockheed's B-1 Burbank, California, plant. *Steve Pace Collection*

In keeping with the patriotic parades and rallies that flourished all across America during WWII, UAW-CIO union employees of Champion Spark Plug sponsored this float extolling their wartime contributions. It is being towed by another Toledo contribution, the Jeep. From 500,000 aviation spark plugs per year in 1941, production soared to 24 million per year by 1943. From 1941 to 1945 Champion, as the major contractor, provided 78 million ceramic spark plugs to the US military aviation services. *Cooper Industries Champion Spark Plug*

Employees of the Maytag Company in Newton, Iowa, burn German dictator Adolph Hitler in effigy to celebrate the end of the war in Europe in May 1945. Awaiting his turn is an effigy of Japanese Emperor Hirohito. Both enemy leaders, as well as Benito Mussolini of Italy, were savagely caricatured by the American media and the US government, part of the propaganda effort endemic to all international conflicts. *Maytag Archives*

Chapter VI

Naval Aviation

While he was assistant secretary of the Navy in 1898, Teddy Roosevelt recommended that his service study the ramifications of military flight. Although no action was taken for several years, the Navy did stay abreast of aviation developments, and in 1910 a civilian pilot named Eugene Ely flew a Curtiss biplane off a wooden platform built over the bow of an anchored US cruiser, the *Birm-ingham*. He was the first man in history to fly off a ship. A year later the Navy bought its first two aircraft. In 1911, Lt. T. G. "Spuds" Ellyson became the first naval aviator, and a tradition was born. A Marine officer, Lt. Alfred A. Cunningham, became Naval Aviator No. 5 in May 1912, marking the beginning of Marine Corps aviation.

The Navy was interested in several aspects of aviation including lighter-than-air (LTA) craft, amphibious aircraft, and both ship-based and land-based planes. Aircraft were catapulted from existing ships to perform scouting duties. They would land alongside their ships upon completion of their missions and be hoisted back aboard. Flying boats operated from facilities on shore, performing scouting, rescue, convoy, and anti-submarine duties. In June 1915 the Navy ordered a nonrigid airship, and in 1919 acquired its first rigid airship from Great Britain. The British method of differentiating between the two types (*a* for rigid and *b* for limp) led to the name blimp for nonrigid airships.

The American automobile industry, prevented by government decree from building cars during the war, became a major supplier of military equipment to all the services. General Motors was the largest producer of any American corporation, and built Grumman F4F Wildcats (as FM-1s and FM-2s) and TBF Avengers (as TBMs) at five of its plants in the Northeast. Featured here is the Linden, New Jersey, plant, which produced the first FM-1s. Employees and civilians are obviously mesmerized by some special event at the plant, very possibly that first Wildcat. The FM-2 was a lighter version of the Wildcat that was usually assigned to the smaller escort, or "Jeep," carriers. The other GM plants involved in building Grumman aircraft were located in Tarrytown, New York; Baltimore, Maryland; and Trenton and Bloomfield, New Jersey. *Northrop Grumman Archives*

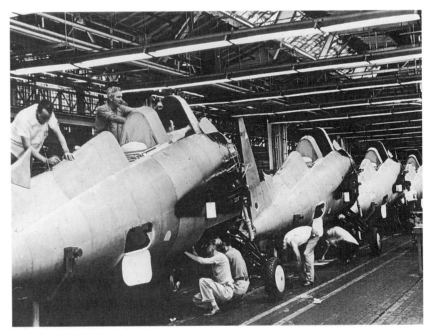

General Motors employees were accustomed to finishing a car every minute of the work day; Grumman workers built six planes every 24hr and had a personal level of pride invested in their finished product that was not necessarily true of the mass-production auto workers. It took some time for the competing philosophies of manufacturing to be merged into a cohesive production plan.

In order to facilitate construction, Grumman gave Eastern Aircraft, which was the name GM assigned to its aviation division, several F4Fs for production study. They were known as PK planes because they were held together by Parker-Kalon temporary fasteners, allowing their deconstruction for training purposes. *Northrop Grumman Archives*

The F4F was powered by an air-cooled Pratt & Whitney R-1830-86 fourteen-cylinder radial engine that generated 1,100hp. The plane's top speed was 298mph and it had a service ceiling of 33,500ft. The production needs of the Navy once the war began resulted in the manufacturing agreement between Grumman and GM. Also in evidence was pressure from the War Production Board to work out such an arrangement. General Motors' Eastern Aircraft produced

its first FM-1 on August 31, 1942. Interestingly, a compilation of aircraft production in the United States by total pounds of airframe ranked the Trenton plant nineteenth and the Linden plant twenty-seventh out of a total of thirty-five plant facilities. Another auto manufacturer, Ford Motor Company, built the B-24 bomber and ranked 4th in total weight production. Grumman ranked 11th at Bethpage. *Northrop Grumman Archives*

When the United States entered WWI in April 1917 the Navy had one training station at Pensacola, Florida, and fifty-four planes. Total personnel were forty-eight pilots and students, and 239 enlisted. By the end of the war nineteen months later, there were eight naval air stations in the United States and twenty-seven overseas, 2,000 airplanes, and fifteen LTA craft. Personnel increased to 3,049 pilots and 43,452 enlisted men. David Ingalls, a pilot from the First Yale Unit who flew with an RAF squadron, was the Navy's only ace, shooting down an observation balloon and four enemy aircraft. Two Marine aviators, Lt. Ralph Talbot, pilot, and Gunnery Sgt. R. G. Robinson, observer, received the Medal of Honor for their part in a raid over Belgium on October 14, 1918.

After the war the Navy continued its aviation programs. Three Navy-Curtiss flying boats departed Newfoundland in May 1919 for Lisbon, Portugal, and one of them, NC-4, completed the journey, becoming the first aircraft to cross the Atlantic Ocean. In 1922 a coal ship, the *Jupiter*, was converted into the Navy's first carrier and renamed the *Langley*,

The Linden, New Jersey, plant's production line in operation. GM's manufacturing techniques were to some extent adopted by Grumman's planners, and the opposite was also true. The automobile industry used semi-skilled workers in car production, while the aviation industry had always hired highly-skilled workers. The military call-up of large numbers of workers, coupled with the suddenly increased demand for an enlarged work force, resulted in a serious shortage of workers with the skills necessary for the precision building of aircraft. Thus, the aviation workers became more automated and the auto workers became more skilled, although these conversions certainly took time. One major difficulty facing the car manufacturers was their inexperience working with aluminum, a major component of all modern aircraft. Executives at the two companies referred to the joint learning experience as The Battle of the Production Line. *Northrop Grumman Archives*

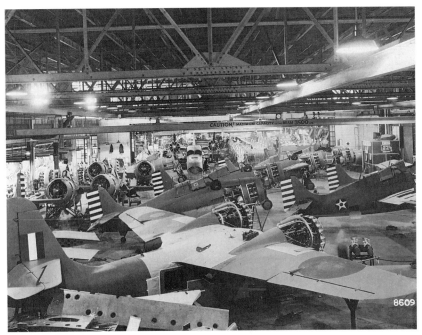

Grumman F4F-4s in early 1942 markings on the Plant One floor at Bethpage. The plane in the foreground is a twin-engined Grumman JRF-6B Goose in British markings. Grumman built 345 of these transport amphibians before production ceased in 1945. In the extreme foreground is a wing leading edge for the F4F. *Northrop Grumman Archives*

and in October of that year the first carrier takeoff and landing were made. Just eleven months later, in September 1923, the Navy's first rigid airship, named the *Shenandoah*, completed its initial flight. During the ensuing fifteen years, technology and technique improved, as did the quality and performance of naval aircraft. Dive bombers and torpedo planes were developed, as were scout and patrol planes, and fighters to operate off carriers. There was great reluctance on the part of the "battleship" Navy to share its premier position with the flying Navy, and public relations and publicity took on deeper meaning for professional Navy men from both schools of thought as they fought for their programs in the midst of economic depression, isolationism, and peace.

There were setbacks to some aspects of naval aviation, especially to the rigid airship program, which was disbanded after the 1935 crash of the USS *Macon* off the California

Grumman Wildcats, wings folded for compact storage, are lined up for fly-away at the company's Bethpage, Long Island, airfield, which was located between plant buildings. During the war years it was the busiest airfield in the New York area, with more traffic than La-Guardia Field, which at the time was New York's principal airport. Before the war Grumman employed 6,500 workers; by September 1943, when employment peaked, the payroll had expanded to 25,527 employees. Most of them were native Long Islanders from various civilian occupations who were retrained by Grumman. *Northrop Grumman Archives*

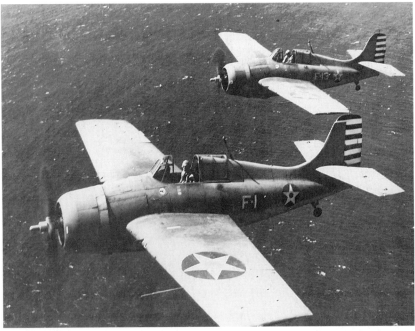

Navy Lt. Comdr. John S. "Jimmie" Thach and Lt. Edward H. "Butch" O'Hare of VF-3 training in Hawaii during early 1942 in F4F Wildcats. Thach devised the "Thach Weave," a defensive flight maneuver that helped offset the advantages of the Japanese Zero in combat. O'Hare earned the Medal of Honor for shooting down five Japanese bombers in one engagement at Bougainville in February 1942. He disappeared during a night-fighter engagement in November 1943. Chicago's International Airport was named in his memory. *National Archives*

The F4F's engine was attached to the engine mount and also covered with its cowling, after which the entire unit was secured to the aircraft's fire wall, as this photograph illustrates. The plane's retractable landing gear had to be hand-cranked up and down on takeoffs and landings, creating an extra burden on the pilot as he executed these critical maneuvers. The wheels and brakes were built by Bendix, and special Bendix air-oil struts were incorporated into the landing gear. *Northrop Grumman Archives*

coast. While only two men died in the accident, seventy-three crew members had been lost two years earlier in the crash of the USS *Akron* off the New Jersey coast in the Atlantic Ocean. In addition, the USS *Shenandoah* had crashed in Ohio in 1925 with the death of fourteen Navy men. The rigid airship program was shelved. However, fixed winged aircraft continued to improve, and on the eve of WWII, the Navy was clearly moving into the era of modern aviation. In addition, two modern aircraft carriers, the *Lexington* and the *Saratoga*, had been commissioned in late 1927, followed by *Ranger* in 1934, *Yorktown* in 1937, and *Enterprise* in 1938. Inexorably, air power was being recognized as an essential element of the US Navy.

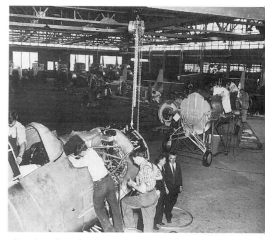

Workers link cables and electrical connections after the installation of the engine on this F4F, while two uniformed employees prepare the plane's under fuselage for attachment of the single wing. In 1940 the US Navy ordered 759 F4F Wildcats from Grumman, and deemed this plane the Navy's front-line fighter. *Northrop Grumman Archives*

The aircraft in the foreground has just received its Pratt & Whitney engine, while the plane opposite is being prepared for the same procedure. Grumman executives liked to consider their employees as "one big family," and employee turnover was very low. In May 1943, according to the War Labor Board, Grumman's turnover percentage was 2.4 percent, while the aircraft industry as a whole had a 5.5 percent turnover rate. The company had its own 40-acre produce farm, which helped in the preparation of 30,000 hot meals a day, and guest musicians as well as employee bands provided music in the cafeterias. Express trucks delivered the food to remote plant locations. Even with food rationing in place, Grumman maintained its tradition of giving every employee a turkey at Christmas. *Northrop Grumman Archives*

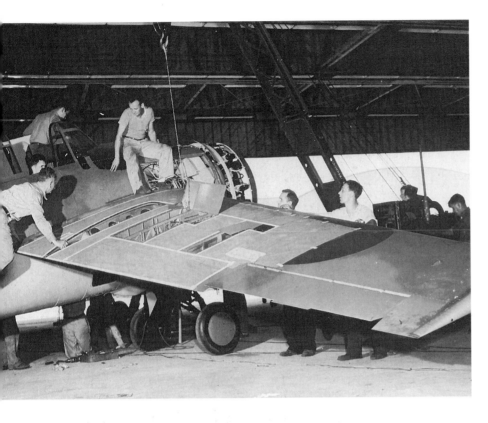

An F4F-4B Martlet IV (note British roundel) undergoing wing installation in Bethpage. The Fleet Air Arm received an initial order of F4Fs in the summer of 1940. The plane was also employed extensively by the US Marine Corps. By 1943 there were twenty-six Marine squadrons flying the Wildcat, and there were thirty-four Marine Wildcat aces during the war. When the Japanese attacked Wake Island in December 1941, there were twelve Wildcats from Marine Fighter Squadron 211 on the island. They lacked ground-based radar and none of the pilots had more than 30hr in the new planes. The aviators had no gunnery or bombing experience, but for two weeks they maintained a spirited defense of the island, sinking or damaging several enemy ships and necessitating Japanese reinforcements before the enemy was able to overrun Wake. *Northrop Grumman Archives*

A flight of FM-1s built by GM's Eastern Aircraft Division fill the New Jersey sky during the summer of 1943. While the color is not discernible in this photograph, the blue-and-white national insignia is surrounded by a red circle. These markings were used briefly from June to September 1943. The Wildcat incorporated a Curtiss Electric constant-speed three-bladed propeller, and was started with a Breeze Type II cartridge starter. *Northrop Grumman Archives*

An FM-1 at the Linden, New Jersey, plant is painted white and decorated with a red cross during a drive to raise money for the hospital ship *Mercy*. The Red Cross posters are requesting a donation of $5 from each employee, and the money collected has been attached to the aircraft, with the obvious intent of covering the entire plane with $5 bills. The names of battles already fought have been inscribed on the fuselage, with Tokyo prominently displayed on the tail. American workers donated millions of dollars to charitable and medical causes during WWII. *Northrop Grumman Archives*

The outmoded *Langley* was reconverted, this time as a seaplane tender for long-range patrol aircraft. Stationed in the Philippines when the war started, she was sunk in February 1942 by Japanese dive bombers while attempting to deliver a shipment of Army P-40s, including pilots and maintenance personnel, to assist the Dutch in Java. However, the *Wasp* was commissioned in April 1940 and the *Hornet* in December 1940, bringing American carrier strength to seven on two oceans when WWII became a reality for the United States.

Great strides forward had been made in the development of naval aircraft, strides that included retractable landing gear, enclosed cockpits, improved radio communications, self-sealing fuel tanks, increased armor and armament, wing flaps, and variable pitch propellers, not to mention more powerful engines and all-metal, monoplane construction. Major manufacturers of naval aircraft just prior to the war were Curtiss, Douglas, Vought,

Three male employees completing the installation of a Pratt & Whitney R-2800-10W (the W represents water injection) in an F6F. During 1942 and 1943 more than 5,000 male workers entered military service, resulting in significant female hirings by Grumman. After two years of war, a third of the company's 25,527 member work force was female, and most of the male employees were older with families. *Northrop Grumman Archives*

These employees are giving an F6F a final washing and polishing before it is painted and rolled out of Plant Three for flyaway. The Hellcat carried six .50cal machine guns in its wings with 500 rounds of ammunition for each gun. Later models of the F6F were equipped with bomb and rocket racks for ground-support work. *Northrop Grumman Archives*

The sign on the back wall identifies the work being done in this shop. Employees are fastening and riveting "skins" for the aft fuselage of the F6F. They were cut from flat sheets, rolled, wrapped around, and riveted. Because there was no double curvature, no presses are needed. The Hellcat fuselage had a teardrop shape, so the seams between sections, or "rings," were actually overlaps. These sections were then slipped over the structural frame in size sequence and riveted to the frame. *Northrop Grumman Archives*

These two young women poised on the wing of a Grumman F6F look enough alike to be sisters, which is probably why they were photographed. Many of the company's 8,000 female employees were housewives from the surrounding communities, and as such often had domestic emergencies that could interfere with work schedules. In order to cope with these inevitable difficulties, Grumman maintained the Green Car service, which would be dispatched to assist with problems in the home or on the road. Grumman also operated three nurseries for the small children of mothers working the day shift, as well as a professional psychological service for employees with personal problems. *Northrop Grumman Archives*

Grumman, Martin, Brewster, and Consolidated.

As much as the Navy improved, however, it still was far behind the Japanese in ships, equipment, and personnel, and it was against the Japanese in the Pacific that the majority of naval air would be employed. Having said that, it should be noted that there was a significant and successful effort by naval aviation in the Atlantic against German U-boats, sinking sixty-three of them, but the Pacific Theater was still the main arena for naval air.

While US Navy patrol and scout aircraft were adequate, US Navy combat planes were sadly lacking in quality. The Navy was converting its dive bombers, torpedo planes, and fighters, but when the war started various Navy and Marine units were still operating the Brewster F2A Buffalo fighter, the SB2U Vindicator dive bomber, and the TBD-1 Devastator torpedo plane. Whenever and wherever these planes were committed to combat, including the battles of Coral Sea and Midway, they were annihilated. Their replacements were

Nearly a score of F6Fs await fly-away on the ramp at Grumman's Bethpage location. Behind the planes are temporary blast barriers, which deflected exhaust gasses and possible debris upward and away from company personnel working in the area when engines were started. In the center rear of the photograph is a twin-engined F7F Tigercat. Although it was test-flown in late 1943 and ordered by the Marines to be used in a ground-support role, it was not operational in time to be of consequence during WWII. The F7F had tricycle landing gear and was the Navy's first twin-engined aircraft planned for carrier operations. Originally designed as a two-seat night-fighter, the F7F evolved into a single-seater and then back to the two-seat version by war's end. A total of 363 Tigercats were built by Grumman, and the Marines used the plane in a ground-support role during the early days of the Korean War. *Northrop Grumman Archives*

This view of a highly organized, if deserted, F6F final assembly line in October 1944 is a far cry from Grumman's pre-war style of individual aircraft manufacture. Except for their outer wings, these planes appear just about ready for painting and fly-away. The first Hellcat on the left of the photo has several notes taped to the fuselage for last-minute checks and corrections before the aircraft will be test-flown. *Northrop Grumman Archives*

163

A few of the 12,275 Hellcats built by Grumman Aircraft between June 1942 and November 1945 at Bethpage await fly-away by Navy ferry pilots. Grumman employed three women pilots during the war who performed test flights in rotation with their male counterparts. These flights were undertaken as soon as an aircraft cleared the manufacturing facility to ascertain any problems or irregularities. Pilots maintained a "crab" list of these difficulties for the ground crews to review and correct before final delivery was made. One woman, Teddy Kenyon, totaled 1,000hr performing these tests and made approximately 4,000 landings and takeoffs from the small Grumman airport. There were also five women plane captains, who moved planes from place to place on the ground. One of them was killed in an aircraft accident in January 1944. *Northrop Grumman Archives*

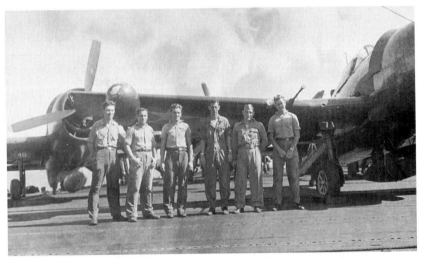

Several members of Air Group Six aboard the USS *Hancock* (CV-19) pose in front of an F6F-5N night-fighter near the end of the war. There were four of these special planes in the group. Suspended from the aircraft wing behind them is the radar bubble, designated APS-6 and built by Westinghouse. Also visible behind the man on the right is the barrel of a 20mm cannon. Late models of the F6F-5N carried two cannon and four .50cal machine guns, while earlier aircraft were armed with six machine guns. Featured left to right are John Talmage, aviation radio technician; George Hoffman, aviation radioman; Leander Benzchawel, aviation radio technician; Donald Walsh, aviation electrician; Lt. Comdr. Charles Penner, pilot and commanding officer of Night Fighter Unit 5; Claude Young, aviation ordnanceman. *Talmage Collection*

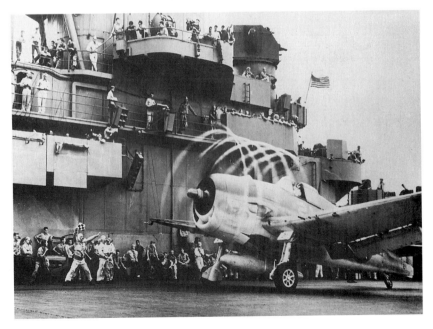

An F6F pilot, poised for takeoff aboard a US carrier in the Pacific, runs up his engine in anticipation as the deck officer prepares to drop the checkered flag. The crewmen observing the action seem very relaxed, even bored with the whole procedure. The pilot keeps his sliding cockpit open to allow quick exit in case the aircraft malfunctions on takeoff and crashes into the sea. *United Technologies Archives*

The F4U-1 with three-bladed propeller in front of the Chance Vought hangar in Bridgeport, Connecticut, in 1943. Second from the left in this photo of the pre-flight work crew (plus two female workers from the office) is Bill Foster, who worked at the plant from 1941 until the end of the war. Engine qualification consisted of "chock and tie-down, run the engine through prescribed rev tests, prop-pitch tests, manifold-pressure tests, etc.," after which the Navy inspector made a final inspection. This facility was building fourteen Corsairs a day in early 1943 and its cadre of test pilots grew from five men to forty-five. One of them, Bill Boothby, was killed when he bailed out of an F4U-1 and hit the fin and stabilizer. Another was killed in a crash of the XF4U-3. *William Foster Collection*

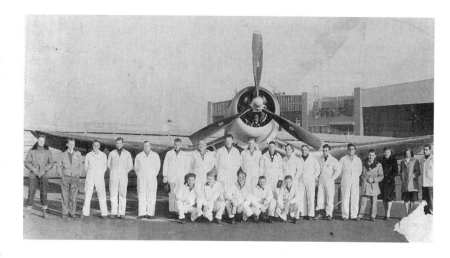

This photograph was taken two days before Christmas in 1942 of the F4U-1 final assembly line at the Vought-Sikorsky plant in Stratford, Connecticut. The wings of most carrier aircraft tilted back along the side of the plane to allow below deck storage. The wing hinges on the Corsair were positioned at the dip, or lowest place, in the wing, thus allowing the wings to fold into the up position while still allowing the maximum 17ft height for below deck storage on the carriers. *Vought Aircraft Company*

Another view of the F4U-1 final assembly line at the Vought-Sikorsky plant. Note the row of cockpits on the left awaiting fuselages and wings. Aircraft aluminum panels of the WWII era were usually riveted together and to the aircraft frame, and the "drag" created reduced the speed of the plane. The Corsair incorporated spot welding instead of riveting, thus reducing the drag, especially on the wings. However, the center section of the outboard wing panels were covered with fabric. *Vought Aircraft Company*

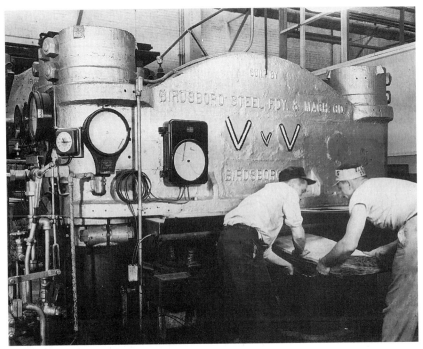

The Armstrong Cork Company of Lancaster, Pennsylvania, was heavily involved in defense production during the war years. These workers are manufacturing wing tips for the F4U in October 1942. Note the "Vs for Victory" painted on the massive Birdsboro processor. *Armstrong World Industries Archives*

The finished product. Armstrong company officials and government inspectors gather around a completed F4U-1 Corsair wing tip in October 1942 at the plant in Lancaster. Because British aircraft carriers had less storage space below decks than their American counterparts, it was necessary to clip 8in off each wing tip, resulting in a square wing tip on the F4U-1Bs supplied to the Fleet Air Arm. *Armstrong World Industries Archives*

solid, high-performance aircraft, especially the SBD Dauntless dive bomber and the TBF and TBM Avenger torpedo plane. The F4F Wildcat fighter was formidable but could not stay with the Japanese Zero in combat. However, American tactics took advantage of the F4F's strengths, and with an experienced pilot, the Wildcat could carefully compete with its adversaries.

The next generation of US Navy fighters, the F6F Hellcat and F4U Corsair, were truly superior aircraft. Their "kill" ratio against the Japanese was astonishing, and once they were deployed in force across the Pacific, there was very little doubt about the outcome of the aerial war in that theater. The exception to that statement was the onslaught of Japanese "kamikaze" aircraft, but as these were essentially flying bombs that were committed to suicide missions from which there was no return, they could not really be considered naval aircraft in the sense of fighting with the goal to inflict damage, survive, and return to fight another day.

While the Avenger remained the main torpedo plane of the US fleet, the Dauntless dive bombers were replaced later in the war by the Curtiss SB2C Helldiver, a massive and powerful aircraft that performed adequately, but never with the same panache or confidence that the Dauntless had provided to its crews.

While it can be argued that every asset in one's arsenal is necessary for victory, the Navy won its air war with essentially four planes: the Hellcat, the Corsair, the Avenger, and one of the two major dive bombers, the Dauntless or the Helldiver. Certainly patrol planes and scouts and land-based bombers played an important part, but these four aircraft were the essence of carrier aviation in WWII.

In 1941, the Navy had seven carriers, 5,233 aircraft including trainers, ten airships, 5,900 officers, and 21,678 enlisted men. By the end of the war, this force had increased to more than one hundred carriers, 40,900 aircraft, 168 airships, 60,095 pilots, and 370,760 aviation support

With engine and propeller installed, the length and angle of fuselage in front of the cockpit is apparent in this side view of an F4U-1 in final assembly. This version has a bubble canopy, rather than the earlier bird-cage canopy, which seriously limited the pilot's rearward vision. *Vought Aircraft Company*

An excellent view of the Pratt & Whitney R-2800 engine that powered the F4U-1 and the three-bladed Hamilton Standard propeller, which was 13ft, 4in in diameter. Both the landing gear and folding wings are being "cycle-tested" in this photograph. The landing gear is being rotated back into the wheel wheels, an interesting innovation. The printed sign on the prop blade says, "Don't rotate propeller after installation." One of the last wartime versions of the Corsair, the F4U-4, was equipped with a four-bladed propeller. Quite visible on this aircraft are the three cut-outs on the starboard wing for three .50cal machine guns. Also prominent is the starboard air scoop for the oil cooler and engine. The national insignia on the wing panel indicates that this plane was built after June 1943, when the star and bar was adopted. *Vought Aircraft Company*

personnel. Navy and Marine pilots sank 174 Japanese ships and destroyed 15,000 enemy planes. There was no doubt in anyone's mind that naval aviation had come of age during WWII, and played a vital role in the defeat of the Axis.

F4F Wildcat

Grumman Aircraft Engineering Company of Bethpage, New York, provided the US Navy with three of its premier airplanes during WWII. While the F4F Wildcat fighter was in many respects inferior to other American fighters and also some enemy aircraft, it played a very important role as part of America's first

The cockpit of Vought-Sikorsky's dive-test plane contains special instrumentation in addition to the normal controls. On the right side is an electrical distribution box containing the switches for the starter, primer, and emergency fuel pump. On the same side are the radio controls and the arresting-hook control for carrier landings. On the left are engine and fuel selection controls as well as wing and landing gear locks and tabs for all control surfaces. The main instrument board is in the center of the cockpit, and the control stick contains buttons to fire the machine guns and release bombs and rockets. *Vought Aircraft Company*

Awaiting fly-away at Vought-Sikorsky's Connecticut plant are ten F4U-1s. Pre-flight foreman Bill Foster remembers that "Sometimes as many as 150 aircraft would accumulate before the Navy sent a transport up from Floyd Bennett [Navy field on Long Island] with hot-to-trot young pilots ready to take delivery and fly them back to Floyd Bennett. It was always a treat to see this many leaving together." It must also have been a treat to observe the landing pattern when 150 planes reached their destination and all wanted to land. *Vought Aircraft Company*

Goodyear Aircraft in Akron, Ohio, started production of the Corsair in early 1943 and flight-tested the first FG-1 in February of that year. More than 10,000 workers were hired and trained to build the Corsair at Akron. This production team proudly poses in front of the third aircraft completed at the plant. The four men wearing neckties are probably the engineers. *Loral—Goodyear Aircraft Archives*

line of defense early in the war, when that line was very thin indeed.

In 1936 Grumman proposed a new biplane fighter to the Navy, and designated it the XF4F-1, but the Navy wanted a monoplane aircraft, and chose the Brewster Buffalo, the F2A-1. Grumman responded by scrapping its previous design completely, replacing it with the XF4F-2 all-metal monoplane. It was accepted for testing in 1937 and a year later had evolved into the XF4F-3 which flew at 333mph and reached 33,500ft of altitude. In August 1939 the Navy ordered the first fifty-four F4F-3s. France also ordered eighty-one of these aircraft but was overrun by the Germans before delivery could be made, so the British government took over the order. The British Fleet Air Arm name for them was Martlet Mk 1. By August 1940 the F4F-3 was coming into the US fleet, and began operating off the *Wasp* and the *Ranger* in March 1941. It was now the Navy's premier fighter, but at the

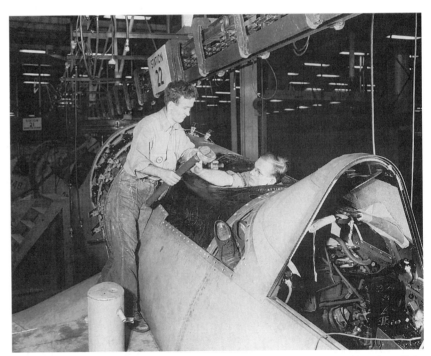

This dedicated Goodyear employee has removed his shoes and tucked them under the windscreen before clambering inside the self-sealing fuel tank located forward of the cockpit. Capacity of the internal tank was originally 237gals, but later versions carried a 160gal external drop tank on the centerline of the fuselage. Goodyear built 4,006 Corsairs during WWII, while Brewster Aircraft in Johnsonville, Pennsylvania, produced 735 Corsairs designated the F3A-1. However, after one year of production, the Navy closed Brewster's assembly line in July 1944 due to management problems, according to aviation author Robert F. Dorr. *Loral—Goodyear Aircraft Archives*

Goodyear built Plant D at its Akron location to accommodate construction of the FG-1 Corsair and incorporated some modern assembly line techniques into the new building. With what the engineers called "conveyorization," each plane under construction moved over a mile of track as the process continued. Speed varied from 1in per minute to a maximum of 8in per minute. More than 2,000 parts and 11,000 nuts, bolts, wires, washers, pins, clamps, and other vital connectors, not counting thousands of rivets, were attached at dozens of assembly stations. If a plane needed major re-work, it could be switched off the main line and switched back after the changes were completed. Power and pneumatic lines were suspended from the overhead to lessen clutter on the factory floor. *Loral—Goodyear Aircraft Archives*

Workers attach a three-bladed Hamilton Standard propeller at Station Forty-three, where the plane was also unhooked from the conveyor. The prop diameter was 13ft, 4in. Hamilton Standard was located in Connecticut and shipped the propellers to Akron. Other subcontractors used by Goodyear were the Briggs Company in Detroit for outer wing panels, Willys of Toledo for some center wing sections and Pratt & Whitney for engines. *Loral—Goodyear Aircraft Archives*

time of Pearl Harbor, only 230 F4F-3 and -3As had been delivered.

The F4F-4 incorporated changes resulting from British combat experience and included six machine guns in the wings, self-sealing fuel tanks, and better armor. This model also had folding wings for improved carrier storage. The F4F performed creditably in the Pacific, although it was not as maneuverable as the Japanese Zero and could not stay with the enemy plane in a climb. However, under the leadership of men such as Lt. Comdr. John Thach, who developed a defensive maneuver known as the "Thach Weave," American pilots were able to fight the enemy on fairly even terms until the next stage in carrier aircraft development.

That next stage was the F6F Hellcat, the design and production of which absorbed Grumman's energies, so most F4Fs were manufactured by the Eastern Manufacturing Division of General Motors (GM). General Motors Wildcats were designated FM-1s and FM-2s. Grumman

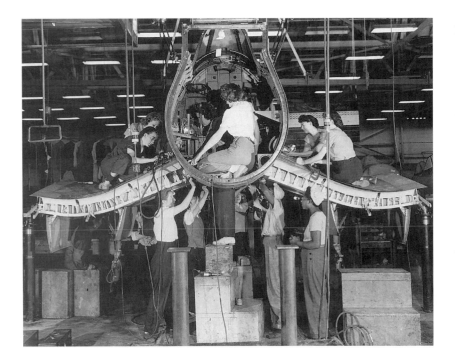

An excellent view of the main beam of the FG-1 being joined to the center fuselage, which includes the cockpit. The landing gear was attached to the center section at the lowest point in the wing bend. In addition to allowing shorter landing gear while still allowing propeller clearance, the gull inner wings joined the fuselage at right angles, an arrangement that minimizes aerodynamic drag. No less than twelve women are busily engaged in this posed photo in Plant D. During the war the Goodyear work force rose from 3,000 to 31,000 workers, including 12,000 women. In 1942 alone the company trained 8,500 women and 4,000 men. *Loral—Goodyear Aircraft Archives*

ceased production of the Wildcat in May 1943, having manufactured 1,978 aircraft. General Motors continued production until the end of the war, as the Wildcat was deployed on "jeep carriers" in both the Atlantic and Pacific. The company's final production total was 5,927 planes.

F6F Hellcat

The Grumman F6F Hellcat did not enter combat until August 1943, but it had tremendous impact on the war in the Pacific. Its kill ratio was more than 19:1, unmatched by any other fighter in the conflict, Allied or Axis. Navy and Marine Hellcat pilots shot down 5,156 Japanese planes in aerial combat while losing only 270 of their own in just two years of warfare. In the Battle of the Philippine Sea, known as the "Mariannas Turkey Shoot" to the American participants, Hellcats shot down more than 300 enemy aircraft, while losing only thirty planes to enemy action. A total of 12,275 F6Fs were delivered to US forces during WWII.

In the first few months of war against Japan, it was readily apparent that the US Navy's front-line fighter, the F4F Wildcat, could not match the Japanese A6M Zero fighter in combat. Pilots who had benefited from regular Navy training for months or years before the war used well-thought-out defensive tactics and were able to hold their own against the enemy, but certainly no

A row of Pratt & Whitney R-2800-10 engines await installation in the line of fuselages in the next row. After being uncrated, they were positioned on a sixteen-stop assembly line where various systems and parts were attached. These included the engine cowling, solenoid, starters, generators, diaphragms, thermo-couple leads, vacuum pump, tachometer, generator, and exhaust lines, to name only part of this sophisticated procedure. The engine would also be inspected before the plane returned to the main assembly line. *Loral—Goodyear Aircraft Archives*

The Marines were the first American service to fly the Corsair in combat. Featured here is Maj. Greg "Pappy" Boyington, commander of the famous VMF-214 Black Sheep squadron, a collection of individuals who did not fit comfortably into standard military organizations. However, they performed admirably under the guidance of Boyington, the Marine Corps' top ace during WWII, who shot down twenty-eight Japanese planes before being shot down himself and taken prisoner. Although he received the Medal of Honor for his exploits, it was not announced during the war for fear that the Japanese would retaliate against Boyington. In this photo he appears to be giving his crew chief a stack of Rising Sun decals, possibly to attach to his plane in recognition of his kill total. *Vought Aircraft Company*

After control riggings, hydraulics, and other systems were inspected at Station Sixty, first by the production department, then by the inspection department, and finally by the Navy, the plane entered the paint shop. Each Corsair received the approved Navy paint scheme and the national insignia before the aircraft moved on to the service hangar. Here the ship's armament would be added and tested before the plane was again inspected and then turned over to the test pilots. The service hangar, designated Plant E, accommodated seventy aircraft with wings folded. *Loral—Goodyear Aircraft Archives*

An example of integrated fuel tanks attached to the wings of a Marine F4U-1D at Guadalcanal in February 1944. Ultimately, the Marines operated thirty squadrons of Corsairs in the Pacific, with several of them based on Navy aircraft carriers, including the *Essex*, the *Bennington*, and the *Bunker Hill* in the last year of the war. *National Archives*

advantage accrued to the Americans and the F4F early in the Pacific air war. The Zero was clearly a superior aircraft in speed, maneuverability, and rate of climb, all of which were so important to a fighter pilot. The nation was now faced with turning out a quality carrier-based aircraft in the shortest possible time, and training pilots within the same parameters.

Fortunately, the F6F Hellcat was initially ordered by the US Navy in 1941, and first flew in June 1942. While the F4F held the line in the early perilous days of the Pacific war, American naval aviators received in-depth training on the F6F before being deployed against the enemy. In contrast, the Japanese lost hundreds of irreplaceable front-line pilots in the battles of the Coral Sea and Mid-

A Marine ground crew on Pelelieu attaches a tank of napalm to the centerline of an F4U-1D for an attack on Japanese ground positions. The product name is an amalgamation of the names of two of its chemical components, naphtha and palmitic acid, which were mixed with gasoline to create a devastating incendiary weapon. *Vought Aircraft Company*

way. They never recovered from these losses, and the quality of Japanese pilots declined as the war progressed.

The Grumman Hellcat started life in Bethpage in September 1940 as the G-50, and in January 1941 the Navy reviewed a mock-up of the fighter, which then led to a contract award in June 1941. It is interesting to note that one Navy requirement was increased structural strength because the plane would be facing Japanese fighters armed with cannon rather than just machine guns.

It can be said that though the nation was asleep, some military professionals were trying to prepare for what was to come. Only five months after its first test flight, a production-line F6F-3 was available for further testing and modifications. Astonishingly, there were very few changes made even though more than 12,000 F6Fs were built. As aviation author Robert F. Dorr has written, "Grumman's approach was to keep it simple, build it rugged, and turn it out in mind-boggling numbers."

The F6F-3 was powered by a Pratt & Whitney R-2800-10W two-stage radial engine that generated 2,000hp. Top speed was 386mph, with a range of 1,040mi and a service ceiling of 37,300ft. There were 4,402 aircraft manufactured in this series, including two night-fighter variants. The F6F-4 was planned as a lighter version for escort-carrier operations but was never produced. This was followed by the final production model, the F6F-5, most of which were equipped with water-injected engines as well as a redesigned bullet-proof windshield. The next version, the F6F-6, flew at 417mph (some say 440mph), powered by an R-2800-18W engine and a four-bladed pro-

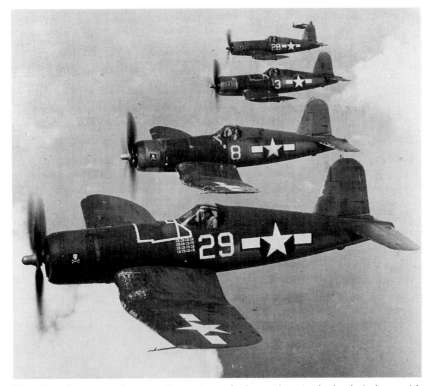

The Navy's most famous Corsair squadron was VF-17, led by Lt. Comdr. John "Tommy" Blackburn and known as the Jolly Rogers due to their skull and crossbones insignia. The unit shot down 302 enemy aircraft, including 156 Japanese planes in seventy-six days in the Solomons in 1943–44. There were fifteen aces in the squadron, led by Lt. Ira Kep-ford, seen here in the lead airplane, with sixteen air-to-air victories. During three years of combat, Navy and Marine Corsairs flew 64,051 missions, of which 9,581 were from aircraft carriers, destroying 2,140 enemy aircraft while losing only 189 of their own for a kill-to-loss ratio of 11.3:1. *Vought Aircraft Company*

The Grumman TBF-1 Avenger, still wearing pre-war national insignia. Visible in the cockpit are the pilot and radioman/rear gunner. If the bombardier is on board, he is hidden within the fuselage. The device on the starboard wing tip is the pitot tube, which measures air speed. This print was probably made from a reversed negative because the standard position of the pitot tube is on the port wing of the TBF. *Northrop Grumman Archives*

Twin lines of TBF fuselages await wing and cockpit installation at Grumman's Plant Two in Bethpage, Long Island, New York, in February 1943. To the left are F6F Hellcat fuselages, some of which have already received their landing gear. Due to problems and delays occurring in Chance Vought's production of the F4U Corsair, the Navy pressed Grumman for greater production of the F6F fighter to replace aging F4F Wildcats in the Pacific theater. The direct result was the shifting of Avenger production to GM, allowing Grumman to concentrate on F6F Hellcat manufacture. *Northrop Grumman Archives*

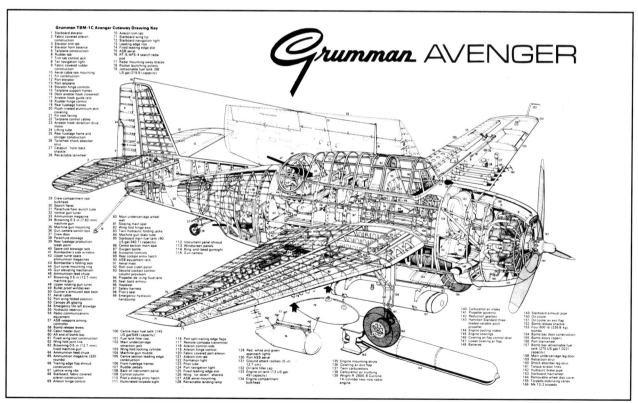

A schematic of the Grumman Avenger. While difficult to read due to the small print, there is a wealth of detailed information in this illustration. *Northrop Grumman Archives*

While "dispersal" solved some of Grumman's production difficulties, it was also necessary to subcontract the manufacture of certain parts to other companies. Grumman subcontracted 27 percent of its total output during WWII. Featured here are employees of the John Deere Company in Iowa building bomb-bay doors for the TBF. The Avenger was the first torpedo plane to carry its Mk 13-2 torpedo inside the fuselage, thus reducing drag on the plane in flight. *Deere & Company*

Four female workers busily rivet and fasten aluminum sheets to the forward fuselage frame of a TBF-1. New workers were given six-week courses at night in local high schools to learn the new skills required for precision aircraft production. College women recruited for the Engineering Unit were given a two-month course at Columbia University in New York City. The woman inside the bomb bay in this photograph is working on the bulkhead panel. As her left foot is dangling below the aircraft, it would appear the bomb-bay doors have not yet arrived from John Deere. The company coveralls were available for $2.50 each. *Northrop Grumman Archives*

This collection of finished and unfinished TBFs crowds the floor of Plant Two on October 31, 1943, only a few months before production ceased at Bethpage. The British roundel is prominently displayed on the wing of the aircraft to the right in this picture; the Fleet Air Arm purchased 958 Avengers during the war. The poster on the back wall of the building urges employees to contribute to the 3rd War Bond Drive, exclaiming "Let's Put Plant 2 Right Over The Top!." *Northrop Grumman Archives*

Grumman's Plant Two in Bethpage, New York, was the manufacturing home of the TBF-1 Avenger. The great majority of these fuselages have been mated with cockpits, tail sections, engines, and pro- pellers but still lack outer wings and landing gear. No-smoking signs are prominently displayed on the plant walls. However, Grumman executives, who showed an extraordinary amount of con- cern for their workers, gained conces- sions from fire-insurance underwriters to open certain areas of the plant facilities to employee smoking. *Northrop Grumman Archives*

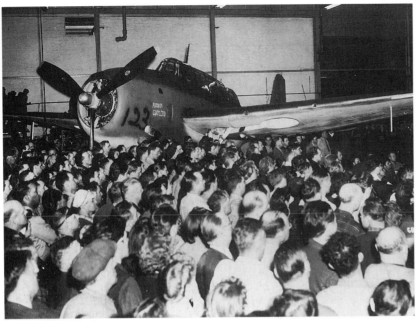

Grumman employees, having built 2,293 TBFs, celebrate the closing of the Avenger assembly line in December 1943. Painted on the fuselage of the display aircraft are the words, "Mission Accomplished." General Motors' Eastern Aircraft Division continued production of the Avenger at its plants in New Jersey and by war's end had manufactured 7,546 aircraft designated the TBM-3. *Northrop Grumman Archives*

peller. Production was to begin in September 1944. However, there was an engine shortage as F6F-6 used the same engine as the F4U-4 Corsair, and the -6 never went into production. In addition to US Navy and Marine squadrons flying the Hellcat, the British Fleet Air Arm procured 1,177 F6Fs and used them in Europe and the Pacific organized into fifteen squadrons.

F4U Corsair

One of the most distinctive aircraft in WWII due to its unusual inverted gullwing design, the F4U Corsair was descended from a long line of naval aircraft built by the Chance Vought Aircraft Company. Chauncey Milton "Chance" Vought was born in 1890 and studied engineering at New York University and the University of Pennsylvania. His intense interest in aviation led to his pilot's license in 1912. Five years later he and fellow aviation pioneer Birdseye Lewis started their own air-

Grumman TBF-1s painted in the Navy's classic blue and gray camouflage pattern await flight testing. Employees called this test strip "Sun Valley" after the famous Idaho ski resort, rather apt on a day when snow covered the ground. Grumman's flight-test area was congested, and one pilot landed short on top of a car in an adjacent parking lot, bounced and relanded successfully on the strip. Another was forced to put down with a dead engine in an empty lot between two buildings, stopping just short of a busy pedestrian and vehicle intersection. *Northrop Grumman Archives*

craft manufacturing company on Long Island, New York. Their VE-7 was purchased by the Army as a two-seat trainer and the VE-7SF, known as the Bluebird, made the first takeoff from an aircraft carrier in October 1922.

During the next eight years the company grew to be the second largest manufacturer of military aircraft in the country.

Chance Vought produced the VE-9H trainer and the UO-1 observer in 1922, an early Navy fighter known as the FU-1, the O2U-1 in 1926, and the O3U-1 in 1930 followed by the SU-1 and SU-4 scouts. In 1933 the SBU-1 dive bomber was delivered to the Navy, and in 1936 the SB2U-1 Vindicator monoplane dive bomber joined the fleet. All of these aircraft were obsolete by the beginning of WWII, except the OS2U Kingfisher reconnaissance plane, which had been designed in 1937, was operational in 1940, and gave excellent service for the duration of the war.

An Avenger takes off using jet-assisted takeoff (JATO). Four 330hp jet units were attached to the underside of the fuselage, creating additional power and reducing needed runway space by 50 percent. *General Tire Archives*

The Avenger was a very rugged aircraft in the Grumman tradition and often managed to return to base when badly damaged by enemy action. In this photo the pilot has managed to land his plane safely on his carrier; unfortunately his rear gunner was killed in action. The man was left at his post, and the aircraft became his shroud and coffin, as the deck crew pushed it into the ocean after a memorial service was read over his remains. *Northrop Grumman Archives*

A row of SBD-2 Dauntlesses await fly-away from the Douglas Aircraft factory at El Segundo, California, in February 1941. The first two models of this aircraft did not have self-sealing fuel tanks. Two .50cal machine guns were fitted in the engine cowling and fired by the pilot. The SBD-1 and SBD-2 weighed 7,698lb and were powered by the R-1820-32 engine that generated 450hp. *McDonnell Douglas Aircraft*

In this photograph several A-24s, the Army version of the SBD, await delivery, their engines hooded over as protection from dirt and ramp debris. They were usually employed in a ground-support role by the Army, either as a low-level bomber or as a smoke layer. In carrying out the latter mission, the A-24 was equipped with a 50gal belly smoke tank and two 18gal smoke tanks on the wings. *McDonnell Douglas Aircraft*

In 1929 Chance Vought Aircraft had joined the Boeing Airplane Company, Boeing Airlines, and Pratt & Whitney Aircraft to create United Aircraft and Transport Company located in East Hartford, Connecticut. Unfortunately Chance Vought died in that city of blood poisoning shortly after the merger in July 1931. In 1939 the Chance Vought Division combined with Sikorsky and moved to Stratford, Connecticut. In January 1943 Chance Vought got its name back when Sikorsky moved the helicopter division to Bridgeport, Connecticut.

Design of the F4U Corsair was started in 1938 when the US Navy requested proposals for a new carrier-based fighter comparable or superior to land-based planes then under development for the Army. From its inception the F4U promised to be a very different plane. Its inverted gull-wing was a radical departure from existing design doctrine, and its four-bladed propeller was the largest of its time. These innovative conceptions were the brainchild of Vought's chief

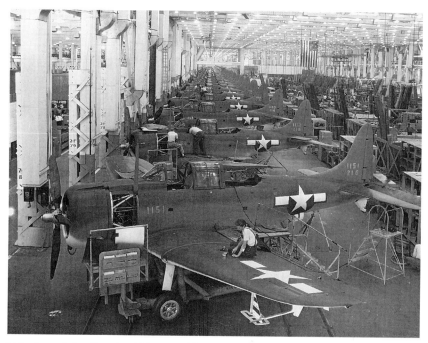

This view of the Douglas SBD assembly line is almost exactly the same as in the previous photo, as the position of the young lady on the port wing will attest. These aircraft are nearly complete but appear to be lacking finishing work in the rear gunner's position. The SBD was given various names by its crews, including the "Barge," the "Speedy D," the "Clunk," and "Slow But Deadly." *McDonnell Douglas Aircraft*

A seemingly endless row of SBD fuselages stretch across the Douglas factory floor in El Segundo. Unlike the carrier-based fighters and torpedo planes used by the Navy during WWII, the Dauntless did not have folding wings, and two aircraft with wings extended used as much storage space on the hangar deck as five planes with wings folded. The SBD was a rugged aircraft, and its airframe could handle excessive stress as well as battle damage. On occasion, pilots experienced 9g when pulling out of dives and were able to bring the aircraft home. *Northrop*

Douglas men and women working in the engine shop at El Segundo. The SBD-3 was powered by a Wright radial that generated 1,000hp, and the -4s and -5s carried a more powerful 1,200hp Wright R-1820-60. The -6, which was the final version of the SBD, was equipped with the Wright R-1820-66 engine generating 1,350hp. *McDonnell Douglas Aircraft*

designer, Ted Beisel. He wanted to join the largest available engine, the Pratt & Whitney XR-2800 Double Wasp, with the smallest airframe to maximize speed and power. First flown in May 1940, the F4U became the first US fighter to exceed 400mph when it reached 404mph in October 1940. Difficulties delayed operational status for the Corsair, including the near total destruction of the only prototype on its fifth flight when a fuel shortage and bad weather resulted in a controlled crash on a golf course by test pilot Boone Guyton.

In addition, the repositioning of fuel tanks resulted in the cockpit being moved 4ft further back on the

An interesting view of the camouflage protection over the Douglas El Segundo plant as seen from below. The house is simply framed and covered with burlap or light canvas and borders a grove of trees. Note the realistic chimney on the far side of the building. *McDonnell Douglas Aircraft*

An SBD-3 from VB-3 is transported by elevator from the hangar deck to the main deck of an American aircraft carrier prior to May 1942. Most of its cockpit is still protectively hooded. Barely visible on the covered tail are the painted red and white horizontal recognition stripes that were removed from Navy planes by official directive early that month. The red ball in the middle of the white star on the wing and fuselage was removed at the same time. *National Archives*

fuselage. This caused vision problems for the pilot. Although the Navy ordered 584 F4U-1s in June 1941, it was reluctant to initiate carrier operations due to the plane's high landing speeds and the pilot visibility problems. Thus the F4U made its debut in the hands of land-based Marine fighter squadrons in February 1943 at Guadalcanal, and these Leatherneck Corsairs made an immediate impact on the war in the Pacific. Within a few months the eight Marine fighter squadrons in that theater of war were flying Corsairs.

Vought built 1,550 F4U-1s before modifying and raising the cockpit on the F4U-1As as well as adding water injection and more power to the engine. The F4U-1Bs were manufactured for the British and their wing tips were 8in shorter so they would fit into the low-ceilinged hangar decks of the Royal Navy carriers. The F4U-1Cs were armed with four 20mm cannons instead of the standard six .50cal machine guns. The F4U-1Ds were manufactured as fighter-bombers, and had factory-fitted bomb and rocket racks as well as

An SBD-3 in mid-war markings (May 1942 to June 1943) takes off from an American carrier in the Pacific. Very visible are the "Swiss cheese" dive brakes on the trailing edges of the wings. These were deployed when the aircraft was diving on its target, helping to steady and slow the plane's descent in order to bomb accurately. *McDonnell Douglas Aircraft*

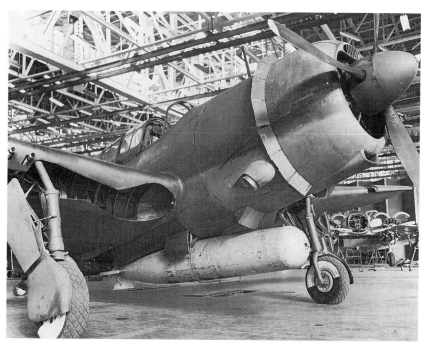

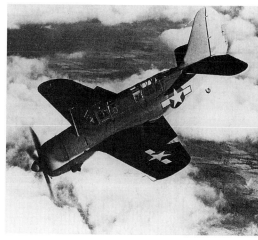

The SB2C Helldiver dive bomber was the last of this type aircraft designed and used by the American military. The initial version, the SB2C-1, was 36ft, 4in long; its wingspan was 49ft, 9in; it stood 13ft, 2in off the ground; it was powered by a Wright R-2600-8 engine that developed 1,500hp; and its top speed was 278mph, considerably larger and faster than the SBD Dauntless it replaced during the last eighteen months of the war in the Pacific. Later models reached top speeds of 294mph. *Chrysler Archives*

The landing gear on the SB2C folded into the leading edges of the wings, a rather unique feature. A door, or hatch cover, sealed the gear well, maintaining smooth airflow over and under the wing. Although the aircraft was designed with an internal bomb bay and was primarily a dive bomber, the aircraft shown in this photograph carries a practice torpedo attached to the centerline as well. Early versions of the Helldiver featured a three-bladed propeller. *Pete Bowers Collection*

Due to previous contract commitments, Curtiss was unable to build the SB2C at its Buffalo, New York, plant and constructed a new facility in Columbus, Ohio, incorporating 1.1 million square feet of factory floor space. The center wing section of the aircraft was built by Chrysler Motors at two plants. This section, which contained the landing gear, bomb bay, and hydraulic controls, as well as miles of wire and cable, was able to withstand stress tests of more than 100,000lb. In this photo, a row of A-25As are near completion. The engine is a Wright radial R-2600-8 rated at 1,500hp. *Pete Bowers Collection*

fittings for fuel drop-tanks. The plane's engine was upgraded to the R-2800-8W. Vought produced 4,102 of the -1Bs,-1Cs, and -1Ds. Goodyear Aircraft built 3,808, designated FG-1, while Brewster built 735 Corsairs, designated the F3A-1.

A night-fighter version of the Corsair was developed and designated the F4U-2, but only twenty-two of them became operational. The F4U-3 was a high-altitude version, but only one was ever built and it was not tested until after the war. The F4U-4 was powered by a water-injected, supercharged R-2800-18W engine that powered the aircraft to a top speed of 448mph with the aid of a four-bladed propeller. The F4U-4 did not become operational until March 1945, so comparatively few of them saw combat. However, this version was heavily involved in the Korean War that began in June 1950, and is the Corsair most familiar to the public.

It was not until April 1944 that the Navy approved the Corsair for

The Army variant of this Curtiss aircraft was designated the A-25, the first ten of which retained the folding wings of the Navy version. The upper rear section of the fuselage just behind the gunner was known as the turtledeck and could be lowered, as shown in this photograph, to offer an improved field of fire for the gunner. His weapon was a single .50cal machine gun. *Pete Bowers Collection*

An A-25A painted with both US and RAAF markings. In addition to the rear gunner's .50cal machine gun, the SB2C carried two 20mm cannon or four .50cal machine guns in the wings. The SB2C-4, used for night operations, incorporated factory-built external bomb racks on the wings. *Pete Bowers Collection*

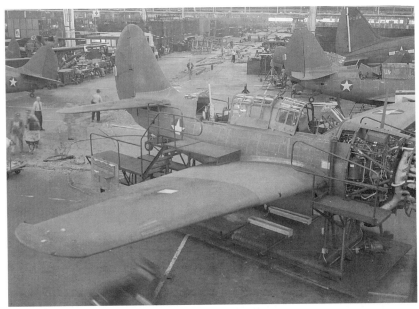

Army A-25s under construction at the Columbus, Ohio, plant. The aircraft's massive tail is very evident in this photo but is dwarfed by the even larger tail of a C-46 Commando in the background, also built by Curtiss. Because the Navy required that two SB2Cs fit on a hangar elevator and that each aircraft be capable of carrying two bombs internally, the engineers designed a shorter plane with a broader fuselage than originally foreseen. The large tail was necessary to rectify flight instabilities resulting from these design changes. The A-25s featured here carry the national insignia used between May 1942 and June 1943, while the star and bar in place on the C-46 was standard after the latter date. *Pete Bowers Collection*

carrier operations. While the Grumman Hellcat was in service for a longer period of the war and had the best "kill" ratio, the F4U could carry more weapons, had a greater range, and was the more powerful plane. Its Japanese opponents called it "Whistling Death."

TBF and TBM Avenger

The US Navy's Avenger torpedo plane, designed by Grumman, was the premier American aircraft of its type in WWII. In fact, it was really the only American torpedo plane in the war after the crippling losses incurred by the obsolete Douglas TBD-1 Devastator during the June 1942 Battle of Midway. Chance Vought Aircraft did manufacture the TBY-2 Seawolf, but only 181 were procured by the Navy, and the aircraft had no impact on the war. The Avenger was the heaviest carrier-based aircraft in the American inventory with a gross weight of 13,813lb. It was also used in a level bombing role in the later war years.

The Navy had procured its first torpedo plane in 1925, and along with the British and the Japanese, foresaw an important role for it against an opponent's capital ships. In most instances a plane could get much closer to its target and also make speed and course adjustments before releasing its torpedo. The Douglas TBD-1 Devastator was the first monoplane, all-metal torpedo plane and the first to be carrier-based, but its top speed was only 192mph. Just 130 of them were delivered to the Navy between 1935 and 1939, and at the time of Pearl Harbor only sixty-nine of them were combat-ready. When three squadrons of TBDs attacked the Japanese fleet at Midway, thirty-five out of forty-one were shot down, including the entire fifteen planes of VT-8 from the USS *Hornet*, and recorded no hits on the enemy ships. Fortunately, the TBF was just coming on line. Several of them participated rather inauspiciously in the battle as shore-based aircraft flying out of Midway Island, as five of six TBFs were lost to enemy action. Ironically, they were also assigned to VT-8 but had not caught up with the carrier-based squadron and were also still going through training on the new plane.

This SB2C-3, undergoing engine run-up, is painted in the classic Navy blue above and gray below camouflage scheme. The folded wings offer an excellent view of the electrical mechanism used to accomplish the vital wing storage function. For all of its size and weight, the SB2C was able to operate off the smaller US escort carriers, designated CVEs, but known as "Jeep" carriers or "baby flat-tops." In the background of this photo is a row of twin-engined AT-9 trainers, also built by Curtiss. *Pete Bowers Collection*

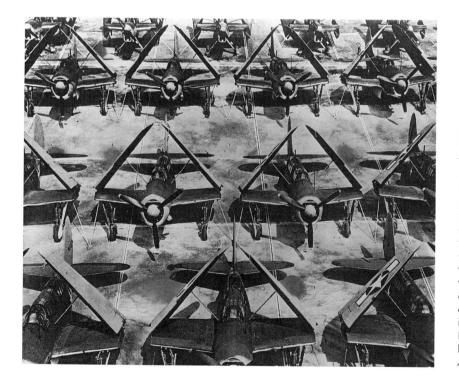

Rows of SB2C-3s wearing post-June 1943 national insignia await fly-away. The SB2C used electrical circuits exclusively for flap and landing gear control, as well as wing-folding, while most WWII aircraft had hydraulic systems. Even after the plane was operational, the electrical circuits caused many problems, and aviators were very distrustful of the system. On occasion, only one flap would open when activated, or only one landing gear would fold up into place, events that could cost the pilot his life. Although considered a superior aircraft in comparison with its predecessor—the SBD Dauntless—the Helldiver was never popular with American aviators. *Chrysler Archives*

An SB2C dives at a 45deg angle on its target with dive brakes on the trailing edges of the wings extended and bomb bay doors open. The turtledeck has been lowered and the rear gunner is ready to engage enemy planes. *Pete Bowers Collection*

A-25As in early-war markings flying in formation on a training mission. Protruding from the rear cockpits of the three aircraft in the foreground are the barrels of the .50cal machine guns used by the planes' enlisted gunners, although the gunners themselves do not appear to be in place. A-25s were employed by Marine Corps pilots as well as Army fliers. *Chrysler Archives*

Planning for the Avenger began in the summer of 1940, and it first flew on August 1, 1941. It was initially delivered to the Navy in January 1942, but several months passed before enough planes were available and enough pilots were trained to make an operational difference. Powered by a Wright R-2600-8 engine that produced 1,700hp, the TBF-1 flew at a maximum speed of 270mph, 80mph faster than its predecessor. It carried a 2,000lb torpedo internally or the same weight in bombs. The Avenger had a power-operated dorsal turret facing rearward and occupied by a radioman/gunner armed with a single .50cal machine gun. Another .50cal, which was fixed forward, was fired by the pilot, and on some models a .30cal machine gun was aimed downward from the rear of the cen-

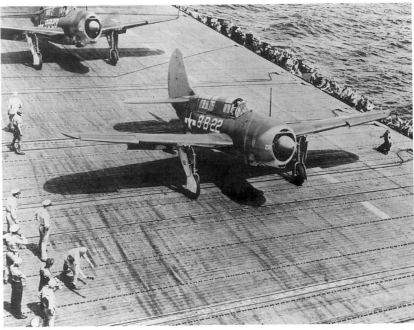

An SB2C begins its takeoff roll on a US aircraft carrier somewhere in the Pacific, while a second aircraft awaits its turn. The Helldiver's service ceiling was 29,300ft and its range was 1,925mi. The -3, -4, and -5 models incorporated a Wright Cyclone radial engine, the R-2600-20, that generated 1,900hp and drove a four-bladed propeller. *Chrysler Archives*

The twin-engined PBY was developed in the late 1930s and was the Navy's first modern amphibious patrol bomber. The PBY-2, of which fifty were manufactured, had no armament. The plane's range was 2,350mi, and it was a PBY that first sighted the Japanese Imperial fleet at the beginning of the pivotal Battle of Midway. The PBY was flown by the British, Canadians, and Australians during WWII, and the Soviets built approximately 200 PBYs under license, designating the plane the GST. *Pete Bowers Collection*

NAS North Island, San Diego, was home to these PBY-3s and was located just across the bay from Consolidated's factory. Note the cut-out hatch on the rear fuselage used for observation and the placement of a .30cal machine gun. Unfortunately, the PBY did not have self-sealing gas tanks, making it a tempting target for Japanese fighters. Consolidated built sixty-six PBY-3s. Top speed for this model was 191mph. *San Diego Aerospace Museum*

PBY-5 fuselages await wings and tails on the Consolidated assembly line in San Diego. Evident are the improved "blisters" on both side of the fuselage, each of which housed a .30cal machine gun. The plane's wingspan was 104ft and its wing area was 1,400sq-ft. Length of fuselage was 63ft, 10in and it stood 18ft, 10in off the ground. The PBY could carry 4,000lb of bombs. A total of 1,486 PBY-5s and PBY-5As were built during the war. *San Diego Aerospace Museum*

The PBY-5 was powered by two Pratt & Whitney R-1830-92 radial engines that developed 1,200hp each. Before the war there were fourteen active Navy PBY squadrons, with five of them stationed in the Hawaiian Islands. The planes were called "Cats" or Dumbos" by their crews. In the Atlantic, PBYs were used to shadow Allied convoys, perform rescue and patrol work, and also in an anti-submarine role. The US Army procured 359 PBYs, redesignating them OA-10s. *Pete Bowers Collection*

A PBY-5 in early-war markings over Lindbergh Field in San Diego. Due to its lack of speed, the PBY was considered very vulnerable to the superior Japanese planes and pilots in the early months of the Pacific war. With the advent of airborne radar in 1942, however, these patrol planes became lethal hunters of enemy shipping at night. Ground crews mixed soap and lamp black to coat these nocturnal bombers, making them very difficult to distinguish against the tropical night sky. The "Black Cats," as they were known, racked up impressive numbers of enemy ships sunk and damaged on these nighttime forays. During the critical early days of the Guadalcanal campaign. Maj. Gen. Roy Geiger (US Marine Corps) used a PBY as his personal transport, naming it the *Blue Goose*. His pilot, Maj. "Mad Jack" Cram, borrowed two torpedoes, suspended them from the fuselage of the PBY, and attacked Japanese resupply ships, hitting one that was beached while unloading supplies. He won the Navy Cross for his actions. *Pete Bowers Collection*

Seeking a four-engined replacement for the PBY, the US Navy contracted in 1935 with Consolidated for the PB2Y, which first flew in 1937 and became operational in 1940. The primary version was the PB2Y-3, of which 210 were built. In this photo, the aircraft is awaiting engine nacelles and propellers, while farther down the flight line five Martin PBMs appear ready for fly-away. *Martin Marietta*

Above and left
Goodyear Aircraft in Ohio was a major subcontractor for the PB2Y, building flight decks as well as the very large and impressive twin-tail empennage at its new plant in Arizona, as featured in these two photographs. Most PB2Y-3s were used as transports and carried five crewmen. When employed as a patrol bomber, it carried ten crewmen and 12,000lb of bombs or depth charges at 225mph. The wingspan of the PB2Y was 115ft, and it was powered by four 1,200hp radial engines. *Loral—Goodyear Aircraft Archives*

tral torpedo compartment and could be fired by the bombardier.

Because Grumman was caught up in the production of F6F Hellcats, it ceased production of the Avenger in December 1943, having completing 2,293 units in Plant Two at Bethpage. General Motors started production of the Avenger in January 1943 at its idle automotive plant in Trenton, New Jersey. General Motors Avengers were designated TBM-3, and GM built 7,546 out of the 9,839 Avengers produced during WWII. Before WWII, Grumman had built 300 aircraft for the US military; between December 1941 and V-J Day in September 1945, this company produced 17,013 planes for America and her Allies.

The Avenger was also used in an anti-submarine role and for recon-

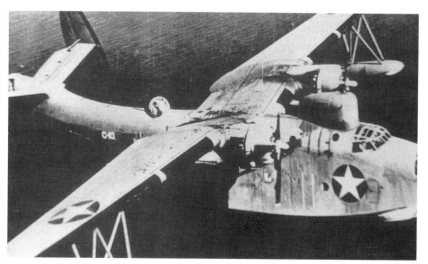

The Martin Mariner flying boat, designated the PBM, was another attempt to replace the venerable PBY. First flown in February 1939, the twin-engined aircraft commenced mass production in 1942 with the PBM-3 model. A total of 1,365 were built during the war, although production continued until 1947. *Loral— Goodyear Aircraft Archives*

Workers at the Martin plant near Baltimore, Maryland, complete rib and stringer construction on the nose, or bow, section of a PBM. The man on the right is affixing temporary clamps to hold the skin to the frame prior to riveting. In the rear of the photo is a completed bow section awaiting attachment to the fuselage of a PBM. *Martin Marietta*

An impressive row of PBM fuselages await the next step in construction. The PBM was the largest, heaviest patrol bomber in the US arsenal with a range of 3,450mi. It was able to carry 4,000lb of bombs and was powered by two 1,700hp Wright R-2600 fourteen-cylinder radial engines. *Martin Marietta*

naissance missions. As mentioned earlier, it was used on a regular basis as a level and glide bomber against entrenched Japanese positions in various Pacific island campaigns. The Fleet Air Arm of the Royal Navy procured 958 Avengers, and New Zealand's air force purchased sixty of them. While the date of final deliveries to the Navy was September 1945, the Avenger continued in service for several years after the war, employing radar in an anti-submarine role.

SBD Dauntless

One of the true workhorses of the Navy's carrier war, the SBD dive bomber, known as the Dauntless, played an integral part in the aerial campaign against the Japanese Imperial Navy, especially in the first two years following Pearl Harbor.

In 1932 Northrop Aircraft was a subsidiary of Douglas Aircraft. The SBD was based on the design of the former's BT-1 trainer, but as a result of their corporate relationship, it was built by Douglas. In April 1938 the US Marines ordered fifty-seven SBD-1s, followed by a Navy order for eighty-seven SBD-2s. They were delivered in 1940 and 1941. The plane was considered obsolete when America entered the war, but there was little alternative as the next generation dive bomber was not yet operational.

During the opening stages of the Battle of Midway in June 1942, three squadrons of obsolete Douglas TBD-1 Devastator torpedo planes attacked the Japanese fleet and were destroyed by enemy planes and ships' guns without registering a single torpedo hit. However, their low-level attacks had brought the enemy's combat air patrols over its fleet down to sea level to engage the Americans, and allowed three squadrons of SBD-3s from *Enterprise*, *Hornet*, and *Yorktown* to begin an attack from altitude on the enemy carriers, unmolested by Japanese fighters. The Dauntless was a rock-steady bombing platform, mainly due to the upper and lower dive brakes attached to the trailing edges of the

Because the PBM was a flying boat, it did not have regular landing gear and each plane was fitted with a wheeled dolly for mobility during the production stage. Employee morale was an important factor on the assembly line and in the office, and painting a patriotic message on the fuselages of milestone aircraft was acceptable, especially as the workers would do it anyway. Apparently there is snow slush on the ramp in this picture, but nobody appears to be very bothered by the outside temperature. *Martin Marietta*

Two inspectors check the de-icing equipment on the massive twin tail of a PBM-3 at the Martin's Baltimore plant. Between 1940 and 1945 Martin built an average of one PBM every two days. The Mariner was 80ft long with an 118ft wingspan, and it stood three building stories high at the top of the tail. Martin's Middle River "B" Building was the largest unobstructed aircraft assembly floor in the world. *National Archives*

A row of wingless PBMs await the application of an approved US Navy paint scheme at Martin's Middle River plant. The PBM Mariner was superior to the PB2Y Coronado in most categories, yet it was powered by two engines instead of four, reducing engine maintenance and other support functions by 50 percent, including fuel requirements—important considerations when operating in a war zone. Many East Coast defense plants did not concern themselves with building camouflage, but obviously Martin considered it important, judging from the paint pattern on his factory in this photograph. *Post Street Archives*

wings. In this instance the attacking Navy fliers sank three of the four Japanese carriers. A few hours later, Dauntlesses from *Enterprise* returned to sink the fourth carrier. An enemy heavy cruiser was also sent to the bottom. These tough SBD-3s, which had only become operational three months earlier, in March 1942, were credited with the victory at Midway and in essence, turning the tide of war against the Japanese in the Pacific. SBDs also engaged in extensive operations in the Solomon Islands campaigns. A total of 584 SBD-3s were produced, followed by 780 SBD-4s, 2,409 SBD-5s, and 450 SBD-6s for a grand total of 5,936 Dauntlesses manufactured by the time the SBD assembly lines were shut down in July 1944. Dauntlesses sank more enemy ships in the Pacific war than any other aircraft.

Martin developed the first electric-pow-ered revolving aircraft gun turret in 1937, mounting them on the PBM initially as well as supplying them to Consolidated for use on the PB2Y-3s and PB2Y-4s. The company's most famous turret was the 250CE, which was developed in 1940 and used as a top turret on many US air-craft, including the A-20, A-22, A-30, B-17, B-24, B-25, B-26, the Vega, and Ven-tura, in addition to the British Lancaster bomber. The 250CE incorporated twin .50cal machine guns, with 360deg of horizontal movement and 90deg of verti-cal firing field. More than 40,000 of these turrets were manufactured at a special Martin plant near Baltimore. *National Archives*

SB2C Helldiver

In 1939 the US Navy knew full-well that its primary carrier-based dive bomber, the Douglas SBD Dauntless, was becoming obsolete when compared to aircraft and air defenses then being developed by other nations. Thus, in May 1939 the order for a prototype dive bomber was given to Curtiss Aircraft, and the resulting prototype SB2C first flew in December 1940. One of the gov-ernment's requirements was that the plane be small enough that two could be transported at the same time from the hangar deck to the flight deck on an aircraft carrier's ele-vator. Another requirement was that its internal bomb bay be large enough to carry two bombs. This led

With such enormous areas of factory floor space in several building to oversee, managers and supervisors used various powered scooters to move about fairly rapidly. In this 1945 photo the repair shop handles a tire replacement on a two-man transport, which is licensed for over-the-road travel. *Martin Marietta*

In March 1943 a Navy beaching crew at-taches a bowline to a PBM returning from a patrol at NAS Banana River, Flori-da. The PBM Mariner was the largest twin-engined flying boat ever construct-ed. It held an enviable position as a pa-trol and rescue craft during and after WWII. *National Archives*

to design problems and flight instabilities that delayed testing and deployment to the fleet. The SB2C was
the first US dive bomber that incorporated folding wings.

The gross weight of the first
SB2C was nearly 3,000lb heavier
than the last version of the Dauntless, and the final version of the
SB2C was 1,300lb heavier than the
first version of the same plane. Pilots,
who often referred to the aircraft as
the "Big-tailed Beast," did not love
the Helldiver, but it was faster, better
armed, and could carry a heavier
bomb load than its predecessor. The
prototype SB2C was lost in an accident, which resulted in a lengthy investigation by the Navy. Along with
construction delays, this retarded
first deliveries until December 1942
and the plane's entrance into combat
until November 1943, hardly a manufacturing miracle.

The US Army used a land version of the SB2C and designated it
the A-25. The 900 delivered were
mainly used in Europe in a ground-
support role. By war's end 7,200

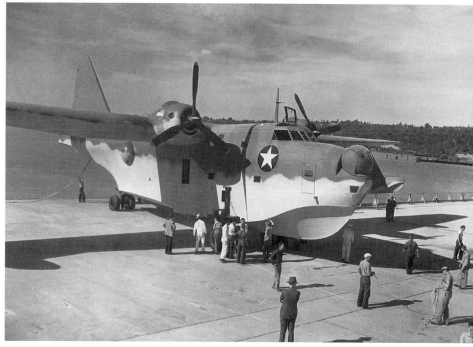

This single Boeing XPBB-1 was delivered
to the Navy in January 1945 but never
went into production. Powered by two
engines, it bears a striking resemblance
to Martin's PBM Mariner. However, the
bow turret is quite different and the aircraft does not incorporate the Mariner's
gull wings, which were designed to place
the engines above waves and spray. The
XPBB-1 also has a single tail compared
the PBM's double tail. *Boeing*

The last of the big flying boats, named
the Mars and built by Martin, was the
world's largest aircraft, weighing eighty-
two gross tons. The fuselage was 117ft
long, and the wingspan was 200ft. However, its slow speed resulted in its redesig-
nation from patrol bomber to transport
as PB2M-1R. The aircraft became operational in 1944 and immediately set
weight and distance records. In addition
to the original XPB2M-1, four JRM-1s
and one JRM-2 were built. *Martin Marietta*

SB2Cs and A-25s were built, with
Fairchild Aircraft Limited of Canada
constructing 300 planes, and the Canadian Car and Foundry Company
Limited manufacturing another 894
Helldivers. Although often deprecat-
ed, the Helldiver remained operational in the Navy until the 1950s.

Patrol Aircraft

Although there was significant
friction between the battleship proponents and the upstart aviation
contingent in the US Navy during
the 1920s and 1930s, both camps
recognized the value of aviation for
patrol and scouting duties. Thus,
single-engined scout planes operated
from airborne hangars within the
cavernous dirigibles, being lowered
and retrieved on a trapeze and hook
system. Other scouts were catapulted
from the decks of battleships and
cruisers to perform their duties, after
which they would land alongside the
mother ship and be winched back on
board.

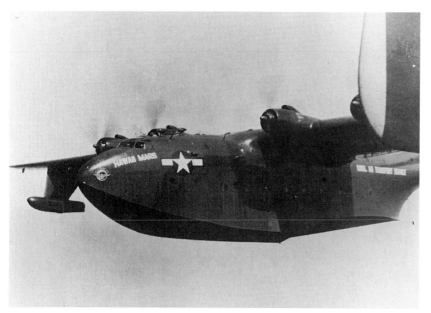

The JRMs were named for Pacific Island chains. The prototype was named the *Hawaii Mars*, but unfortunately it crashed during a flight test on the Chesapeake Bay. This photograph features the second *Hawaii Mars*, which is still in operation as a forest-fire fighter in British Columbia. The *Philippine Mars* is also a fire fighter. The *Marshall Mars* was destroyed by an onboard fire during the war, the *Marianas Mars* crashed while fighting a fire in 1960, and the *Carolina Mars* was demolished by a typhoon in 1962. *Martin Marietta*

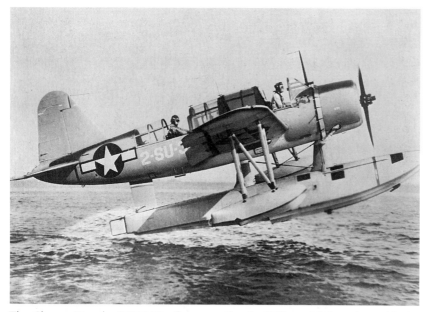

The Chance Vought OS2U Kingfisher was the US Navy's first catapult monoplane. Designed in 1937, it first flew in July 1938. This observation scout plane carried two crewmen and was armed with three .30cal machine guns. It was also equipped to carry small bombs on its wings. The Navy ordered fifty-four OS2U-1s, which were delivered to the fleet in 1940, and followed up with the purchase of 158 OS2U-2s the same year. While the Kingfisher was an excellent scout aircraft, it was most famous for its successful rescue of aviators down in the sea, including Eddie Rickenbacker, WWI ace and race-car driver who went on to become president of Eastern Airlines. *EDO Corporation*

The Navy's first modern long-range patrol aircraft was the twin-engined PBY-1 Catalina, of which sixty were built by California's Consolidated Aircraft beginning in 1935. These were followed in the next two years by PBY-2s (fifty), PBY-3s (sixty-six), and PBY-4s (thirty-two), with each model improving in engine horsepower, range, speed, and altitude. In 1940 the PBY-5, with more powerful engines and greater structural strength, became operational and was followed a year later by the PBY-5A, the first amphibian. Consolidated built 1,486 of these two models. The last PBY was the -6A, with 175 manufactured before the assembly line closed in April 1945. Total production, including those PBYs built in Canada but excluding approximately 200 manufactured under license in the Soviet Union, was 3,290.

Consolidated followed the Catalina with the four-engined PB2Y Coronado, which first flew in 1937 and became operational in 1940. Only 216 PB2Y-2s through -5s were built, and the aircraft never achieved the reputation of its predecessor, the PBY-5. Many were converted into transports able to carry 17,700lb of cargo or forty-four personnel.

Consolidated Aircraft was anything if not persistent, modifying the design of its famous B-24 Army bomber into a Navy land-based patrol craft designated the PB4Y-2 Privateer, on which the B-24's double tail was replaced with a single tail fin and rudder. A total of 739 were delivered to the Navy but very few ever saw war-theater service, and then only in the Pacific.

The other major patrol bomber developed for war service was the PBM Mariner, manufactured by Martin Aircraft. First flown in 1939, the twin-engined PBM-1 featured an unusual twin canted tail. The aircraft became operational in 1941, and over the next four years, 1,289 were manufactured, with production continuing after the war until 1947. While these last several types of planes were designed to replace the venerable PBY, none of them ever succeeded in doing so during the war years. Even Boeing built the XPBB-1, but it never entered production.

However, another WWII American patrol plane that is still in service today is the Mars, six of which were built by Martin Aircraft. Reclassified as a general transport, the aircraft's designation was changed from XPB2M-1 to the JRM in 1943. Initially the Navy ordered twenty of these behemoths, which were powered by four 2,500hp Curtiss-Wright Cyclone radial engines, but Japan's surrender reduced the Navy's needs to six planes. The double-decker JRM was 120ft long, had a 200ft wingspan, and weighed 162,000lb. It could carry 300 passengers or 68,195lb of cargo. The Mars stayed in service until 1956. Two had been lost in accidents but the remaining four were sold to a forest-service company in British Columbia, and two of them are still operating today, capable of dropping 7,200gals of water per sortie on remote forest fires.

Existing records indicate that 100 OS2Us were used by the Royal Navy, and it appears that at least one of them was flown by the Royal Australian Air Force (RAAF), according the markings on this plane in 1942. Another 300 of these aircraft were manufactured by the US Naval Aircraft Factory and shipped to nine inshore patrol squadrons, newly formed in 1942. They were designated OS2N-1s. *Vought Aircraft Company*

A row of OS2U-3 Kingfishers, equipped with Pratt & Whitney R-985-AN-8 Wasp Junior radial engines, await fly-away. Earlier versions were considered underpowered with Pratt & Whitney 450hp -4 Wasp Juniors. The plane's pontoons could be removed and replaced by wheels for regular runway operations. The Kingfisher protected the pilot and gunner with 187lb of armor plating around their positions. During 1941 368 OS2U-3s were delivered to the Navy, followed by 638 deliveries in 1942. A total of 1,519 of these versatile aircraft were manufactured before the production line closed in 1942. *EDO Corporation*

The EDO Corporation in College Point, New York, began operations in 1925, and produced nearly every aircraft float, or pontoon, procured by the military during WWII. The company built 1,200 floats, designated Model 68, for the OS2U and also manufactured the C-47's Model 78 float. In this photo, military officers and civilian managers work on future plans, most likely for the "Flying Dutchman" lifeboat partially visible to the left rear of this image. It was carried under the fuselage of specialized B-17s and B-29s and dropped to aircrews down in the ocean. The self-righting lifeboat was equipped with provisions, sails, and an engine to transport the survivors to safety. *EDO Corporation*

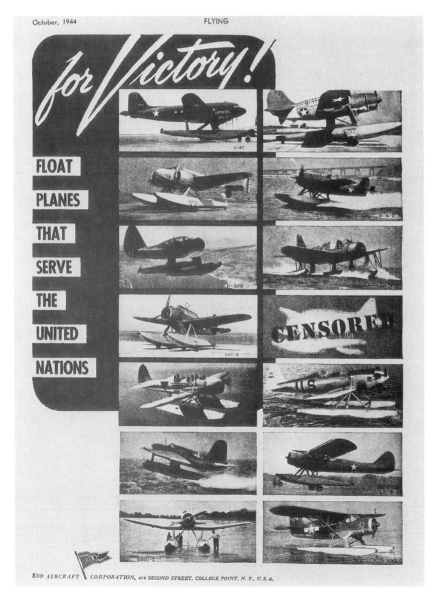

This advertisement portraying EDO's contributions toward victory in WWII was displayed in the October 1944 issue of *Flying* magazine. The upper left picture is of a C-47, and the picture next to it portrays an experimental Curtiss aircraft. The second row features the AT-7 trainer and the Grumman F4F Wildcat fighter! The OS2U is under the F4F, and the same plane designated an SB, or scout bomber, is shown in the bottom photo on the left. EDO employed 2,440 workers during the war and is still flourishing today as the major manufacturer of aircraft floats. *EDO Corporation*

A ship's crewman is positioned on the wing of this OS2U-3 to facilitate the cable hook-up, which will winch the aircraft back on board. Saving the lives of US pilots and crewmen who were forced down at sea was of prime importance, and search and rescue procedures using ships, submarines, and aircraft became quite sophisticated. The Kingfisher earned a fine reputation for landing on the water in hazardous circumstances and rescuing these fortunate survivors. In some instances the small planes would pick up so many men that they would be unable to take off, and taxied back to their ships or to rendezvous with other friendly ships or submarines. The rescued aviators rode on the wings. In July 1944 an Avenger from the aircraft carrier *Cabot* was shot down in a raid on Yap in the Caroline Islands. All three crewmen were injured and in the water within range of enemy shore batteries. An OS2U-3 from the cruiser *Columbia* landed and picked up the three men and taxied 5mi under fire to rendezvous with an American submarine, which took the two crewmen aboard. Then, with the seriously wounded pilot in the rear seat, and the gunner sitting astride the fuselage, this intrepid OS2U pilot took off and flew back to his mother ship. All in a day's work for the Kingfisher. *Vought Aircraft Company*

The famous Goodyear "K" ship tethered to a movable mooring mast. The ship was 250ft long; its helium capacity was 425,000cu-ft, and in later models it was 456,000cu-ft. Armament was upgraded from .30cal machine guns to .50cal machine guns, and depth charge racks were affixed to the bottom of the control car. Goodyear built 134 "K" ships during WWII. When ready for deployment, the airships were first flown to Lakehurst, New Jersey, for East Coast operations and Moffet Field, California, for West Coast operations. Substations were started in Boston, Norfolk, Savannah, Miami, New Orleans, Galveston, Los Angeles, and Portland. At certain fields the blimps could be hangared, but in most cases they were moored to a mast and withstood the elements magnificently, averaging 87 percent "on-line" readiness throughout the war. *Loral—Goodyear Aircraft Archives*

Goodyear employees in Akron, Ohio, stretch out the envelope, or bag, of a non-rigid airship, or blimp. The British Air Ministry had categorized airships as type A–rigid and type B–limp, which resulted in the popular nickname for these giant balloons. It required several acres of fabric, rubberized and paraffined, to make it not only gas-tight but also resistant to water and sunlight, to create the bag for a blimp, which for a "K" ship weighed four tons. After various sections were patterned, cut, and cemented together, the bag was inflated with air and the work continued. Along the interior roof line, four curtains, known as catenaries, were positioned with a total of twenty-four suspension points. Cables were attached to the ship's car from these points and its weight distributed evenly over the bag. *Loral—Goodyear Aircraft Archives*

The interior of the envelope being prepared for a Goodyear "M" ship, the largest blimp ever built. Initially the M-1 contained 625,000cu-ft of helium, which was increased to 647,000cu-ft in the M-2 and ultimately to 725,000 in the last series of "M" ships. Carrying a crew of ten in three attached cars in train, the "M" ships were 308ft long, longer than a football field. The first car housed the pilots, navigator, flight engineer, observer, and gunner, as well as radio and radar equipment. The second car accommodated a gunner and the bombardier, and also the engines, while the third car contained an observer and fuel and cargo. With electric propellers with controllable and reversible pitch, the "M" ships could land in a smaller area by reversing the props and using them as brakes. In 1946 an "M" ship completed an endurance flight of 177hr and 4,000mi. *Loral—Goodyear Aircraft Archives*

Although not strictly a patrol plane, the Chance Vought OS2U Kingfisher was one of the most famous Navy aircraft of its time, due to its dramatic record for rescuing downed fliers at sea. There were many memorable incidents in which an OS2U recovered so many air crew that the plane was unable to take off from the sea and taxied to safety with men actually sitting on the wings. Other valuable single-engined scout aircraft such as the Grumman J2F Duck and the powerful Curtiss SC Seahawk performed admirably during the war, but the Kingfisher is the plane remembered by the naval aviators of WWII. In the Aleutians Campaign it even served as a dive bomber against Japanese land targets.

Any discussion of patrol aircraft operated by the US Navy during WWII must include the admirable records of the blimps, or lighter-than-air ships. Not to be confused with barrage balloons, which were unmanned, tethered, helium-filled balloons used to frustrate low-level enemy air attacks, blimps were used as sea convoy escorts and for antisubmarine patrols.

Goodyear Aircraft had been building airships since 1913 and produced observation balloons, blimps, and free balloons for training during WWI. In 1928 the company started its own blimp fleet, and during the next fifteen years, this fleet carried more than 400,000 passengers without a mishap. In 1940 the Navy decided to build a blimp fleet and, after Pearl Harbor, increased the projected number of ships to 200. "L" and "G" ships were designed as trainers, while "K" and later "L" ships were assigned to active patrolling. A "K" ship was 253ft long and stood 80ft high. The total wing area of America's largest WWII bomber, the B-29, was less than the area of the fins and movable surfaces of a "K" ship. Airships took off and landed on a single retractable wheel, and when carrying additional fuel, could taxi across the field to get extra lift on takeoff, allowing an "M" ship to depart 6,000lb overloaded. Inside the balloon bag were two ballonets filled with air, used to maintain the tautness of the bag as the helium gas in the main chamber contracted and expanded due to outside temperature variations.

"L" ships were based on pre-war design and were 150ft long, carried a crew of seven and their helium capacity was 125,000cu-ft, while advance trainer "G" ships were 190ft long, also carried seven crewmen and had 200,000cu-ft of helium capacity. The "K" ships carried depth charges and were 250ft long, carried eight

Airship cars were framed with welded tubular steel and covered with aluminum alloy and fabric. The two engines were mounted on tubular steel outriggers on each side of the car. Oil tanks were also built into the outriggers, while the fuel tanks were attached to the roof of the car. The "K" ships also had two "slip" tanks on the bottom of the car, which carried extra fuel and could be dropped free in an emergency. Airships were often aloft for 20hr, and the cars included living quarters for those crewmen not on duty. In addition, all the other equipment needed to maintain these ships in flight and in mission performance, from radios to parachutes, were stored in the car. *Loral—Goodyear Aircraft Archives*

The assembly line in Goodyear's Plant B was 1,100ft long, and thirty blimp cars were usually under construction at one time. When a car was halfway through the line it was turned upside down so work could be performed on its top half.

Platforms on rollers were built around the cars and moved with them along the assembly line. The "L," "G," and "K" ships carried a single car, while the "M" ships incorporated three cars attached in tandem. *Loral—Goodyear Aircraft Archives*

The "K" ships needed a 300 by 100ft space for inflation, with another 100ft of head space. As the bag was inflated with air prior to a leak inspection, a large net was draped over it and anchored by hundreds of sandbags so it would not float to the hangar ceiling. After the top fin was attached and the interior cables were connected, the air in the bag was replaced with helium. The car was then rolled under the bag and attached to the catenaries. A fairing was installed to mate the bag and the car. Men on special ladders and suspended from the ceiling in boatswain chairs completed the exterior connections. Wooden battens were laced to the ship's nose so it would not "cup in" during flight. More than 16,000 parts and pieces of equipment were required to build a "K" ship, and an "M" ship was half as big again. *Loral—Goodyear Aircraft Archives*

The airship hangar at Wingfoot Lake was the site used for final construction. When the cars and outriggers were delivered to this location they needed a police motorcycle escort. The building was doubled in size during WWII, and could house three "K" ships at one time, but could not handle "M" ship construction, which was completed in the Airship Dock in Akron. That facility was 1,175ft long and 325ft wide. Blimp production peaked in July 1943, when fourteen ships were delivered to the Navy in July, and thirty-four in the three summer months. Wingfoot Lake was the most attractive of Goodyear's industrial establishments, and even had flower beds around the buildings. Located 10mi from the downtown headquarters, its employee absentee rate was only half that of the company as a whole during the war. *Loral—Goodyear Aircraft Archives*

crewmen and helium capacity was 425,000cu-ft. The queens of the fleet, "M" ships, were 308ft long and had 725,000cu-ft of helium capacity, while carrying ten crewmen. As cutbacks in military planning occurred in 1944, the Navy's "O" ship, which was due to be built by Goodyear and had a helium capacity of 1,500,000cu-ft, was canceled. It would have been twice the size of the "M" ships.

Goodyear manufactured 154 airships during WWII. Nearly 90,000 US merchant ships in convoys were escorted by blimps during the war years without the loss of a single ship. As for the blimps themselves, only one was lost to enemy action, and only one crewman lost his life. The airships fulfilled an incredible, if little known, mission during WWII, providing security and saving countless lives.

On occasion, unavoidable production delays resulted in free time for employees, and Goodyear people often held an impromptu dance on the factory floor. Goodyear employed 3,500 workers before the war, and only one woman was doing factory work in January 1942. The men recruited or already working were constantly being drafted off the assembly lines into the military services. In 1942 Goodyear lost 2,700 men in this fashion, followed by 3,000 in 1943 and another 1,000 in 1944. As a result, women were heavily recruited, and by the end of 1944, 44.6 percent of the company's employees were women and 56.3 percent of all production workers were female. Goodyear's peak employment was 33,500, but in order to achieve and maintain the levels needed for continued production, the company hired a total of 81,222 during the war. Although the War Manpower Act froze men in their jobs, it was not very enforceable as every company needed workers. Goodyear estimated that only 5 percent of its male employees who left voluntarily received the necessary release from the company. The rest just walked away. With cutbacks in production, the work force numbered only 18,500 on V-J Day. The abrupt end to the Pacific war resulted in the cancellation within 24hr of 15,000 equipment and parts orders valued at $120 million. *Loral—Goodyear Aircraft Archives*

During WWII, Goodyear blimps escorted 87,000 Allied merchant ships without the loss of a single vessel to enemy action. Only one blimp was lost and one man was killed in combat. They were able to operate at night and under adverse weather conditions and could spot an enemy submarine 90ft below the ocean's surface. The blimp was then able to track the underwater enemy and accurately drop bombs or depth charges from this steady platform in the sky. In 1942, 454 ships were sunk by the enemy in the Atlantic, but in 1944 that number was reduced to just eight. Much of the credit goes to the Navy's airship patrols in conjunction with Allied surface vessels. Blimps patrolled a 5,000mi sea frontier, and left an unprecedented record of mission accomplishment. *Loral—Goodyear Aircraft Archives*

Epilogue

By the summer of 1945, most Americans had been confident for some time that the Allies were going to win the war. However, they also expected that an invasion of the Japanese Home Islands and the total defeat of the enemy's military forces and civilian auxiliaries were required to achieve this goal. Fanatical resistance, resulting in very heavy casualties, was anticipated,

and Japan's sudden surrender after the atomic bomb attacks on Hiroshima and Nagasaki came as a complete surprise to just about everybody except, of course, the inner circle of government and military officials who had been aware of these new weapons.

Many defense contracts had been terminated or reduced during the twelve months prior to August 1945 as victory seemed assured, but now the cancellation of military programs assumed gigantic dimensions immediately, and resulted in massive layoffs. The "last hired," usually women and minorities, were the "first fired." Many women happily re-

verted to their pre-war roles as homemakers, eagerly awaiting the return of husbands and boyfriends from military service, but significant numbers were reluctant to surrender their new economic independence. For black Americans, the war had offered a glimpse of equality in both the social and economic arenas, and they were impatient to continue these developments. Some of these problems were self-correcting, in that civilian manufacture replaced military contracts very quickly in many industries, and accorded new opportunities to some of those wishing to continue employment. However, another negative vocational aspect

Many Americans had never known any US president except Franklin D. Roosevelt, who was elected chief executive four times. When he died on April 12, 1945, of a cerebral hemorrhage in Warm Springs, Georgia, less than a month before the end of the war in Europe, his countrymen everywhere mourned his passing. At Great Ashfield Air Base near Stowmarket, England, the 385th Bomb Group of the USAAF flew the nation's flag at half-mast in his memory. President Roosevelt was sixty-three years old when he died. *Jim Dacey Collection*

Grumman Aircraft employees in Bethpage, New York, gather to listen to President Harry Truman's radio speech announcing the surrender of Germany to the Allies, May 8, 1945. Women and older men predominate in this photo as those males of military age were in the armed services. As most Grumman production went to the Navy in the Pacific war, the end of the conflict in Europe did not immediately result in employee layoffs. Those would occur when the Japanese capitulated in August 1945. *Northrop Grumman Archives*

from the civilian point of view was the return of millions of soldiers, sailors, airmen, and marines, both male and female, eagerly seeking to re-enter the job market. Again, some of this occupational opportunity pressure was alleviated by the GI Bill, which offered educational alternatives to the returning veterans, but there is no discounting the disappointment encountered by significant numbers of Home Front workers when faced with a peacetime economy.

Although this veritable army of defense workers faded from the center stage with the end of the war, their accomplishments remained as steadfast testimony to their prodigious efforts, and nowhere was this more apparent than in the US aircraft industry. Aircraft production of all types in the United States rose from 2,141 planes in 1939 to 19,433 in 1941. These numbers were dwarfed in 1942 when the nation produced 47,836 planes and again in 1943 when 85,898 aircraft flew forth from dozens of factories across the land. Top production was reached in 1944 when 96,318 planes were manufactured in the United States. With the end of the conflict in sight, production dropped to 46,001 aircraft in 1945.

Great Britain and the Soviet Union both out-produced the United States in 1939, 1940, and 1941, but Britain's top year for the rest of the war was 1944, when it manufactured 26,461 aircraft. The Soviet Union reached 40,300 planes the same year, less than half of the American production in 1944.

Examining the enemy's production of aircraft, Germany's best year was 1944, with 40,593 units manufactured. Japan also reached its maximum effort in 1944, when its factories supplied 28,180 planes to Imperial Japanese forces. Between 1939 and 1945 the United States manufactured 303,713 aircraft, followed by the Soviet Union with 158,220, and Great Britain with 131,549 planes. For all of its economic efficiency, Germany managed to build only 119,871 planes, and

In an area of New York's Manhattan Island known as "Little Italy," a group of Italian-Americans enthusiastically celebrated the end of the war in the Pacific on V-J Day, August 15, 1945. Even though their ancestral land had surrendered unconditionally to the Allies on September 8, 1943, it was badly battered for the remainder of the war because the Germans defended the northern sectors of Italy desperately, retreating very slowly and inflicting heavy casualties on Allied troops right up to the termination of hostilities. *National Archives*

Japan's total aircraft production for the war years was a paltry 76,320 units. The Soviet Union never released its WWII loss figures, but the United States lost 59,296 planes and Great Britain lost 33,090, compared to the destruction of 95,000 German and 49,485 Japanese aircraft.

In retrospect, it appears logical that when Germany invaded the Soviet Union in 1941 and Japan attacked China several years earlier, their military planners realized that the nations they were attacking were physically vast and had large populations in comparison to their attack-

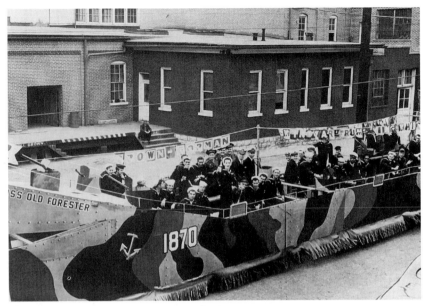

One of the most famous pictures of WWII was taken by *Life* magazine photographer Alfred Eisenstaedt in New York's Times Square on V-J Day, August 15, 1945. It is reputed that the sailor and the nurse involved in this embrace were not known to each other, but were drawn to Times Square to celebrate Japan's surrender. *National Archives*

The cocktail flag flies from the bow of the CSS *Forester* during a Brown-Forman Distillery employee victory parade in Louisville, Kentucky, after the end of WWII. The liquor industry produced alcohol for medicinal use during the war, and also as fuel for torpedoes, creating a scarcity for the man on the street. To

make matters worse, American consumption of alcohol increased from the pre-war level of 140 million gallons to 190 million gallons annually during the war years. In August 1944 the government allowed one month of production for civilian use to ease the shortage. *Brown-Foreman Archives*

ers. What is astonishing is that the Axis powers did not seem to comprehend that this same condition existed in their war with the United States, which also was protected by two huge oceans. They attacked a colossus, but seemed unprepared for the consequences.

American manufacturers experienced production setbacks due to scarcities in raw materials, unavoidable changes in equipment design, and unwarranted governmental interference in the manufacturing process, as well as shortages of experienced workers when and where they were needed. The airplanes needed to defeat the Axis powers had been mainly designed prior to Pearl Harbor, and America's aircraft manufacturers were eager to enter full-scale production. That they successfully overcame the difficulties of the existing marketplace, just as they successfully confronted the nation's enemies abroad, is a matter of record.

From 1940 to 1945 the United States spent $185 billion on arma-

Pratt & Whitney was a major manufacturer of wartime aircraft engines, but production dropped dramatically as the government abruptly canceled contracts after V-J Day in August 1945. This desolate assembly line reflects that status most poignantly. The dropping of the

atomic bombs on Japan that resulted in the Japanese surrender caught most defense companies unawares. They and most Americans expected the war to last much longer, requiring the actual invasion of the Japanese Home Islands to achieve victory. *United Technologies Archives*

Suddenly, the United States no longer needed its enormous fleets of military aircraft. At Willow Run Airport near Detroit, where so many B-24 Liberator four-engined bombers had been manufactured by the Ford Motor Company, four dozen survivors are parked alongside an unused runway, awaiting their fate. Some were sold to friendly nations, but most became scrap. Only two B-24s survive in flying condition today. *Yankee Air Force Museum*

ments, and approximately $46 billion of that was dedicated to aircraft and their support requirements. More than 750,000 Americans were directly employed by aircraft manufacturers during peak production (1944), and another 250,000 workers were working for subcontractors. The end result of this production juggernaut was overwhelming Allied air power. In modern warfare an interdependent mixture of air, ground, and sea power is necessary to triumph over the enemy, and no one service can claim utmost priority. However, one element can often provide the decisive factor, and American air power fulfilled this role in WWII. The modest industry that rose to the occasion and provided the thousands of planes necessary for victory performed an economic miracle, which is still evident today in America's superior aircraft design and production, both military and civilian.

Great fleets of warplanes will never again darken the skies as they

The *Renaissance*, a famous B-26 Marauder twin-engined bomber from the European Theater, was offered for sale in January 1946 in Ontario, California. Note the rows of bombs painted on the fuselage denoting completed missions over enemy territory. The swastikas represent German planes shot down by the plane's gunners. The organization handling disposal and sale of most surplus military aircraft was the Reconstruction Finance Corporation. *Phil Kaplan Collection*

The carcasses of obsolete P-40s are stacked nose down on a remote California airfield awaiting the scrap pile. The engines and propellers have been removed, and in most cases the national insignia has been painted over. The jet age become a reality in the last year of the war, and most propeller-driven aircraft were no longer able to compete in combat. Several WWII American planes performed creditably in the Korean War, and the C-47 and A-26 were used in combat roles during the Vietnam conflict, more than two decades after their baptism of fire during WWII. *National Air & Space Museum*

did during WWII. Missiles, rockets, the jet age, and nuclear weapon systems have made those formations obsolete. Many of the average citizens of this nation who built these aircraft are gone as well, but their prideful legacy remains as an example of a people united in sacrifice and patriotism.

In November 1945 more than 4,200 heavy bombers awaited destruction at the Reconstruction Finance Corporation storage depot in Walnut Ridge, Arkansas. The great majority featured here are B-17 Flying Fortresses, but a few B-24 Liberators are also visible in this rather overwhelming vision of the end of an era. *Phil Kaplan Collection*

Arlington Cemetery in Virginia, across the Potomac River from the nation's capital, is the most famous repository of America's war dead, and WWII was a major contributor to that dismal total. During three years and nine months of conflict, the United States suffered 292,131 dead and 671,278 wounded. These figures do not include those men missing in action and never recovered. While the sacrifice of all these men helped achieve victory, it is little remembered, except by those members of that generation still with us today, and some few others who still revere our nation's past... Lest We Forget.

Bibliography

Magazines and Government or Official Publications

USAAF: The Official WWII Guide to the Army Air Forces. New York: Bonanza Books, 1988

American Fighters of World War Two. Garden City NY: Doubleday & Company 1969

Fact Sheet - World War II 50th Anniversary of WWII Commemoration Committee Washington, D.C. 1992

"How Many Planes When?" Fortune August 1940

Naval Aviation 1911 - 1984 GPO Washington, D.C. 20402

"Night Fighters" Air Force Magazine January 1992

"Production Wars" Wings Magazine October 1991

"War Comes to San Diego" San Diego Historical Society 1993

"Willow Run" Air & Space Magazine August/September 1992

Books

Allen, Hugh "Goodyear Aircraft" Corday & Gross Co. Cleveland OH 1947

Bavousett, Glenn "Combat Aircraft of WWII" Bonanza Books New York NY 1989

Biddle, Wayne "Barons of the Sky" Simon & Schuster New York NY 1991

Birdsall, Steve "Log of the Liberators" Doubleday & Company Garden City NY 1973

Dorr, Robert "US Fighters of World War Two" Arms and Armour Press London UK 1991

Gurney, Gene "War In the Air" Brown Publishers New York NY 1964

LeMay, Curtis E. (with Bill Yenne) "Superfortress" McGraw-Hill Book Company New York NY 1988

Lingeman, Richard "Don't You Know There's A War On?" G.P. Putnam's Sons New York NY 1970

Morrison, Wilbur H. "Point of No Return" Times Books New York, NY 1979

Pawlowski, Gareth "Flattops and Fledglings" Castle Books New York NY 1971

Rogers, Donald "Since You Went Away" Arlington House New Rochelle NY 1973

Rosenbaum, Robert A. "Aviators" Facts on File Oxford UK 1992

Sonnenburg, Paul & Schoneberger, William Allison "Power of Excellence 1915-1990" Coastline Publishers Malibu CA 1990

Stoff, Joshua "Picture History of WWII American Aircraft Production" Dover Books Mineola NY 1993

Wilmott, H.P. "B-17 Flying Fortress" Bison Books Greenwich CT 1983

Index